# Shakespeare on Prejudice

RELATED TITLES

*The Merchant of Venice: Language and Writing*
Douglas M. Lanier
978-1-4725-7148-9

*Othello: Language and Writing*
Laurie Maguire
978-1-4081-5659-9

*Shakespeare's Artists: The Painters, Sculptors, Poets and Musicians in his Plays and Poems*
B. J. Sokol
978-1-3500-2193-8

*Shakespeare's Legal Language: A Dictionary*
B. J. Sokol
978-0-8264-7778-1

# Shakespeare on Prejudice

'Scorns and Mislike' in Shakespeare's Plays

*B. J. Sokol*

THE ARDEN SHAKESPEARE
LONDON • NEW YORK • OXFORD • NEW DELHI • SYDNEY

THE ARDEN SHAKESPEARE
Bloomsbury Publishing Plc
50 Bedford Square, London, WC1B 3DP, UK
1385 Broadway, New York, NY 10018, USA
29 Earlsfort Terrace, Dublin 2, Ireland

BLOOMSBURY, THE ARDEN SHAKESPEARE and the Arden Shakespeare logo are trademarks of Bloomsbury Publishing Plc

First published in Great Britain 2022
Paperback edition published 2023

Copyright © B. J. Sokol, 2022, 2023

B.J. Sokol has asserted his right under the Copyright, Designs and Patents Act, 1988, to be identified as author of this work.

For legal purposes the Acknowledgements on pp. ix–x constitute an extension of this copyright page.

Cover design: Tjaša Krivec
Cover image: Titian, *Allegorie der Zeit* (Wikimedia Commons)

All rights reserved. No part of this publication may be reproduced or transmitted in any form or by any means, electronic or mechanical, including photocopying, recording, or any information storage or retrieval system, without prior permission in writing from the publishers.

Bloomsbury Publishing Plc does not have any control over, or responsibility for, any third-party websites referred to or in this book. All internet addresses given in this book were correct at the time of going to press. The author and publisher regret any inconvenience caused if addresses have changed or sites have ceased to exist, but can accept no responsibility for any such changes.

A catalogue record for this book is available from the British Library.

A catalog record for this book is available from the Library of Congress.

ISBN:  HB:    978-1-3501-6839-8
       PB:    978-1-3502-9614-5
       ePDF:  978-1-3501-6841-1
       eBook: 978-1-3501-6840-4

Typeset by Integra Software Services Pvt. Ltd.

To find out more about our authors and books visit www.bloomsbury.com and sign up for our newsletters.

*For my teachers
(including many of my marvellous students)
In memory of Sean Elliott, poet and scholar*

# CONTENTS

*List of Illustrations*  viii
*Acknowledgements*  ix

Introduction  1

1  Prejudices against learning: envy, resentment and presumed omniscience  17

2  Shakespeare and prejudices against art  47

3  Shakespeare on prejudices against 'strangers'  87

4  Prejudices against peace  131

5  Prejudices against 'Anteros' or mutual erotic love  177

Afterword: interpreting chapter overlaps  225

*Appendix: Renaissance and modern takes on false and true knowledge*  229
*Notes*  234
*Bibliography*  274
*Index*  301

# ILLUSTRATIONS

1.1 Title page of Erasmus, *A deuoute treatise vpon the Pater noster*, trans. Margaret More Roper (London, [1526?]) 30

4.1 'O WORMES MEATE: O FROATH O VANITIE: WHY ART THOV SO INSOLENT', in *Vincentio Saviolo his practise: in two bookes: the first intreating of the vse of the rapier and dagger, the second, of honor and honorable quarrels* (London, 1595), 2 vols, book 1 sig. k3  144

5.1 Engraving by Vinceno Cartari of Eros and Anteros made after a painting by Guiseppe Salviati (*c.* 1502–*c.* 1575) in Vinceno Cartari, *Le imagini de i dei de gli antichi* (Venetia, 1571) 183

# ACKNOWLEDGEMENTS

My debt to colleagues, friends and collaborators is so extensive as to be hard to specify within a reasonable scope. My first and greatest thanks are to my wife and frequent co-author, Dr Mary Sokol. Among the very many others who have been immensely generous, supportive and helpful I would like to mention first Inga-Stina Ewbank and Anne Barton, critics and scholars whose excellent legacy lives on. The psychoanalyst and W. R. Bion scholar Chris Mawson very recently gave me most generous assistance – he is greatly missed by his friends and colleagues. David Crystal has also supplied most generous help, as have Gabriel Egan and Ronald Britton. I am most grateful also to Paul Taylor at the Warburg Institute, Kelly Marshall at the University of London Senate House Library and Jackie Brown at the British Library. I have had valuable and enlightening conversations with a multitude of others over the many years in which this project has been brewing. These include David Bell, Francesca Armour-Chelu, David Black, Lisa Hopkins, Robin Headlam Wells, Roger Kennedy, Barbara Kreps, Jeanne Magagna, Thomas Mcalindon, William McCormack, Ruth Morse, Simon Reynolds, Quentin Skinner, Lyn Stephens, Elizabeth Urban, René Weis and many more. Of course, all errors and misapprehensions in the following – and most especially all deficiencies and shortcomings – are entirely my own, despite the excellent help and encouragement that I have received.

I also want to credit the generosity of the English Department at University College London, where I have been a research associate throughout the preparation of this work. Without the excellent facilities at UCL, and those at the libraries of the University of London where I am Emeritus, it would have been impossible to complete this work during a time of pandemic and lockdown. I also particularly want to thank Tony Trowles and David Burden for arranging for me to examine the tomb of Richard II at Westminster Abbey.

# Introduction

## The boundaries of the present study

Prejudices may be positive as well as negative, natural or inevitable,[1] helpful or invaluable,[2] etc. The discussions here will not deny such possibilities but will be restricted deliberately to considerations of only those prejudices that involve irrational and unsupported distastes for, aversions to, exclusions of or condemnations of selected institutions, groups, persons or things. That is to say, my topic will be what King Edward in Shakespeare's *3 Henry VI* calls '*your scorns and mislike*' (4.1.23).

Unsupported and unsupportable negative prejudices have always flourished, and always will, despite requiring denials of reality and distortions of truth. Hereafter, for brevity, such *mislikes* will usually be labelled 'negative prejudices' or just 'prejudices'. This study will not simply decry such prejudices as depicted by Shakespeare, although in many instances they have miserable or destructive consequences. This is because indignant demonizing of elements of mental life to which we are all subject does not advance an understanding of them. And so, my aim will be to explore Shakespeare's insights into how negative prejudices arise and become harmful or destructive.

This study will be divided into five chapters, each addressing 'scorns and mislike' directed against one of five differing sorts of prejudicial targets. This division does not produce a comprehensive categorization of all prejudices, or of all prejudices treated by Shakespeare – and some others will be noted (for instance, prejudices against illegitimate birth, or against physical disability). It will be seen, additionally, that several specific prejudices considered here overlap my convenient five categories. Some reasons for this will be discussed in an Afterword, but also it will be noted throughout that quite often an ostensible target of 'scorns and mislike' depicted by Shakespeare stands in place of another more occluded target. This is to say that Shakespeare was well aware of the psychological mechanisms now known as projection, and those mechanisms will receive considerable attention hereafter.

# Which prejudices will be addressed here?

The five chapters of this book will address respectively Shakespearian portrayals of prejudices against teaching and learning, against what we now call the 'arts', against decent and generous relations with outsiders or 'strangers', against peaceable social arrangements, and against erotic mutual love. It will be seen that Shakespeare's treatment implies significant insights into the causes and processes of such unwarranted rejection or despising.

In 1582 the writer and schoolmaster Richard Mulcaster (a figure probably well known to Shakespeare)[3] offered a definition of 'prejudice' as follows:

> Prejudice, when he that misliketh doth know the thing well, but is so wedded unto, naie rather so bewitched with his own fantsie, which it self is seduced by som foren allurement, as he will rather mislike against knowledge, then withstand against fantsie.[4]

The elements of prejudice named here – stubborn 'fantsie', 'allurement' and a disavowal of 'knowledge' (as opposed to simple ignorance) – all raise issues that Mulcaster enlarges upon later, and those are issues that will be important in the following discussions. Especially interesting is Mulcaster's term 'mislike' which implies wilfulness rather than judgment, and also Mulcaster's insistence that the 'thing' misliked is something known well. It will be argued here that such knowing may be situated where disowning of knowledge meets projections of that which is disowned onto another person or thing.

# Prejudices and values

Mulcaster also notes that *misliking* that 'commeth upon desert, when the thing is such, as for verie naughtinesse it is to be misliked' differs wholly from an ill-founded *misliking* 'upon opinion, when error in the partie misliketh that thing, which is of it self well worthie the liking'. He then divides the second sort of misliking, the sort that is erroneous, into two varieties: in one of those the misliking arises from 'mere ignorance', and in the other it arises from 'prejudice'.[5] This means that, for him, a prejudice is an adverse opinion that is 1) not justified by fact, 2) not driven by simple ignorance, and 3) directed against something that is 'of it self well worthie the liking', which is to say something *good in itself*. To some degree notions of just what is good are culturally determined (and also may be culturally contested, as they were in Shakespeare's time at least as much as in ours). Nevertheless, an *idea* of the good is not in the same way subject to variability, relativity or vicissitudes. On the contrary, as will be discussed presently, notions dividing goodness from badness may have deep psychological origins connected with human survival and growth; some hold that 'goodness' is crucial for being itself.[6] Moreover, the desirability of the specific good things that Shakespeare that alludes to – the desirability of learning, art, peace, civil amity and mutual love – is not easily dismissed.

The above threefold division proposed by Mulcaster wherein only one of the three branches indicates a 'prejudice' resonates with a division of 'discriminations' made in our time by Thomas Sowell. Sowell holds that persons or groups of persons may be differentiated from one another in one of three ways. These are labelled 'discrimination 1a', 'discrimination 1b' and 'discrimination 2', and refer respectively to decisions based on accurate assessments of individuals, based on group statistical evidence (which may not accurately reflect individual cases) and based on 'unsubstantiated notions or animosities'.[7] A recent review of Sowell's scheme identifies his third, wholly unwarranted, type of discrimination as 'what economists refer to as "taste-based discrimination" or "animus"', but questions Sowell's contention that state interventions may exacerbate rather than ameliorate the harms done by this.[8] Although this reviewer adopts a different political perspective from Sowell, it is certain that for them, as for hopefully for any other right-minded person, Sowell's bigoted 'discrimination 2' (closely resembling Mulcaster's 'prejudice') is socially and morally harmful and bad.

Mulcaster next expands that 'Ignorance' that 'knoweth nothing' and is an 'infirmitie ... not bolstered with ill will' differs from 'prejudice' that 'knoweth and will not, and therefor is a great fo to a not favored good' (46). Calling the target of a 'prejudice' a 'not favoured good' is a lovely Elizabethan locution in accord with which Shakespeare represents good things misjudged to be bad on account of what Mulcaster further calls 'cankred and a corrupt opinion' (46).

Although my topic, and Mulcaster's, is prejudice *against* persons or things, a curious overlapping may arise because badly conceived preferences or enthusiasms (positive prejudices) may sometimes support unwarranted mislikes or scornful rejections. Thus, for instance, I will be considering several Shakespearian men whose keenness for military life associates with their scorning or misliking women's love. Likewise, several young men who exhibit fashionable 'intellectual' enthusiasms (in *The Taming of the Shrew* and *Love's Labour's Lost*) also, initially, reject links with women. Shakespeare's satire of such attitudes could have been topical, for he may well have been aware of the high-minded coterie surrounding the 'wizard' ninth Earl of Northumberland which included poets, mathematicians and a visiting Italian philosopher. Northumberland himself wrote a diatribe against women that is catalogued in the Public Records Office as 'On the entertainment of a Mistress being inconsistent with the pursuit of Learning'.[9]

My first chapter will mention Shakespeare's pseudo-intellectual men in connection with their shallow commitments to educational ideals, but these same men will be considered more closely in my final chapter in connection with prejudicial rejections of mutual loving commitments. There it will be argued that Shakespeare depicts mutual erotic love as gratifying, desirable and worthy, although often beset by difficulties. Because such love is good in itself, any belittlement of it or attack upon it indicates ill-founded negative prejudice.

These and many more instances illustrate a pattern that pertains to *all* the negative prejudices to be discussed here – all involve adverse views of things that are perceived in their contexts to be 'a not favoured good'.

# Varied definitions of 'prejudice'

The following discussions will rely on the uses of certain 'terms of art'. For example, the term 'stranger' will be used here in an Elizabethan sense whereby it denotes a specific 'other', a social 'outsider' or member of an out-group. This usage is in not in accord with modern parlance, but will serve a useful purpose. Likewise the term 'object' will frequently be used in the following to refer to one of the internal psychic objects studied in psychoanalytic object-relations theories – this usage is remote from the senses that the word 'object' takes in ordinary discourse. Likewise, a highly specific but now unfamiliar classical and Renaissance concept known as 'Anterotic love' will be defined in and then deployed throughout Chapter 5 – there is in fact no equivalent compact term for this type of an affectionate relation now available.

In accord with the fact that new explorations sometimes require new delimitations of terms, there is a need to differentiate uses in this study of the word 'prejudice' from other senses or emphases attached to that term elsewhere and over time. Particularly of late there has been a tendency to use the term 'prejudice' in ways that are implicitly restricted or narrowed in application to instances of racism, xenophobia or chauvinism. However, greater insights will emerge in this study of Shakespeare's work if 'a prejudice' is allowed to convey a wider meaning according with Richard Mulcaster's position that 'prejudices' include all unsupported adverse views of any kinds of 'thing' where these opinions do not arise from mere ignorance, but derive rather from fantasies and delusions eschewing experience and clear thinking. Therefore the following five chapters will address a wider range of negative biases than do many other recent considerations of negative prejudices.

Shakespeare himself used the term 'prejudice' only in another manner,[10] but a near synonym for *to be prejudiced against* sometimes used by Shakespeare and other Elizabethans was *to mislike*.[11] So, in *The Merchant of Venice* 2.1.11 the Prince of Morocco pleads 'Mislike me not for my complexion', while in *3 Henry VI* 4.1.23, as is noted just above, the king asks his courtiers to consider their objections to Lady Grey 'Setting your scorns and mislike aside'.

There have been some very interesting vagaries in the understanding of the term 'prejudice' over time. The Oxford English Dictionary significantly varies the contents and ordering of its sub-definitions of 'prejudice, n.' between the second edition of 1989 (here called OED2) and the 2007 third edition (here called OED3). In the more recent OED3 the first sub entry (I.1.a) of the definition of 'prejudice' is 'Preconceived opinion not based on reason or actual experience; bias, partiality', but then this sub-definition continues: '(now) *spec.* unreasoned dislike, hostility, or antagonism towards, or discrimination against, a race, sex, or other class of people'. That specification in this first sub entry corresponds to a recent shift of meaning that is problematic for the current study because it narrows the main definition in a way that would preclude the discussions to follow of five different targets of prejudice. Only one of those five targets ('strangers') falls within the OED3 specification.

Alternately, the first entry for 'prejudice n.' in the earlier OED2 conveys only the legal overtones of the term by defining prejudice as 'Injury, detriment, or damage, caused to a person by judgement or action in which his rights are disregarded; resulting in injury; hence, injury to a person or thing likely to be the consequence of some action'. In fact, there is *no* exact parallel in OED2 with OED3's leading definition of 'prejudice n'. The closest OED2 gets to that appears under the sub-heading OED2, II.3.a beginning 'Preconceived opinion; bias or leaning favourable or unfavourable; prepossession'.[12] Following this OED2 adds 'when used *absolutely*, usually with unfavourable connotation' (thus emphasizing negative prejudices). In OED2 there is no specification that races, sexes or other classes of persons are the definitive targets of a prejudice.

Thus the differences between the OED editions of 1989 and 2007 suggest there was a shift over two decades to a narrower use of the term *prejudice*. Since 2007 such a tendency to specialization has progressed further, and racism in particular has become a prominent topic of discussion and debate. Also recently, as noted above, Thomas Sowell has examined the social and economic implications of racial discrimination in the United States while more broadly the psychoanalyst M. Fakhry Davids has argued that such xenophobic prejudices as racism correlate with permanent aspects of the human psyche. In his book *Unconscious Racism* Davids also cites and agrees with a culturally and historically specific study suggesting that 'slavery remains embedded in the minds of British [psychoanalytic] patients from an African-Caribbean background'.[13] Very important topics such as these surely warrant further research and discussion. However, Sowell and Davids are concerned with present-day matters (e.g. modern USA social and economic policies and questions pertinent to the current day psychoanalytic profession) and take no note at all of Shakespeare specifically.[14]

How such recent researches as the above might be brought to bear on Shakespeare studies is an important question. One approach to this might be to follow the dictates of 'presentism', which is a school of literary criticism that attempts to align older texts with impassioned views occasioned by prominent issues or widespread beliefs of the present moment.[15] Gabriel Egan describes how present-day debates or convictions may drive this critical mode and overwrite Shakespearian texts and contexts: 'Presentism has become a way of doing literary criticism by explicitly evoking the present concerns that motivate a desire to reread old literature (especially Shakespeare) to discover resonances that it could not have had for its first audiences or readers, because these only became possible as a consequence of what happened between then and now'.[16] In common with others, I have elsewhere discussed at some length the possibility that fallacies or anachronisms may arise from such approaches.[17]

However, there are also areas of study concerned with 'Shakespeare and race' that are historically founded and of great interest. Such studies examine how, through successive periods of history, cultures evolve to produce varying appreciations of, interpretations of, productions or performances of, and teachings of Shakespearian texts.[18] Some among such studies investigate perceptions of Shakespeare that vary in response to the cultural dynamics surrounding the complex and shifting issues of a widely defined concept of race.[19] Recent leading proponents of such an approach include Ayanna Thompson and her colleagues.[20]

The house of Shakespeare studies should have many mansions, which is to say that giving space to multiple perspectives on Shakespearian topics can only enhance our appreciation and understanding. In the perspective selected for study here various forms of prejudice portrayed by Shakespeare (including but not restricted to prejudices against 'strangers' or disliked groupings) are placed side by side in the light of carefully investigated Elizabethan historical contexts. Due note will be taken that those contexts may have involved debates or ambiguities. In relation to those contexts, then, the speeches, interactions and behaviours of Shakespearian figures are interpreted in an attempt to delineate the patterns of reaction or the implied drives of adherents to unsupportable beliefs.

## Another difference

This study will differ from some others in the same subject area not only because it will consider a wider range of prejudicial targets than have mainly been addressed recently, but also because it will reject as prejudiced in themselves the not infrequent claims that Shakespeare shared (for alleged social or psychological reasons) the vicious biases of his prejudiced characters. I will occasionally describe and challenge some of the more complex of those attacks on Shakespeare's personal integrity and humanity, not to castigate 'Bardophobic' speculations but rather to demarcate and test my own methods and views by contrasting them with those speculations.

## Further characteristics of prejudice

Although negative prejudices preclude or destroy impulses to tolerance, the kinds of prejudice studied here are neither the inverse of nor the simple absence of *tolerance*. The non-reciprocal relation between prejudice and tolerance is analogous to the fact that ugliness and beauty are not so much opposites as they are incommensurables. This is to say that beauty is not simply a lack of ugliness nor ugliness a lack of beauty – because beauty involves elements such as symmetry, integrity and harmony while ugliness involves features other than the lack of such elements. Likewise, the sort of 'tolerance' that I among others have previously discussed involves positive elements such as generosity, good will, good humour, curiosity and a wish to empathize with others[21] – while the simple *lack* of such elements, if not also accompanied by scorn or malice, may indicate merely dullness, ignorance, indifference or unawareness, rather than prejudice.

In a further differentiation, possessing the kind of prejudices of concern here is distinct from an entertaining of hypothetical 'mental models' or 'preconceptions' that some theorists suggest always precedes constructive thinking.[22] This is because prejudicial beliefs are held with an unfounded certainty that is immune to investigation or revision. In consequence, those beset by prejudices cannot employ logic or reality testing, and in that sense cannot think. It might be objected that prejudices *are* thoughts, but that paradox is resolved by the psychoanalyst W. R. Bion's 1962 'A Theory of Thinking', which distinguishes between 'thoughts' and 'thinking'. Indeed, Bion maintains that 'thinking' might occur, but also might *not* occur, after 'thoughts' arise in a mind,[23] and holds further that 'thinking has to be called into existence to cope with thoughts'. Thus he continues that his theory 'differs from any theory of thought as a product of thinking, in that thinking is a development forced on the psyche by the pressure of thoughts and not the other way around' (111).

Bion adds that when thoughts are not subjected to thinking, 'the assumption of omniscience [becomes] a substitute for learning from experience', and in such cases:

> Omniscience substitutes for the discrimination between true and false a dictatorial affirmation that one thing is morally right and the other wrong ... There is thus potentially a conflict between assertion of truth and assertion of moral ascendancy. The extremism of the one infects the other.
>
> (114)

In line with such notions, I believe that being prejudiced is a particular kind of *thoughts*-propelled *non-thinking* that produces the illusion that thinking has taken place when thinking has not occurred at all. Such processes lead to unshakeable certainties accompanied by scornful rejections of alternatives.

The flourishing of prejudicial certainties entails gross overlooking of actual perceptions, palpable mismatching of words and things, rank failures of logic and indifference to demonstrations of falsehood. As a result, 'it is harder to crack prejudice than an atom' (as Albert Einstein reputedly said).

## Psychoanalytic concepts useful here

W. R. Bion's just-mentioned theory about 'thoughts' arising without 'thinking' subsequently taking place is one among several ideas drawn from psychoanalytic studies that will be especially useful and pertinent here. Thus I will be citing some psychoanalytic thinkers who focus directly on questions of prejudice,[24] and others, like Bion, who more generally investigate distortions of thinking.

When psychoanalytic concepts are made use of here these will never be taken to be the emanations of oracles, but understood rather as products of close observations followed by interpretations subject to continuing debate, revision and development. For instance, over his career Freud himself more than once radically altered his thinking. Psychoanalysts have always primarily sought therapeutically useful insights, but also, from the start, there has been fruitful two-way traffic between psychoanalytic thinking and literary studies. Of course, it is wrong to imagine that Shakespearian characters may be psychoanalysed, for they are impersonations that cannot be encouraged to free associate, report dreams or fantasies, or be responded to empathically in controlled settings over a long term. Nonetheless, the following studies of Shakespearian representations of prejudices against persons or things will benefit from considerations of a number of psychoanalytic concepts that have been developed following interactions with adults, then children, and more recently with infants and carers. Here at the outset I would like to mention briefly some important psychoanalytic concepts that will help to advance the present study.

With apologies to readers familiar with the complexities and the still-evolving understanding of them, let me offer a truncated account of some such concepts. One is the concept of 'splitting' in unconscious 'phantasy' of a subject's psychic 'objects' (which are the foci for real or imagined relationships). According to Melanie Klein and her followers such splitting is universal in normal infant development, and also recurs cyclically – in an attenuated form except in psychosis – later in life. The process of splitting in infancy allows for invaluable realizations of differences between self-things and other-things, but also entails Klein's 'paranoid-schizoid position'.[25] This is a 'constellation of anxieties, defences and internal and external object relations that Klein considers to be characteristic of the earliest months of an infant's life and to continue to a greater or lesser extent into childhood and adulthood'.[26] Early in life the self-things and other-things divided may be an infant's hungry mouth and the mother's feeding breast, and slightly later a child's dependency on their mother in contrast to their parents' creative-couple relationship. In healthy development a working through of the terror, envy and hatred arising from fear and frustrations experienced in the paranoid-schizoid position gives rise to vital growth and learning. This learning allows the child to gain awareness of good things and therefore of goodness, of their own personal identity and of other identities in bilateral or triangular configurations.

In primitive splitting a subject's internal and external objects are divided into fragmented objects that are perceived to be wholly good or wholly bad. As mental growth progresses such splitting of objects into unrealistically good or bad 'part-objects' is replaced by subtler and more integrated assessments of selves and others. However, splitting of objects followed by projections outward of unwanted bad part-objects can result in prejudicial thinking, even in adult life. Thus the psychoanalyst John Steiner has written of the connections between splitting, idealization, projection and prejudice:[27]

> Splitting off and projecting undesirable aspects of one's self and of one's objects is the basic mechanism of prejudice. Free of flaws, the ideal couple can enjoy superiority and solidarity while the recipient of the projections becomes the flawed and unacceptable object, often treated as if he is not fully human. In this way, the prejudice can sustain an idealization, but if the idealized object fails to live up to expectations, the idealization may collapse and the now degraded, formerly ideal, object becomes unacceptable and is treated with prejudice. Indeed, the mechanism underlying prejudice is fundamental to the need to sustain idealized objects and is fundamental to the hatred of the idealized objects when they disappoint.

According to Melanie Klein and her followers, in opposition to splitting there is a further process in which the repairing of part objects and making them whole occurs in the so-called 'depressive position'.[28] The challenges, risks and pains of whole-object relations notwithstanding, entering this position allows for otherwise unobtainable connectedness and realism. Thus it may enable the overcoming of former prejudices even after those have done regrettable damage, as is seen in a number of Shakespeare contexts to be considered in the following chapters.

# Texts used

Shakespeare quotations will be from the 1989 Oxford Shakespeare (Electronic edition) unless they bear 'tln' references taken from Charlton Hinman's facsimile edition of the First Folio.[29] The Oxford edition supplies several passages from alternative editions or sources of Shakespeare's work and the lineation of these takes forms resembling 'A.C. 3–7', meaning lines 3–7 in additional passage C. The notes (but not the main text) will use title abbreviations adopted from the *Oxford Electronic Shakespeare* as follows:

| | |
|---|---|
| 1H4 | Henry IV, part 1 |
| 1H6 | Henry VI, part 1 |
| 2H4 | Henry IV, part 2 |
| ADO | Much Ado About Nothing |
| AIT | All Is True (Henry VIII) |
| ANT | Antony and Cleopatra |
| AWW | All's Well That Ends Well |
| AYL | As You Like It |
| COR | Coriolanus |
| CYL | The First Part of the Contention (Henry VI, part 2) |
| CYM | Cymbeline |
| ERR | The Comedy of Errors |
| H5 | Henry V |
| HAM | Hamlet |
| JC | Julius Caesar |
| JN | King John |
| LLL | Love's Labour's Lost |
| LRF | The Tragedy of King Lear (Folio) |
| LRQ | The History of King Lear (1608 Quarto) |
| LUC | The Rape of Lucrece |
| MAC | Macbeth |
| MM | Measure for Measure |
| MND | Midsummer Night's Dream |
| MV | The Merchant of Venice |
| OTH | Othello |
| PER | Pericles, Prince of Tyre |
| R2 | Richard II |
| R3 | Richard III |
| RDY | Richard, Duke of York (Henry VI, part 3) |

| | |
|---|---|
| ROM | Romeo and Juliet |
| SHR | The Taming of the Shrew |
| SON | Shakespeare's Sonnets |
| STM | Sir Thomas More |
| TGV | The Two Gentlemen of Verona |
| TIM | Timon of Athens |
| TIT | Titus Andronicus |
| TMP | The Tempest |
| TN | Twelfth Night, or What You Will |
| TNK | Two Noble Kinsmen |
| TRO | Troilus and Cressida |
| VEN | Venus and Adonis |
| WIV | The Merry Wives of Windsor |
| WT | The Winter's Tale |

# 1

# Prejudices against learning: envy, resentment and presumed omniscience

## Wider and narrower concepts of 'learning'

In his *Learning from Experience* the psychoanalyst W. R. Bion wrote, 'If the learner is intolerant of the essential frustration of learning he indulges phantasies of omniscience and a belief in a state where things are known'.[1] In that wider sense of 'learning' all of the prejudices to be considered in this study depend upon a refusal to learn or a failure to learn from experience.[2] Hence Shakespeare's prejudiced characters all espouse and act on baseless convictions that 'things are known'; for that reason the cover of this book reproduces an allegorical painting by Titian bearing a Latin motto translating 'From the experience of the past, the present acts prudently, lest it spoil future actions'.

The present chapter, however, will depart from the wider meaning of the gerund 'learning' where it denotes *any* act of acquiring knowledge (meaning 1.a in OED3), and adopt instead the narrower sense in which learning must involve education or formal study. Thus it will consider the 'learning' that involves knowledge 'acquired by systematic study' (in accord with meaning 3.a in OED3). So, in particular, it will consider Shakespearian representations of prejudices against schooling or its equivalents, or against knowledge acquired through schooling, or against those possessing, seeking or offering education.

This narrower sense of the term 'learning' is implied in all but a couple of the thirty-five appearances of that word in Shakespeare's work. Variants of the lexeme based on 'to learn' appear as well in nearly all of the play-texts and poems in the Oxford Shakespeare,[3] indicating an area of fascination.

Shakespeare's responses to the acquisition and possession of learning were of necessity conditioned by the circumstances of his time. His culture, for instance, took a great interest in 'the new learning', a phrase that referred to humanistic studies of classical literature and philosophy ('learning' 3.b in OED3). Perhaps because education was becoming more widely available than before, Shakespeare frequently presented the possession of elements of that 'new learning' as normative rather than innovative, and as widespread rather than confined to the few. For instance, familiarity with Ovid's poetry is exhibited not only by the pedant Holofernes in *Love's Labour's Lost* (4.2.123–5), but also by the fool Touchstone in *As You Like It* (3.3.5–6) and the servant Tranio in *The Taming of the Shrew* (1.1.33). In *Titus Andronicus* 4.1.42–50 the raped and gruesomely mutilated Lavinia proves her familiarity with the contents of Ovid's *Metamorphoses* when that book is carried in by her schoolboy nephew. In *The Taming of the Shrew* 3.1.28–43 Bianca exchanges wittily coded mistranslations of Ovid's *Heroides* with her tutor, and in *Cymbeline* 2.2.44–6 Giacomo spies on Imogen who is privately reading Ovid's *Metamorphoses*.

Thus Shakespeare's clowns, young women, servants, all sorts, seem to know their classics, conveying a vision of learning that is not, using a modern term, 'elitist'. Indeed, a coterie of fashionably pedantic Renaissance courtiers in *Love's Labour's Lost* who fancy themselves a social, cultural and intellectual elite are first mocked, and then defeated, by far wiser female heads.

It is unlikely that Shakespeare would have directed such witty gestures at only a small part of his audiences, or would have deployed his numerous classical allusions for the benefit of only a few of his readers or spectators. Thus, it seems that Shakespeare assumed his audiences had some learning.

To that I would add that they must also have been aware of resistances to formal learning. The harsh conditions that scholars met in Elizabethan schools may have fed such awareness. Additionally, Shakespeare's capacity to convey what Bion calls the 'essential frustration of learning' probably also underwrites his many portrayals of ambivalences regarding education. Taking into account these and other factors, I will next discuss how education and educators are portrayed both positively and negatively in varied Shakespearian contexts. In particular, I will consider how Shakespeare repeatedly refers to pupils' reluctance to be taught and repeatedly presents their schoolmasters in an ironic or farcical light, although sometimes he reflects on valued and successful interactions between teachers and students, too.

# Shakespeare's depictions of schools and schooling

The words 'school', 'schoolboy', 'schoolmaster' and allied terms appear seventy-one times within thirty-four of the forty-three texts in the second Oxford Shakespeare edition (in 79% of the works). Words belonging to lexemes based on 'pupil', 'pedant', 'teacher' and 'tutor' are also very frequently used. Shakespeare often conveys positive valuations of education or being educated. For instance, being a 'scholar' is viewed positively in twenty-two Shakespearian contexts, as opposed to ambiguously in two contexts and negatively in two more.[4] Thus high praise is offered when a Shakespearian figure is identified as 'a scholar and a soldier', 'a scholar, a statesman and a soldier' or as possessing 'The courtier's, soldier's, scholar's eye, tongue, sword'.[5]

Moreover, the term 'learning' when used to designate an educational acquisition is positively valued in many Shakespearian contexts.[6] An affirmative connection is made as well between 'Degrees in schools' and social cohesion in Ulysses' famous disquisition on 'degree' in *Troilus and Cressida* at 1.3.104. Several of Shakespeare's characters refer to the lasting bonds of friendship they have forged at school, evoking positive images of the social aspects of schooling.[7]

All this may suggest that Shakespeare remembered his school days with gratitude and pleasure, but there is no way to be sure of that. In fact, there is no certainty about as much as the place or duration of Shakespeare's schooling. Some have speculated whether Shakespeare 'had been in his younger years a schoolmaster in the country',[8] or whether he had first encountered the theatrical profession through the intervention of a Stratford schoolmaster,[9] but knowing answers to those questions might not greatly illuminate his widely varied artistic representations of teachers, teaching and learning. For, as always, credit must be given to Shakespeare's extraordinary powers of intuition, imagination and observation.

Nevertheless, it is important to note the high probability (without documentary proof) that Shakespeare received an Elizabethan grammar school education at the King's New School on Church Street in Stratford-upon-Avon. This is supported by several circumstances, including the social position of Shakespeare's artisan/merchant father (who was appointed Chief Alderman of Stratford in the early 1570s), the fact that nearly all of Shakespeare's fellows in his profession were products of Elizabethan grammar schooling, and that the typical grammar school curriculum accounts for many features of Shakespeare's work.[10] On the other hand, there are no signs of Shakespeare having progressed to either of the Universities where records have survived reasonably intact. Thus it is highly likely that Shakespeare acquired his intellectual formation from grammar schooling, and that alone.

It is easy to imagine that young Shakespeare was an apt pupil resembling Olivir's brother who in *As You Like It* 'keeps at school, and report speaks goldenly of his profit' (1.1.5–6). In *Cymbeline* the young Posthumus is said to have been an even brighter pupil who absorbed

> all the learnings that his time
> Could make him the receiver of, which he took
> As we do air, fast as 'twas ministered,
> And in 's spring became a harvest. (1.1.43–6)

Nevertheless, even such a very receptive child might encounter Bion's 'essential frustration of learning'. He might, for example, find school as ego-bruising as did the art historian Michael Baxandall whose memoirs describe a bright student's chagrin at not being the best among his peers.[11] A related possibility is a superior student's discomfort upon learning that they are not as wise as they imagine. As W. R. Bion put it in a 1975 talk:

> the individual person hates housing or developing a new idea, because if you do, it is inevitable that you feel you *should* have got it right the last time. The inevitable discovery that you have been mistaken is a dreadful thing to discover. It also carries with it the feeling that if your own ideas change, then all the problems that you have ever solved are re-opened because they have a relationship of things-not-oneself with oneself.[12]

Conversely, a less talented student for whom lessons are baffling will experience painful befuddlement, humiliation and frustration. Thus, although other readings have been offered, the frustration and resultant rage of an inept pupil may also be implied when Miranda recalls how she 'taught thee each hour / One thing or other' and Caliban replies, 'You taught me language, and my profit on 't / Is I know how to curse. The red plague rid you / For learning me your language!' (*The Tempest* 1.2.356–7, 365–7).

Additionally, on a level applicable to all learners, W. R. Bion describes widespread vicissitudes of the 'impulse to be curious on which all learning depends', and also the problem that any communication of new ideas 'may arouse feelings of persecution in the receptors of the communication'.[13]

The young Shakespeare would have met with very long study days at his grammar school, and harsh demands made on his attention and retention. He also most probably witnessed threats of corporal punishment and the meting out of it, perhaps experiencing such punishment himself. The beating of schoolboys was evidently widespread, as is indicated, for example, in the quip made by Benedick in *Much Ado About Nothing* that the Count is 'worthy to be whipped [for] … The flat transgression of a schoolboy' (2.1.206–8). A similar metaphor is used by the Queen in *Richard II* when she chides her husband that he will 'pupil-like / Take correction, mildly kiss the rod' (5.1.31–2). Falstaff of *The Merry Wives of Windsor* also recalls being beaten when a schoolboy: 'Since I plucked geese, played truant, and whipped top, I knew not what 'twas to be beaten till lately' (5.1.24–6). Moreover, when the schoolmaster Gerald in *The Two Noble Kinsmen* introduces himself as 'I, that am the rectifier of all, / By title *pedagogus*, that let fall / The birch upon the breeches of the small ones, / And humble with a ferula the tall ones' (3.5.111–13) he unashamedly states that he beats his charges.

Roger Ascham's famous 1570 treatise *The Schoolmaster* conversely recommends educational methods based on gentleness, patience, cheerfulness, kindness and an atmosphere of play. This book begins by recounting a debate following 'newes brought … that diuerse Scholers of Eaton, be runne awie from Schole, for feare of beating'.[14] That introduces Ascham's own view that 'yong children, were soner allured by loue, than driuen by beating, to atteyne good learning' (B2r). Ascham later describes merely sadistic child beating (C4r–v):

> whan the scholemaster is angrie with some other matter, then will he sonest faul to beate his scholer: and though he him selfe should be punished for his folie, yet must he beate some scholer for his pleasure: though there be no cause for him to do so, nor yet fault in the scholer to deserue so. These ye will say, be fond scholemasters, and fewe they be, that be found to be soch. They be fond in deede, but surelie ouermany soch be found everie where.

Although Ascham reports that 'ouermany' did not, some Elizabethan schoolmasters are known to have adopted the advice of Erasmus, Vives and Ascham himself to rely on persuasion rather than resorting to inflicting physical pain.[15] It is not known if Shakespeare's teachers were of one sort or the other, but is certain that when he became a poet he consistently evidenced a despising of cruelty, especially to children.

Yet, despite its possible tedium or terrors, young Shakespeare's own schooling gave the future author access to a wealth of learning from which he greatly profited. Thus a boy whose father probably could not write his own name acquired a lifelong fascination with literature and learning that shines through all of his works.

Shakespeare's remarkable generation of poets and playwrights included many who had no more than middling-class backgrounds, and almost all of those attended an Elizabethan grammar school. These included Spenser, Peele, Greene, Lodge, Kyd, Daniel, Marlowe, Jonson, Heywood, Marston, Webster, Middleton and almost certainly Dekker.[16]

Helen Hackett's assessment of the impact of the rigorous, strenuous and regimented grammar school regime on such an extraordinary cohort of Elizabethan writers concludes:

> Forms of psychological damage inflicted at school might have been paradoxically productive of great writing; and

the repressive and tedious aspects of Elizabethan pedagogy might have created habits of resistance and 'swerving' that were also conducive to later literary originality. Thinking about just what it was that happened in the Elizabethan classroom, and the various processes by which this might have been connected to the later literary achievements of former grammar-school pupils, highlights the extreme complexity of the relations between education and creativity in general, a continuing issue for us today.[17]

This complexity may help explain why Shakespeare often reflected somewhat wryly on the pains and absurdities of being educated.

I say pains *and absurdities* because there were not only uncomfortable rigours, but also unconscionable rigidities in the schooling experienced by, and later depicted by, Shakespeare. Collin Burrow has argued intriguingly that the latter may have served Shakespeare well when he became an author:

> there were a number of failings, both practical and theoretical, in how Shakespeare was trained to read the classics in his early years, and, oddly enough, those failings were part of what made his later responses to his reading so powerful. Emrys Jones is correct to say that 'Without humanism ... there could have been no Elizabethan literature: without Erasmus, no Shakespeare'; but ... the quirks of and failings within humanist methods of responding to the classics mattered for Shakespeare as much as, or perhaps more than, their successes.[18]

Thus Burrow suggests that Shakespeare 'learned as much from the failings of his masters, and from the unintended consequences of the way they taught, as from their successes' (24). If so, this might help account for the very peculiar mixture of gratitude tempered by scepticism that informs many of Shakespeare's depictions of schoolmasters.

Shakespeare's powers of observation prompted acute portrayals of children, and thus he describes schoolboys who prefer to have time to themselves and the wide outdoors for their playground rather than be cooped up in a classroom for long hours. A vivid portrayal of their type is heard in Jaques' 'seven ages of man' speech in *As You Like It*:

Then the whining schoolboy with his satchel
And shining morning face, creeping like snail
Unwillingly to school. (2.7.145–7)

The boy's whining and creeping indicate his reluctance to arrive at school, while his shining face may indicate not only that his face has just been washed, but also his wish to spend the fresh morning outdoors, or anywhere else away from the narrow and demanding schoolroom. The latter is all the more likely if Shakespeare had a model in mind of the 'tiny school ... crammed into an upstairs room in the Guildhall in Stratford'.[19]

In another portrayal of reluctance to study, Shakespeare shows a young woman resenting impositions upon her leisure and attention when she is privately tutored. So Bianca in *The Taming of the Shrew* testily defies her suitors disguised as tutors with 'I am no breeching scholar in the schools. / I'll not be tied to hours nor 'pointed times, / But learn my lessons as I please myself' (3.1.18–20). Rebellious or balky scholars are often referred to figuratively by Shakespeare as well. *Romeo and Juliet*, for instance, contains the similes 'Love goes toward love as schoolboys from their books, / But love from love, toward school with heavy looks' (2.1.201–2). Likewise, in *The Taming of the Shrew* Gremio describes his relief in departing from Petruchio's mad wedding in terms of going 'As willingly as e'er I came from school' (3.3.23). In *2 Henry IV* Hastings describes an army 'dispersed' as being 'like a school broke up / Each hurries toward his home and sporting place' (4.1.329–30).[20]

Such images may convey only light-hearted wryness, but a closer look at Jaques' account of the second of his seven ages of man may uncover something deeper. This depends on noting that Jaques' seven life stages are implicitly linked in a chain so that, for instance, the Elizabethan schoolboy seen in the second 'act' will have learned enough about poetic and rhetorical tradition to enable him to become the derivative poetaster of the third 'act', the 'lover, / Sighing like furnace, with a woeful ballad / Made to his mistress' eyebrow' (2.7.147–9).[21] Jaques refers to here how humanist educational pursuits are connected with the creation of callow love lyrics.

Shakespeare illustrates this same theme in *Love's Labour's Lost* when courtiers schooled in the grammar school exercise of *imitatio* (imitation 'in the style of') are transformed (or deformed) into poetical lovers. At first, each of them writes stilted and derivative love lyrics (which will be considered further in Chapters 2 and 5), but near the play's end Biron attempts to repudiate his insincerity, and thus forswears 'the motion of a schoolboy's tongue' (5.2. 403).

Returning to the whining schoolboy of Jaques' second act who becomes the 'Sighing' lover of his third act, I would suggest that this schoolboy evolves in turn from the 'mewling' infant in Jaques' first act. The chain of linkage in Jaques' 'strange, eventful history' (2.7.164) works, I believe, as follows: the schoolboy's bright-faced morning wish to be free from all duties and constraints is associated with the freedoms of infancy. On the other hand, Jaques' image of an 'infant, / Mewling and puking in the nurse's arms' indicates that the first stage in life also entails discomforts and distress. But Shakespeare also several times refers to nurses who are adequate to the task of containing an infant's distress, thus producing a comfortable venue allowing for growth and development.[22] Likewise, adequate schooling and teachers may be able to contain natural difficulties with learning, again allowing for growth and development.

Shakespeare was certainly familiar with the concept of a school as a nursery or Alma Mater (this phrase, meaning 'fostering mother', referred to universities from the fifteenth century, according to OED3). So when young Lucentio reaches Padua intending to pursue 'A course of learning and ingenious studies', he identifies the place as 'fair Padua, nursery of the arts' (*The Taming of the Shrew* 1.1.9, 1.1.2). Vice versa, Shakespeare's Mowbray negatively conflates 'fawn[ing] upon a nurse' with being 'a pupil' (*Richard II* 1.3.164–5). In the same play the Duchess of York identifies a nurse with an educator in her 'if I were thy nurse thy tongue to teach' (5.3.111).

Thus Shakespeare sometimes images excellent educators, although, as will be seen, many of his depictions of teachers are at least mildly satiric. Regarding this, it has been suggested that one 'cannot determine from Shakespeare's comical or serious treatment of individual professional men just how seriously he regarded the professions they represent' because such depictions fell in line with a 'decorum' governing most theatrical treatments of teachers, doctors, lawyers or clerics.[23] Convention therefore may have partly underwritten the more or less mild ridiculing of many of Shakespeare's educationalists. But sometimes Shakespeare's teachers are more complexly depicted, as will be seen next.

# Shakespeare's schoolmasters: ridicule, praise and unconventionality

The misadventures of the would-be exorcist identified as 'a schoolmaster called Pinch' in a stage direction in *The Comedy of Errors* (tln 1321–2) might be due to a convention of ridiculing teachers as well as other professionals, or perhaps to a more serious reaction against superstition.[24] An irreverent view of an authority figure may also inflect the farcical misadventures of the unnamed 'Pedant' who is a stalking horse for Tranio's schemes in *The Taming of the Shrew* 4.2, 4.3, 4.4 and 5.1. Similarly, the carping, Latin-spouting and risibly sententious schoolmaster Gerald in *The Two Noble Kinsmen* pompously lays claim to knowledge of 'learned things' (3.5.14), and yet gains scant respect from the country folk whose Mayday revels he directs in the hope of gaining rewards from the Court (3.5.1–160). Thus one countryman sarcastically identifies Gerald, 'the dainty dominie, the schoolmaster', as a know-all (2.3.41–3).

In another case made more complicated because of probable topical allusions,[25] the bombastic schoolmaster Holofernes is only one among a gallery of wild abusers of Euphuistic constructions and inkhorn terms in *Love's Labour's Lost*. Yet, especially when he presents a stilted theatrical performance, Holofernes tops the others in the absurdity of his posturing. When disguised as tutors, humiliations also rain on the well-born Hortensio and Lucentio in *The Taming of the Shrew*. Thus the pantaloon Hortensio has a lute broken over his head (2.1.148–59), and young Lucentio is self-misled into becoming the successful suitor of the actually shrewish Bianca. Moreover, both of these pretended tutors exhibit anti-teacher prejudices, each remarking that they have degraded themselves socially by occupying a teacher's role. So, Hortensio proclaims that he mimics a mere 'cullion' (4.2.16–20) in his ruse, while Lucentio identifies his assumed identity as that of 'some Florentine, / Some Neapolitan, or meaner man of Pisa' (1.1.202–3). A Folio stage direction backs this up by identifying the fake tutor Cambio as 'Lucentio, in the habit of a meane man' (tln 897 after 2.1.38). Other examples of social disdain for pedants are seen when both Gerald and Holofernes receive sarcastic acclaim from the higher-ups when they present overblown speeches introducing their rehearsed entertainments to assembled courtiers.

Moreover, when Shakespeare's teachers are thrust into political situations that require them to 'speak truth to power', their impact is consistently unsuccessful. Thus Shakespeare's Artemidorus is rudely rebuffed with 'is the fellow mad? ... give place' when he attempts to give Caesar a warning about the conspiracy against him (*Julius Caesar* 3.1.3–12). That is Shakespeare's invention, altering the account in Plutarch's 'Life of Caesar' (65.1) where Artemidorus is identified as a 'teacher of Greek philosophy', and where his missive is accepted (but not read).[26] Similarly, in *Antony and Cleopatra* an unnamed 'schoolmaster' acting as Antony's political emissary to Caesar (3.11.71) is scoffed at in 3.12.2–6[27] on account of his social standing (his role corresponds with that of Plutarch's Euphronius, the tutor to Antony and Cleopatra's children).

Likewise, in *3 Henry VI* the pleas of the young Earl of Rutland's compassionate 'Tutor' are simply ignored when he cries out 'Ah, Clifford, murder not this innocent child / Lest thou be hated both of God and man' (1.3.8–9).

Despite all that, however, the effectiveness of Shakespeare's teachers and the regard extended to them is not always negligible. Several, for instance, are efficient in their secondary roles as arrangers of public theatrical spectacles – just as were a number of actual Tudor schoolmasters.[28] Moreover, Shakespeare's late plays present four extremely highborn characters acting as teachers: these are Pericles and Marina in *Pericles* and Prospero and Miranda in *The Tempest*.[29]

Hiewon Shin proposes a loss of status when Prospero becomes Miranda's tutor: 'For a duke to take on the role of a lowly schoolmaster – a very low-paid, low-status job ... would have been extremely unusual, although the desert-island scenario makes unusual practices necessary to some extent, and the aura of fantasy and fairies should make us cautious about too literal minded a resort to social history'.[30] It should be noted, however, that Shakespeare alludes to a real world social-historical controversy concerning the education of women when Prospero describes the care he has taken to educate Miranda[31]:

Here in this island ...
Have I thy schoolmaster made thee more profit
Than other princes can, that have more time
For vainer hours and tutors not so careful. (1.2.172–5)

This alludes to common Renaissance prejudices,[32] resisted by some, against the education of girls or women. Richard Mulcaster, for instance, advocated the extension of educational opportunities even to 'yong *maidens*',[33] and earlier Sir Thomas More and his humanist circle put this into practice.[34] The pioneering woman-of-letters Margaret Roper, the eldest of More's three very well-educated daughters, produced her first book when she was still in her teens.[35] Its title page shows a young woman reading and surrounded by books (Figure 1.1).

FIGURE 1.1 Title page of Erasmus, *A deuoute treatise vpon the Pater noster, made fyrst in latyn by the moost famous doctour mayster Erasmus Roterodamus, and tourned in to englisshe by a yong vertuous and well lerned gentylwoman of. xix. yere of age*, trans. Margaret More Roper (London: Thomas Berthelet, [1526?]). © British Library Board, C.37.3.6 (1). Image produced by ProQuest as part of *Early English Books Online*. www.proquest.com. Image published with permission of ProQuest. Further reproduction is prohibited without permission.

Elizabethans were also aware of Queen Elizabeth's excellent education under the direction of Roger Ascham,[36] and of the high educational achievements of other privileged Elizabethan women. Shakespeare himself may have followed the literary lead of one of those.[37] Correspondingly, Shakespeare represents many high-spirited and intellectually gifted women, and also depicts fathers providing for the tuition of their daughters. Also, even Shakespeare's most blatantly misogynistic characters, Iago and Thersites, never reproduce the prejudices against female education expressed by some of his contemporaries.

Thus many aspects of the topic of education were evidently important to Shakespeare. However, oddly, only one among all of his many fictional teachers is seen actually teaching a pupil at any length. That one is Sir Hugh Evans, to whom I turn next.

# Shakespeare's tutorial scene

Shakespeare's complex portrayal of Sir Hugh Evans instructing the schoolboy William Page in the 'tutorial' scene 4.1 in the Folio text (only) of *The Merry Wives of Windsor* indicates an intriguing balance between jesting ridicule and sincere appreciation of a purveyor of learning.

In common with other Shakespearian schoolmasters, Evans has a subsidiary role as an organizer of a local theatrical entertainment. Thus he assumes responsibility for 'teach[ing] the children their behaviours' (4.4.66), which is to say rehearsing them in their parts, in preparation for the costumed tormenting of Falstaff at Herne's Oak.

Additionally, and very significantly, Evans has another profession – he is also Windsor's parson. So, in the Folio text of *Merry Wives*, he is ten times called a 'parson' and ten times called a 'priest', and for that reason is thirteen times addressed as *Sir* Hugh Evans, this honorific being attached to clergymen in Shakespeare's time. None of Shakespeare's other schoolteachers, and none among Shakespeare's more than half dozen private tutors,[38] show any signs of having additional priestly professions.

Next I will summarize some complex historical factors involved in Evans's presentation as having this combination of callings.[39] Studies of medieval and early modern English education made by Joan Simon, Jo Ann Moran, Helen M. Jewell and David Cressy refer to several official pronouncements, mainly made before the English Reformation, encouraging clergymen to serve as schoolteachers.[40] However, in reality from the late Middle Ages onwards clergymen teachers were not in the majority and most of the minority of teachers who *were* clergymen were either chantry priests (who no longer featured in England after the Reformation), or else were 'Newly ordained priests and curates [who] frequently took up teaching for a short period before they were preferred to a better paying benefice'.[41] Shakespeare's Sir Hugh Evans fits neither of the above descriptions, for he is not a chantry priest or a non-incumbent priest, but rather the well-established parish priest of Windsor.

Therefore Evans's devotion to teaching the children of his town would be an anomaly even if Shakespeare had intended to indicate an accurate fifteenth-century setting for his play. But in fact (as is characteristic of Shakespeare) *The Merry Wives* contains details defying historical consistency,[42] and moreover many agree that the Windsor in Shakespeare's play closely resembles a late Elizabethan town.[43]

An Elizabethan setting would have made a schoolteacher-priest even more unusual than a fifteenth-century one. In the Elizabethan period priests 'formed only a minority of the teaching force', according to David Cressy. For instance, none of Shakespeare's own likely schoolmasters at the Stratford Grammar School were clergymen.[44] Cressy adds that among that 'distinct minority' most 'were clergy who supplemented their clerical income by teaching, rather than schoolmasters who doubled as priests'.[45] The assertions of Cressy and others that schoolmaster-priests were uncommon in Shakespeare's time, and that most of those were newly ordained priests awaiting preferment, are amply supported by Jay P. Anglin's detailed survey of teachers in Elizabethan London and adjoining counties. Anglin also shows that when those non-incumbents received benefices they usually quit teaching.[46] Anglin concludes that there was a 'numerical preponderance of the laity in the ranks of diocesan schoolmasters' and that there was an Elizabethan 'laicization' of the teaching profession.[47] It therefore appears that the combination in one person of the parish clergyman with a town's schoolmaster would have seemed abnormal in Shakespeare's time, leaving the question of why this is emphasized in *The Merry Wives of Windsor*.

Perhaps an image of the absurdity of a clergyman-teacher explains Maria's rather cryptic allusion in *Twelfth Night* when she remarks on the ludicrousness of Malvolio appearing cross-gartered 'Most villainously, like a pedant that keeps a school i' th' church' (3.2.71–2).[48] Likewise, Evans performing the same two functions in Shakespeare's Windsor may have struck original viewers of *Merry Wives* as laughably peculiar. In any case certain kinds of absurdity do attach to Evans's interaction with his pupil William in Shakespeare's only extended tutorial scene.

This tutorial scene, which is absent from the 1602 and 1619 quartos, does not advance the plot of the play, but it does contribute significantly to its portrayal of Evans. In the play at large Evans is frequently mocked on account of his Welsh pronunciation and locutions, but is otherwise depicted as generally benign, and as intending to serve his community well. So Parson Evans initially attempts to be a peacemaker between the play's antagonists, saying, 'I am of the Church, and will be glad to do my benevolence to make atonements and compromises between you' (1.1.28–30). Later, however, Evans becomes partisan when attempting to promote the marriage of Anne Page to the idiotic but wealthy Slender,[49] and is in consequence challenged to a duel by the irate Doctor Caius (a French 'stranger' in Windsor, where Evans is Welsh). Evans is valiant enough to agree to attend this meeting, but when fearfully awaiting it he cheers himself up by singing his often commented-upon conflation of Marlowe's famous lyric 'Come live with me and be my love' with Psalm 137 (3.1.16–29).[50] This mixture of course undermines the dignity of his clerical status, although his Christian forbearance is redeemed when he later makes peace with Caius.

The tutorial scene arises because, after Evans has suspended Windsor's school for a day, William Page's mother arrives accompanied by her son and Mistress Quickly and asks to hear a sample of William's performance when questioned 'in his accidence' (4.1.11). Evans generously complies with her request, sacrificing part of his own day of freedom. Thus he begins the rote drilling of a reluctant William who has to be told at the start to 'Hold up your head' (4.1.16). Despite this head-hanging, William starts fairly well but, perhaps fatigued by the long solo lesson or perhaps abashed at being asked to perform in front of three adults, he eventually fails to provide the requested 'declensions of your pronouns' and replies, 'Forsooth, I have forgot'. To this Evans responds with a threat of corporal punishment: 'If you forget your [declensions] you must be preeches'. But then kindly Evans quickly retracts this threat to beat William, and rather tells him to 'Go your ways and play; go' (4.1.68–73).

In the most salient aspect of the tutorial scene, the unlettered bystander Mistress Quickly develops a painful sense of her separation from a benign educational encounter. Thus, feeling excluded, Quickly repeatedly attempts to interfere with the Latin grammar lesson, which she hilariously misunderstands. When her ignorant proposals are rejected she is piqued to prejudice, and so speaks wrathfully about the teacher and his mode of education.

Shakespeare's treatment of this motif involves cunning structural arrangements that render it brilliantly comical on several levels.[51] Of greatest significance for the present discussion is that Quickly's first three interjections into William's lesson reveal only her ignorance concerning Latin grammar and vocabulary, but her second trio of interjections introduce increasingly absurd and increasingly obscene misinterpretations of what Evans teaches William. Finally, in the culminating third sally in her second trio of gaffes, Quickly recalls her former ridiculous remarks in order to accuse Evans thus:

> You do ill to teach the child such words. He teaches him to hick and to hack, which they'll do fast enough of themselves, and to call 'whorum'. Fie upon you.
>
> (4.1.59–62)

This hostile attack, a wholly baseless allegation of the teacher's sexual misconduct, signals a sharp anti-educational prejudice.

Alongside her many other malaprop 'Dramatic Quickleyisms', as Barbara Hardy calls them,[52] Quickly's interjections into the tutorial in *The Merry Wives* make it amply clear that she is not one of Shakespeare's women who have benefited from education. The envy of the unlettered may actually be a prevalent if half-buried Shakespearian theme.[53] Certainly, Quickly's envy flares when she feels excluded during a teacher–pupil interaction when her attempted contributions to it are depreciated. Her blunders with a foreign language are not merely comic, as similar ones are in other parallel scenes,[54] but are rather tellingly functional in her play.

So, although she at first seems deaf to repeatedly being asked to desist from interrupting William's lesson both by Evans and by William's education-supportive mother Mistress Page (at 4.1.23, 45, 28, 50 and 4.1.50, 67), Quickly eventually produces the above-quoted accusatory outburst. Until then, although none of Quickly's ignorant suggestions gain concurrence or approbation, she steadfastly persists in offering a string of self-satisfied absurdities. This persistence suggests the mindset in which, as Ronald Britton puts it, 'your desire to believe that you know outweighs your desire to know'.[55] As noted in the Introduction above, the Elizabethan educator Richard Mulcaster held that this is precisely the mindset that typically underwrites prejudice.

Yet another aspect of the tutorial scene in *Merry Wives* relates to the denigration of a particular teacher – and here Shakespeare's comic construction is particularly subtle. In this aspect an at-first almost subliminal implication in the scene at last comes into focus when Quickly asserts that Evans teaches bawdy words to a 'child', concluding 'Fie upon you!'. This vehement accusation provokes no response from Evans other than a reiteration of his comments on her grammatical ignorance, for his sole reply is:

> 'Oman, art thou lunatics? Hast thou no understandings for thy cases, and the numbers of the genders? Thou art as foolish Christian creatures as I would desires.
>
> (4.1.63–6)

Because Evans here wholly fails to note Quickly's explicit accusations of bawdry, audiences are forced to confront the fact that schoolmaster Evans has consistently remained unresponsive to all of Quickly's own prior increasingly bawdy misinterruptions. Here his obliviousness at last becomes so blatant as to arouse a clear suspicion that Evans is wholly unaware of sexuality.

There are other intimations earlier in *The Merry Wives* that suggest the same lack of sexual awareness on the part of Parson Evans. For one, as mentioned, he seems unaware of the sexual content when he conflates Marlowe's famous lyric urging cohabitation, 'Come live with me and be my love', with Psalm 137. His championing of idiotic and seemingly asexual Slender as a match for young Anne Page may have a similar implication. Additionally, a stage direction in the quarto edition of *Merry Wives* mandates that Evans be dressed 'like a Satyre' during the gulling of the seducer Falstaff near the ithyphallic Herne Oak.[56] This costuming of the priest-pedant as a hypersexual 'Satyre' may further suggest ridiculing of Evans's sexual obtuseness.

Evans's blank unresponsiveness to Quickly's cascading bawdy improprieties in the tutorial scene tends to make his character seem ridiculous, thus operating in the mode known as 'derision humour'.[57] But that is not the whole story of Shakespeare's subtle presentation of Evans, for pointing up the sexual 'innocence' of a parson-schoolmaster need not comprise a grand prejudicial slur. It may resemble, rather, a kind of school-boyish japing at 'Sir' who does not get the point of an off-colour joke or remark. Raillery of that sort was probably recognizable by those in Shakespeare's audiences who had experienced Elizabethan school days.

The mild derision of a schoolmaster implicit in *Merry Wives* may mirror as well a certain mode of assuaging 'the essential frustration of learning'. Exposing shortcomings without causing pain thus may resemble using a homeopathic dose of an irritant that can keep at bay the dangers of a poisonous anti-educational prejudice. So, I suggest, Shakespeare's representation of Evans's incomprehension of sexuality aligns with an attitude toward a schoolmaster that is perhaps tinged with disdain, but is still benign. This is an attitude that a slightly resentful yet far more than half-admiring pupil might bear.

Several of Shakespeare's other dramatized educators are presented as ridiculous in behaviour or expression, but the more subtle and complex presentation of the foibles and limitations of his Evans discredits, rather, the wrongheaded anti-educational prejudices of Mistress Quickly. Thus Shakespeare's sole extended depiction of an educator at work mixes some wryness concerning him with a portrayal of kindness and dedication that expresses grateful and affectionate appreciation.

# Shakespeare's Jack Cade's prejudices against learning

Gratitude for education and retrospective affection for one's teachers are, however, not universal. On the contrary, strong prejudices concerning schooling sometimes persist long after an initial adverse experience at school. In consequence, some educated persons may be as liable as uneducated ones to prejudices against learning.

This pattern is shockingly portrayed in *2 Henry VI* where the rebel leader Jack Cade viscerally hates all aspects of teaching or learning. Shakespeare's Cade expresses these prejudices whilst leading a violent rebellion that has been very widely interpreted. However, Shakespeare's Cade's despising of all learning and of the learnèd is not debatable,[58] for he undeniably displays violent spite against any who can read, write, speak foreign languages or those who teach, found schools or provide reading materials.

Cade's spite exceeds even that of the murderous despot Pol Pot, under whose rule 'To avoid being targeted, people did not wear glasses; no one dared speak French; and reading a novel was considered a capital offense'. For, despite that, reading and writing (of the right materials) were actually encouraged in Khmer Rouge Cambodia.[59] Shakespeare's Cade goes much further and would banish all reading and writing.

Shakespeare provides his Jack Cade with a number of characteristics unsupported by historical sources. For instance, his Cade claims to be a Kentishman in *2 Henry VI* 4.9.72–3 but there is no evidence of the birthplace of the historical Cade.[60] Instead the *DNB* suggests that all extant sources are vague about Cade's antecedents, leaving even his true name in doubt.[61]

In addition to allowing his Cade to claim a specific birthplace, history and descent,[62] Shakespeare also supplies details indicating that his Cade has been exposed to a Renaissance education. Those details also suggest that Cade's former school experiences resulted in failure and, as in some instances reported by Roger Ascham,[63] his failure fuelled resentment. (In 1978 the pseudonymous Pol Pot admitted that in 1948 'he had failed the examinations that would have allowed him to pursue a baccalaureate' and 'the following year he was enrolled as a carpentry student'.)[64]

Upon his initial entry Cade vehemently objects to the very existence of written records by declaring that a document written on parchment can 'undo a man'. He adds that 'I did seal once to a thing and was never my own man since' (4.2.79–84). Thus he implies that his hatred of writing derives from an entrapping, irksome and humiliating experience of entering into indentures as an apprentice.[65]

Immediately after Cade expresses this hatred of, especially, legal writing his followers bring in as their captive the unhappy Clerk of Chatham, who 'can make obligations and write court hand' (93–4). The Weaver exclaims that this Clerk 'can read and write and cast account', and Cade replies 'O, monstrous!' (86–8). The outraged Weaver adds, 'We took him setting of boy's copies' (89), indicating that the offence of being an educator compounds that of being literate. This entire sequence (4.2.86–109) ends with Cade's cruel command, 'I say, hang him with his pen and inkhorn about his neck'.

This command is in the mode of a world-turned-upside-down in which possessing ability disables. Accordingly, Cade soon after pronounces the anarchic 'we are in order / When we are most out of order' (4.2.188–9). However, ambiguities arise when in fulminating against Lord Saye Cade links his anti-learning prejudices with allegations of treason against an egalitarian 'commonwealth', thus:

> Fellow-kings, I tell you that that Lord Saye hath gelded the commonwealth, and made it an eunuch, and, more than that, he can speak French, and therefore he is a traitor!
> (4.2.162–5)

Next Cade rationalizes his condemnation of Saye by arguing, 'The Frenchmen are our enemies ... can he that speaks with the tongue of an enemy be a good counsellor or no?' (167–70). These charges are made specific when Lord Saye has been captured by the rebels and Cade asks him: 'What canst thou answer to my majesty for giving up of Normandy unto Monsieur Basimicu, the Dauphin of France?' (4.7.25–7). Here, surprisingly, Cade reveals that he knows French well enough to joke about Monsieur 'kiss-my-arse' (Basimicu). Let me reiterate – Cade jests in French to insult a man condemned to death because he can speak French. This provides an indication that Cade, while championing illiteracy, is himself actually somewhat literate and sophisticated.

Similar incongruities arise when, in his tirades against the educated, Cade merges envious irrationality with rationally framed and rhetorically posed arguments. Cade has, in fact, two modes of address, one wholly irrational and the other semi-rational. In the first mode he plays the blunt tyrant, as when proclaiming specific charges against Lord Saye:

> Be it known unto thee by these presence ... that I am the besom that must sweep the court clean of such filth as thou art. Thou hast most traitorously corrupted the youth of the realm in erecting a grammar school; and, whereas before, our forefathers had no other books but the score and the tally, thou hast caused printing to be used and, contrary to the King his crown and dignity, thou hast built a paper-mill. It will be proved to thy face that thou hast men about thee that usually talk of a noun and a verb and such abominable words as no Christian ear can endure to hear.
>
> (4.7.27–38)

This announces that disseminating knowledge, founding schools or even sourcing materials for book manufacture are abominable offences. Here Cade displays raw prejudices untethered to political rationalizations and unmediated by rhetorical or ironic flourishes. Yet even here a distinction should be noted between Cade's scornful *awareness* of the concepts of 'a noun and a verb' and semi-comical Quickly's full ignorance of all grammatical categories. Hence even here brutal Cade betrays having experienced some education.

Cade's accusation that Lord Saye has promoted printing rests on a typical Shakespearian anachronism, for at the time of Cade's rebellion, in 1450, the first English printing presses had not yet been set up. Despite lapses, however, Shakespeare's construction of Cade is richly and sadly life-like. For instance, again presenting a half-educated demagogue with anti-intellectual prejudices, Cade mixes an attack on a real inequality in a legal system mixed with envy-laced allegations of privilege:

CADE
> Thou hast appointed justices of peace to call poor men before them about matters they were not able to answer. Moreover, thou hast put them in prison, and, because they could not read, thou hast hanged them when indeed only for that cause they have been most worthy to live. Thou dost ride on a foot-cloth, dost thou not?

SAYE
> What of that?

CADE
> Marry, thou ought'st not to let thy horse wear a cloak when honester men than thou go in their hose and doublets.

(4.7.38–48)

Cade's first two sentences refer to the 'benefit of clergy' whereby a criminally accused Elizabethan capable of reading aloud a 'neck verse' written in Latin could have their trial transferred to the Church Courts that could not impose capital punishment.[66] So far so genuine, but after mentioning this legal distinction between educated and uneducated persons Cade slides seamlessly into irrationality. Thus he asserts that illiteracy renders a person '*most* worthy to live', thereby reversing the inequality he complains about, and next he adds a non-sequitur equating certain men with animals, giving vent to trivial material envy.

Lord Saye finally attempts a plea for mercy, addressing Cade's followers as 'You men of Kent' and then quoting Julius Caesar's praises of Kent in his *Commentaries*. Before paraphrasing Caesar's remarks on the civility of this region in English Saye first pronounces the Latin tag: '*bona terra, mala gens*' (4.7.51–73). Not surprisingly, this address fails to win the unlettered Kentish rebels over, but it does make a strong and revealing impression on Cade, for in the Folio text of the play Cade replies to this plea for clemency with, 'Away with him, away with him, he speaks Latine' (tln 2690–1).

The quarto version of the play prints a more pungent collective response to Saye's Latin:

CADE
*Bonum terrum* – zounds, what's that?
BUTCHER
He speaks French.
FIRST REBEL
No, 'tis Dutch.
SECOND REBEL
No, 'tis Out-talian, I know it well enough.

(4.7.54–7)

Following either version, Cade is next disingenuous when ordering Saye's death, for he admits aside that he was moved by the power and grace of Saye's language. However, the same aside reveals that appreciating Saye's admirable pleading gives Cade an even greater impetus to kill him:

I feel remorse in myself with his words, but I'll bridle it. He shall die an it be but for pleading so well for his life

(4.7.102–4)

This aside reveals Cade's despising of refined verbal abilities, but it also reveals his capacity to recognize and respond to such abilities. This indicates that Cade has an educated ability to appreciate the modes of discourse that he finds despicable. Once again Shakespeare's Cade shows signs of having been exposed, very unhappily, to some elements of an Elizabethan education.

In the terms set out by Richard Mulcaster (discussed in the Introduction), Jack Cade thus partakes of a 'prejudice' that 'is a great fo to a not favored good'. Mulcaster also distinguishes between four causes of negative prejudices: the prejudiced 'person himself', writes Mulcaster, is 'either superficiallie learned, and yet loth to seme so: or enviouslie affected and still carping at his better: or ambitiouslie given and presumeth upon countenance: or he measureth knowledge by gain'. Mulcaster then colourfully expounds that 'All which four causes mean learning glad to make great shew, enuious affection glancing at good things: vane presumption plaing the peicok: covetous desire carelesse of great cunning' (47–8). These 'four causes' may be summarized as pretensions to knowledge, envy, social presumptuousness and greedy desire. All four of these correspond with notable aspects of Cade's prejudices. Thus Cade and his followers are without doubt driven by envy and, as just argued, Cade himself is a 'superficiallie learned' pretender to knowledge. Cade also reveals greedy acquisitiveness for power and sex when he declares (as Lord Saye is dragged away to be beheaded):

> The proudest peer in the realm shall not wear a head on his shoulders unless he pay me tribute. There shall not a maid be married but she shall pay to me her maidenhead, ere they have it. Married men shall hold of me *in capite*. And we charge and command that their wives be as free as heart can wish or tongue can tell.
>
> (4.7.117–20)

Shakespeare's Cade furthermore manifests the 'vane presumption plaing the peicok' when he claims descent from the aristocratic Mortimers and Plantagenets (4.2.40–50, 129–44, 4.6.1).

Although he subsequently addresses his followers as 'Fellow-kings' (4.2.162), Shakespeare's Cade is no democrat when he anticipates that in his future commonwealth all will 'worship me their lord' (4.2.77), and he is correspondingly gratified when one of his followers addresses him as 'your lordship' (4.7.3–4). Moreover, when his erstwhile 'Fellow-kings' waver in following him he promptly calls them 'base peasants' (4.7.175). This raises the question of how far he relies upon collective support to instigate, amplify or bolster his prejudices. Does his adherence to *shared* beliefs correspond with the remark of Ronald Britton that a group may 'substitute concurrence for reality testing, and so shared phantasy can gain the same or even greater status than knowledge'?[67] Cade's certainties do begin to fade when he observes the mob's fickleness (4.7.172–209), which he calls 'base and ignominious treasons' (4.7.218–19). Thereafter he has to flee alone, and he is vanquished when weakened by hunger, being ill-nourished by his beliefs. Cade admits at last that he had harnessed his prejudices to his 'ambitions' (4.9.1), but also, I think, he had allowed the prejudices supporting his beliefs and hopes to 'substitute … for reality testing'.

To sum up, I want to consider the inverse of Cade's attempt to use prejudice to vanquish learning. This is a process described by Richard Mulcaster whereby education may overcome prejudice. So, in his *Elementarie*, Mulcaster asserts that one can 'by auoiding of ignorance auoideth all misliking' and then he praises education 'bycause it is the best mean to auoid generall ignorance, the mother to misliking, and to com by generall knowledge, which is the cause of allowance' (44). So, for Mulcaster, knowledge promotes 'allowance', by which he means something like a minimal tolerance that is converse to prejudicial 'misliking'.

The enmity of prejudice and knowledge is such that either may defeat the other, but in Mulcaster's view more strength lies on the side of knowledge (although considerable cunning lies on the side of prejudice). Thus Mulcaster writes that prejudice is 'a deadlie enemie to knowledge, bycause prejudice must giue place, if knowledge com in place, and therefor that it maie not com, he emploieth all his forces, by all cunning, and all well colored shifts to shoulder it out: a professed so, and so much the shrewder, bycause he supplanteth knowledge vnder the opinion of knowledge' (48).

In Cade's case, I have argued, prejudice 'supplant[s] knowledge under the opinion of knowledge' in someone who is not dull or wholly unlearned, or, as Mulcaster nicely puts it, in someone who has 'no heauie head' (48). However, Isabella in *Measure for Measure* exclaims against 'man, proud man, / Dressed in a little brief authority, / Most ignorant of what he's most assured' (2.2.120–2), expressing the dire view that self-assured ignorance, and therefore prejudice, is a universal human tendency.

Other Shakespearian characters holding self-assured 'opinion[s] of knowledge' denigrate art and artists. These will be the topic of my next chapter.

# 2

# Shakespeare and prejudices against art

## The terms 'art' and 'artist'

With some exceptions where our current more limited usage of the word 'artist' seems to have been anticipated,[1] Elizabethans usually applied the word 'artist' to all sorts of skilled or highly trained practitioners, such as medical practitioners, and called their activities an 'art'.[2] This, however, does not mean that they lacked an appreciation similar to our own of the practitioners and products of the imaginative or expressive 'arts'.

In the Hellenistic-era specification of the Nine Muses those nine sisters included seven who personified various kinds of poetry, drama, music and dance, plus two more (Clio and Urania) personifying History and Astronomy. In one of the over two dozen Shakespearian mentions of the 'muses', Theseus in *A Midsummer Night's Dream* is offered a wedding interlude billed as 'The thrice-three muses mourning for the death / Of learning, late deceased in beggary' (5.1.52–4). This proffered performance evidently featured scholars or the like begging for royal patronage, not imaginative artists.

However, Elizabethans did distinguish between the skilled 'artists' who pursued the likes of philosophy, medicine or astronomy and the providers of the musical, literary, visual or dramatic artworks that they highly prized. The question is whether they thought of those latter sorts of expressive artists as inhabiting a single category.

There are many indications that this was the case. For one among others,[3] Shakespeare and other Renaissance writers relayed a sort of debate that was latterly called a *paragone*. Those *paragoni* were disputations in which proponents of one branch of what *we* call the 'arts' argued for its superiority in excellence compared with one or more other arts. *Paragoni* contestants would pit, for instance, poetry against painting, or painting against sculpture.[4] The interest taken in such discussions implies an acceptance of the comparability of differing arts, and that in turn indicates the comprehension of a category within which various expressive 'arts' could be compared. Hence the very existence of *paragoni* points towards a category we would call 'art', and moreover indicates a *positively valued* concept of such art.

This chapter will therefore freely use the terms 'art' and 'artist' when discussing Shakespearian representations of prejudices against artistic culture or the makers or performers of artistic works. It will show that, beyond admiration of what we now call 'art' and 'artists', Shakespeare's works also portray attacks on them.

# Two modes of prejudices against art

Prejudices against art and artists may take the form of active hostility or else of dismissive indifference. The deadly effects of 'indifference', a factor called by T. S. Eliot 'unflowering',[5] may prove more destructive to art and its institutions than explicit hostility expressed through iconoclasm, censorship or suppression. This is because embattled art that defies its enemies (or else wittily circumvents their strictures) demonstrates its seriousness *prima facie*, while art belittled or scornfully degraded may be ignored as irrelevant or jejune.

Illustrating one type of active hostility, Shakespeare's Malvolio priggishly objects to joyous artistic expression. The revellers in *Twelfth Night* then contrive his deserved defeat through ridicule, although mirth may go too far there. With respect to embattled art, Shakespeare in his own artistic practice used indirection or humorous narration to circumvent the dangers inherent in touching on very sensitive subject matters.[6] Although the playwrights Kyd, Marlowe, Jonson, Marston, Middleton, Chapman and Nashe all fell foul of the authorities, cunning Shakespeare never did, showing that suppression and censorship could be dodged.

Shakespeare was concerned about an even more dangerous *indifference* to art and artistic culture when he presented an extended account of historical circumstances in which art-depreciating prejudices accompanied by disruptions of society brought about the demise of a flourishing artistic culture. That dire topic will be treated in detail in the latter part of this chapter, but first I will mention that Shakespeare also treats less destructive types of narrow-minded philistinism. These arise when a number of Shakespearian youths entertain foolish prejudices concerning the supposedly unmanly nature of aesthetic expression. Some of those characters think themselves informed or witty when deriding artistic endeavours, and show preferences for art-deriding *macho* behaviours.

Several such figures will receive extended attention in subsequent chapters of this book in connection with their militarism, chauvinism or misogyny, but for now I will instance one particular Shakespearian youth who exhibits callow prejudices against art, and yet is not so blatantly a swaggering *maschista* as is, for instance, the poetry-deriding Mercutio in *Romeo and Juliet* (2.1.9–10, 2.3.36–41). This figure is the older of the two exiled princes in *Cymbeline* who rejects his younger brother's proposal that they sing the lovely lyric 'Fear no more the heat of the sun' in order to mourn the supposed death of Imogen/Fidele. He squeamishly insists that they rather only 'word' or 'say our song' (4.2.241, 243, 255), and his objection to singing comes on the heels of his scornful comment on the younger one's just-spoken beautiful prose lament for Fidele: 'Prithee, have done, / And do not play in wench-like words with that / Which is so serious' (4.2.219–32). Thus, for him, verbal beauty is effeminizing. These two outdoor-bred youths are martially inclined, as they show when one vanquishes Cloten on sore provocation (4.2.119–23) and then in battle both rescue the King (5.5.1–51), and they are proud of having become recently more 'mannish' in voice (4.2.236–9). As such they present a semi-comic portrayal of male youth complete with anti-art and anti-'wench' prejudices that they will presumably (or hopefully) outgrow.

This maturation, however, does not occur within the scope of the play. Elsewhere Shakespeare's plays do sometimes portray an overcoming of prejudices against art, even by the middling aged. This accords with the general rule that for Shakespeare personal growth is possible at any age.[7] I will next examine two Shakespearian contexts in which post-adolescent learning allows for the overcoming of anti-art prejudices.

# Redeemable prejudices against art

Theseus in *A Midsummer Night's Dream* rejects certain artworks when he selects from among a range of entertainments offered for the celebration of his forthcoming wedding. When he refuses one of those interludes, a presentation of 'The riot of the tipsy bacchanals / Tearing the Thracian singer in their rage' (5.1.48–9), several useful distinctions can be made. Theseus's rejection of this artwork does not resemble Shakespeare's Holofernes' posturing as a would-be connoisseur laying down negative aesthetic opinions (Holofernes promises to entertain a dinner table with this in *Love's Labour's Lost* 4.2.151–7). We are meant only to laugh at Holofernes' vapid literary theorizing, and likewise at the unfounded pretension of the preening figures who gush over 'Julio Romano's' as yet unseen statue in *The Winter's Tale* 5.2.93–102. On the contrary,

Theseus attributes his rejection of the 'bacchanals' interlude solely to a lack of novelty, to the fact that he has already seen it, remarking that 'That is an old device, and it was played / When I from Thebes came last a conqueror' (5.1.35, 48–51).

Shakespeare himself would not have approved of such a novelty-seeking and aesthetics-ignoring dismissal of a theatrical repeat performance. That would have been especially so at the time when he wrote *A Midsummer Night's Dream*, for just about then, in 1594,[8] he also became a 'shareholder' in his theatre company, the Lord Chamberlain's Men. Thus, 'unlike most Elizabethan dramatists',[9] he became the joint owner of the valuable play-scripts used by a repertoire theatre company, and in the light of his investment he must have been very glad that most Elizabethan audiences enjoyed repeat performances.[10]

Repeat performances are mentioned as a selling point, for instance, on the title page of the 1602 quarto, 'A Most pleasaunt and excellent conceited Co-medie, of Syr *Iohn Falstaffe*, and the merrie Wiues of *Windsor* ... By *William Shakespeare*.'[11] Below this and just above the publisher's colophon the title page reads (with my italics added): 'As it hath bene *diuers times* Acted by the right Honorable my Lord Chamberlaines seruants. Both before her Maiestrie, and else-where'.

The wearily knowing tone of Theseus's rejection of an already-seen interlude might provoke a supposition that his unexpected acceptance of the Athenian manual workmen's alternative offer of 'A tedious brief scene of young Pyramus / And his love Thisbe' (5.1.56–76) will make way only for unkind mockery of this script and its performers. Theseus's bride-to-be Hippolyta explicitly expresses such an anxiety, averring, 'I love not to see wretchedness o'ercharged, / And duty in his service perishing' (5.1.85–6). However, Hippolyta's anticipation that the artistic efforts of the 'rude mechanicals' (as Puck calls them in 3.2.9) will be met only with courtly fleering turns out to be unfounded. On the contrary, Theseus first reassures her about this, and in the event enacts an unexpected approval of this artistic effort, as will be detailed below.

Theseus's acceptance of the mechanicals' artistic intentions is especially surprising because, just before commanding the performance of *Pyramus and Thisbe*, he expresses scepticism concerning the imagination generally, saying:

> Such tricks hath strong imagination
> That if it would but apprehend some joy
> It comprehends some bringer of that joy;
> Or in the night, imagining some fear,
> How easy is a bush supposed a bear!
>
> (5.1.18–22)

Earlier in this same famous speech Theseus denigrates the mentality of imagination-wielding poets by bracketing them thus: 'The lunatic, the lover, and the poet / Are of imagination all compact' (5.1.7–8). Theseus's turnaround from dismissing purveyors of imaginative art to defending them represents the overcoming of a prejudice against art.

The transformation of Theseus's attitude to poets is the focus of a recent article in which Donald Carlson holds that Theseus's response to the playlet offered by the manual workers is the key to this change:

> the interlude prompts Theseus to soften his earlier stance on poets. His attitude shifts from dismissive to courteous at least and incipiently charitable at most. To Hippolyta's protest that the mechanicals will embarrass themselves, reminding Theseus that Philostrate has judged that 'they can do nothing in this kind,' Theseus responds, 'The kinder we, to give them thanks for nothing' (5.1.94–95). After seeing the performance, Theseus reveals a changed perspective when he dismisses the wedding party to bed with, ''Tis almost fairy time' (5.1.381). Theseus' imaginative transformation leaves Athens a richer place.
>
> (209)

This seems to me correct, especially since in response to Hippolyta's comment during the mechanicals' play that 'This is the silliest stuff that ever I heard' Theseus offers the insight that 'The best in this kind are but shadows, and the worst are no worse if imagination amend them' (5.1.209–11). That remark conveys Theseus's realization that a crucially important requirement for the proper appreciation of any work of art is the willing contribution of an audience's imaginations, what Ernst Gombrich calls 'the beholder's share'.[12] A realization of this sort signals the overcoming of an initial prejudice against art.

I am, however, dubious of Carlson's allegations that Shakespeare's portrayal of Theseus's changed outlook is part of Shakespeare's reply 'to the recently martyred Jesuit Robert Southwell thoughts about the proper uses of poetry found in the letter prefatory and introductory poem to his posthumous collection *St. Peters Complaint and Other Poems*'.[13] The most impressive detail that Carlson presents to suggest a link between *A Midsummer Night's Dream* and Southwell lies in the similarity of the Jesuit's 'a Poet, a Lover, and a Liar are by many reckoned but three words of one significance' and Shakespeare's 'The lunatic, the lover, and the poet are of imagination all compact'. However, John Clause, who discussed this echo before Carlson did (which Carlson acknowledges), explains that Shakespeare's idea here is 'not quite a perfect match' for Southwell's,[14] and Carlson agrees (198).

Indeed, Shakespeare's and Southwell's sentences contain similar tricolons, but on the semantic level the admonitions made by the Catholic Southwell against sensual love poetry (as opposed to religious poetry) do not at all resemble Shakespeare's Theseus's much broader disparagement of imagination. In fact, Carlson's claimed 'conversation' between *A Midsummer Night's Dream* and the views of 'the recently martyred' Southwell involves a *disjunction* between Southwell's admonitions against erotic poetry and the play's supposed celebration of a 'wonderworld of charm, pardon, and promise'[15] that allegedly existed in medieval Catholic piety.

Carlson's main claim is that by Shakespeare's time such charm had been dissipated thanks to the narrowness of first

Marian Catholicism and then Elizabethan Protestantism. So, according to him, *A Midsummer Night's Dream* reflects the sad loss of an idyllic rural, traditional and ceremonial past. Carlson further claims that pre-Reformation English culture resolved the divisions between 'the secular and spiritual', 'sanctity and festivity', 'prayerfulness' and 'playfulness', 'imaginative exuberance' and 'religious devotion', 'love' and 'conflict', and related antinomies (199, 202–6). This, he says, was spoiled by the narrowness of Protestantism and the Counter-Reformation. However, this interpretation comes up against contrary historical facts. For one, as C. L. Barber's *Shakespeare's Festive Comedy* establishes, England continued to enjoy its traditional popular pastimes and merry festivities long after the split with Rome.[16] Additionally, the English poetic flowering in 'the age of Gower and Chaucer', which is extolled by Carlson as symptomatic of pre-Marian Catholic culture (211), faded more than a hundred years before the English Reformation (that decline will be discussed at length later in this chapter).

Aside from these historical incongruities, Carlson's view that in *A Midsummer Night's Dream* the 'lovers' and mechanicals' entrance into the forest' resembles an enlightening 'mystical experience' (206) overlooks the multiple frightening and discordant elements actually met in the Athenian green world. Even G. K. Chesterton, who holds that the 'sentiment' of this play 'is the mysticism of happiness', admits that 'The events in the wandering wood are in themselves, and regarded as in broad daylight, not merely melancholy but bitterly cruel and ignominious'.[17] This is true: the desperate and ignominious discords of the ill-sorted and estranged couple Queen Titania and King Oberon are reflected in natural disasters (2.1.88–117), while Robin Goodfellow's mischief sows betrayal of friendship, pain and humiliation among the lovers. Worse still, Puck's blessing in 5.2.33–5 on the play's 'best bride bed' (that 'the issue there create / Ever shall be fortunate') sits very strangely with the disastrous future of the 'issue' of Theseus's and Hippolita's union, their miserably fated son Hippolytus.

On the other hand, Chesterton and others[18] have identified aspects of the forest sojourns in the play that are relatively benign. So Chesterton's comment continues with 'yet by the spreading of an atmosphere as magic as the fog of Puck, Shakespeare contrives to make the whole matter mysteriously hilarious while it is palpably tragic, and mysteriously charitable, while it is in itself cynical'. Donald Carlson goes much further and contends that something remarkably positive comes about in Shakespeare's Athenian forest when, as a result of his visit there, Theseus's prejudicial rejections of art and imagination are reformed and reversed. I agree with his claim that the impact of the forest is beneficent when it leads to Theseus's appreciation of the mechanicals' play, contrived and rehearsed in the forest. I agree, that is, if Carlson's contention is stripped of his idealization of 'the imaginal life of the old faith, a life conducive to poetry and sympathetic to poets, unlike the extreme camps of either the Reformation or the Counter-Reformation' (211). Then I would wholly endorse one of Carlson's key insights, his perception that 'the Pyramus and Thisbe interlude illustrates how even badly executed poetry and drama can channel grace to its audience' (208). However, in my opinion, the 'grace' in question does not derive from Carlson's 'bygone age' of medieval Catholicism and Shakespeare's creation of 'a fictional world that evokes the spirit of that age' (202), but derives rather from the revitalization of stultified, conventionalized and timeworn artistic modes resulting from an infusion of popular artistic gestures and genres. Those derive from a living *current* culture, perhaps following tradition but not basically either antiquarian or nostalgic in orientation.

Theseus is only one among several Shakespearian upper echelon characters who reject fashionably sophisticated styles of art that have become unsatisfying or irksome. In Theseus's case distaste is reversed when the art he encounters sets sail for wilder shores – not wilder in the sense of far-fetched, but rather in the sense of touching on the refreshing power of the vernacular. Count Orsino in *Twelfth Night* numbers among others who seek similar refreshment. Orsino is first seen luxuriating in the pumped-up conventional emotions of an unsatisfied lover, but surfeiting on this cliché he soon finds that the sorrowful music he has requested is cloying and 'not so sweet now' (1.1.8). Later, in the presence of his true future love as yet unrecognized, he asks Feste for a rendition of

> the song we had last night.
> Mark it, Cesario, it is old and plain.
> The spinsters, and the knitters in the sun,
> And the free maids that weave their thread with bones,
> Do use to chant it. It is silly sooth,
> And dallies with the innocence of love,
> Like the old age. (2.4.41–7)

This encounter suggests the power of folk-like artwork to rekindle a jaded nobleman's enjoyment of art. Hence a prejudicial *mislike* is disrupted when art breaks barriers of status and taste.

A pattern of aristocrats refreshed by contact with popular culture corresponds with how, in the pastoral literary mode, taking recourse to the art-filled cultures of country folk revives those whose sophisticated lives fail to satisfy or nurture their needs. That very well-studied literary mode, adopted from the classics, was of course repeatedly and knowingly inserted into Elizabethan poetry and drama.

In the pastoral mode or otherwise, Shakespeare frequently shows narrow frigidity melting when meeting with the artistic operations of what William Empson calls 'a community more various, rambunctious, popular, and contrary'.[19] But in their Shakespearian representations such encounters may be only temporarily charming, rather than productive of lasting transformations. For instance, an encounter with art-filled folkways only transiently charms the disguised courtier and King who visit the sheep-shearing festival in *The Winter's Tale* 4.4. Thus this scene concludes with the King's destructive threats to the pastoral lovers and the courtier's selfishly attempted exploitation of them. Viewing the Morris-dancing in scene 3.5 of *The Two Noble Kinsmen* equally only transiently affects Arcite, who immediately after arranges the play's 'honourable' deadly duel. Hearing a popular 'three mens song' in *Twelfth Night* 2.3 does not at all ease the art-despising prejudices of Malvolio, but on the contrary enflames them.[20]

However, other Shakespeare characters do overcome anti-art prejudices, recognizing them to have been wrongheaded. For instance, Lord Biron in *Love's Labour's Lost* falls in love reluctantly, and expresses humorously exaggerated objections to associated modish artistic styles (3.1.169–200). So, disparaging the poetic and emotional posturing of the conventional suffering lover, Biron accuses 'Dan Cupid' of being the 'Regent of love-rhymes, lord of folded arms' (3.1.176). Here he scorns the same conventions that Mercutio mocks in 'Now [Romeo] is for the numbers that Petrarch flowed in' (*Romeo and Juliet* 2.3.36–7). Once smitten, however, Biron attempts to become a Petrarchan lover-poet. Finally, he repudiates his own stale artistic attempts, and in doing so achieves far greater eloquence than he had ever managed before. So he renounces his former uses of:

> Taffeta phrases, silken terms precise,
> Three-piled hyperboles, spruce affectation,
> Figures pedantical
>
> – (5.2.406–8)

and admits 'these summer flies / Have blown me full of maggot ostentation'. He continues:

> I do forswear them, and I here protest,
> By this white glove – how white the hand, God knows! –
> Henceforth my wooing mind shall be expressed
> In russet yeas, and honest kersey noes.
> And to begin, wench, so God help me, law!
> My love to thee is sound, sans crack or flaw.
>
> (5.2.408–15)

As in the movement in his earlier metaphors from taffeta and silk to russet and kersey, so his diction here progresses towards the simplicity of his monosyllabic line 'My love to thee is sound, sans crack or flaw'. But there are two verbal jokes in this passage. One is that while pretending to 'speak broad' – that is with the countrified diction seen in 'God help me, law!' – Biron lapses into the use of the French word 'sans' (witty Rosaline promptly calls him up on that). The other is that Biron's just prior line, 'By this white glove – how white the hand, God knows!' (5.2.411), although also monosyllabic is still exceedingly refined in expression, and thereby conveys something like erotic awe.[21] This is partly due to superb vowel variety and harmony, but in addition to its excellent poetic diction this line stands out by not being drawn from the stale storehouse of tried and tested Petrarchan tropes and flourishes. Instead, being purged of affection, it expresses the lover's un-self-important admiration of the beloved.

Despite its simplicity, this line is to my hearing the loveliest verse line heard in a play-script that is filled with both embedded and exhibited poetry.[22] Its true lyricism framed by self-depreciating humour chimes with the overcoming of a prejudice against artistic endeavours.

# Irredeemable prejudices against art

The remainder of this chapter will explore prejudices against art portrayed by Shakespeare that arise in brutal and strife-filled settings in which art is not just undervalued, but is actually dismissed as if it had no value at all. These prejudices and those settings are represented by him as irredeemably destructive to artists and artistic culture.

Shakespeare's *Julius Caesar* contains two such instances of destructive prejudices. In the first a poet named Cinna is done to death by the bloodthirsty Roman mob simply because his name is the same as that of one of the conspirators against

Caesar. It is of no avail that he repeats 'I am Cinna the poet, I am Cinna the poet' and 'I am not Cinna the conspirator', for a braying prejudice emerges when a plebeian interposes 'Tear him for his bad verses, tear him for his bad verses' (3.3 29–32). This conveys macabre humour, but also indicates that at a time of civil unrest language (in the form of naming) has been stripped of meaning, having been degraded into slogans.[23]

Secondly, in *Julius Caesar* 4.2.178–90 a character repeatedly identified in the Folio's paratext as 'a Poet' is dismissed and derided when he attempts to become a truce-maker between the squabbling conspirators Cassius and Brutus. Prejudice against art is evident when Cassius mocks this Poet's quotation from Homer's *Iliad* with 'Ha! ha! How vilely doth this cynic rhyme',[24] and Brutus adds, revealing a militaristic prejudice against art, 'What should the wars do with these jigging fools?' (4.3.185–9). My next chapter will show that Shakespeare indicates how prejudices against peace and peace-making can become deadly, but here in *Julius Caesar* the unnamed peace-making poet is only humiliated, not done to death. However, (speaking, as Rosalind says in 2.4.53, 'wiser than thou art ware of') Touchstone in *As You Like It* remarks that 'When a man's verses cannot be understood ... it strikes a man more dead than a great reckoning in a little room' (3.3.9–12).[25] The great Elizabethan miniaturist Nicholas Hilliard likewise claimed that the dismissals of artistic work in times of political turmoil may be death-like, so if a talented painter 'live in time of trouble, and under savage government wherein arts be not esteemed ... woe be unto him as unto an untimely death'.[26]

So power politics, mob violence and a great-man mentality arising at a time of civil and political turmoil in *Julius Caesar* result in what may be called the 'dismissive oppression' of two poets. I do not think the scorn that they heap on the 'Poet' is meant to imply that Brutus or Cassius are unlettered or naturally boorish, but rather that their engagement with political struggles causes them to regard art as unworthy of serious attention.

The individual identities of the two poets met in *Julius Caesar*, the one martyred and the one mocked, hardly shine forth, but the dismissal of poetic art is given a human face or faces in Shakespeare's second history tetralogy. Those plays, beginning with *Richard II*, reveal with great subtlety the prejudicial oppression of poets or symbolic representatives of poetry in times of civil turmoil.

## An overview on Shakespeare's *Richard II* and prejudices against art

It will be argued next that Shakespeare's contemporaries associated the deposition of King Richard II and ensuing political instability with the demise of what is now termed 'Ricardian poetry'.[27] Additionally, the long-lasting decline in the quality of English poetry after 1400 may have reminded late Elizabethans of threats arising in their own political and cultural situations in the 1590s.

To investigate these claims I will consider Elizabethan and later views of Richard II's realm and of a decline in artistic culture following Richard's usurpation. I will also examine the possibility that Shakespeare intended his Richard II to resemble a poet-king. My argument will conclude that Shakespeare's second tetralogy not only depicts destructive cultural losses but also suggests that those who prejudicially dismiss artistic expression will become joylessly self-destructive.

## Elizabethan understandings and modern views of Ricardian culture

Richard II's magnificence, elegance and taste would have been immediately visible to Elizabethans who viewed, for example, the architectural and artistic splendours of Richard's rebuilt Westminster Hall (often visited because it housed England's three major law courts), Richard's self-designed grand tomb in Westminster Abbey or Richard's many portraits and other surviving artefacts. However, the cultural achievement of Richard's time most noted by Shakespeare's contemporaries was its poetry.

Although Elizabethans were cognizant of artistic flourishing in the Ricardian period, later opinions have differed widely as to the motives and actual extent of Richard's artistic interests. A brief survey of some modern scholars' widely conflicting views of Richard II's involvement with art or artists will be useful here to indicate polarities between which more nuanced Elizabethan outlooks may have rested.[28]

In his 1941 biography Anthony Steel claims that Richard II 'was undoubtedly himself a connoisseur of buildings, sculpture, painting, books and music, as well as of plate, jewellery, and dress; there is on record plentiful if scattered evidence of these tastes which has never been put together'.[29] Since then many scholars have diligently 'put together' much evidence of Richard's tastes[30] but this has not produced a consensus regarding his commitment to the arts. Rather, a polarization of views has emerged. Before the 1980s most scholars agreed that Richard II presided over a court dedicated to the arts, and especially the art of poetry. For instance, in 1949 Joan Evans wrote that 'Under [Richard's] leadership all the arts of England enter upon a phase of fruition', in 1971 Margaret Aston found Richard II 'a discriminating patron of the arts', and in 1971 J. Taylor wrote that Richard's court was a 'notable centre of the arts, the most notable perhaps since the court of Eleanor of Aquitaine'.[31] In 1968 Gervaise Mathew also lauded Ricardian literary and artistic achievements, and noted especially the rise in his age of an idea 'of the poet in contrast to an earlier medieval conception of the versifying minstrel', linking that with new international notions of the poet as 'essentially a learned man'.[32]

However, at a 1981 conference resulting in a 1983 collection of essays such views were so strongly challenged that Michael Bennett suggested that 'The scholars who assembled at the ... Research Society symposium in Bristol in 1981 came close to staging a second deposition of the king'.[33] In the Introduction to this essay collection one of the editors, J. W. Sherborne, roundly denies any 'great claims ... made for the personal culture of Richard II and that of his court'.[34] The collection's other editor, V. J. Scattergood, offers reasons for caution in making such absolute historical claims,[35] and later remarks:

> There does, however, appear to have been a good deal of literature of one sort or another, religious and secular, old and new, in Latin and in the vernaculars, circulating in and around the court of Richard II. Though there is little evidence of widespread patronage, the circumstances for the production and dissemination of literature were obviously not unfavourable.
>
> (41)

Nonetheless, Scattergood expresses doubt that Richard II was 'at the centre of a literary court culture based on the English language' (30).

After this collection appeared other critics inclined in diverse ways, with some still expressing great admiration for a literary culture 'based on the English language' promoted by Richard II. For instance, in 1992 Michael Bennett found it:

> at once exhilarating and humbling to reflect on the England of Richard II, a country of only two million inhabitants, but with Chaucer, Gower, Langland and the *Gawain*-poet all at the height of their literary powers ... the poets of this time were responsible for a cultural revolution, so enlarging the capacities and enhancing the status of the English language as to accomplish a vital breakthrough or, perhaps even more remarkable, a number of parallel breakthroughs to vernacular eloquence.[36]

Bennett adds that 'In seeking to explain the "rise of English" as a literary language ... it would be most unwise to leave the royal court [of Richard] out of the account' (7), and that: 'If a man can be known by the company he keeps, Richard can certainly be regarded as a man of literary tastes ... [for he] seems to have been close to a number of younger courtiers with known literary interests, most notably Sir John Montagu, Earl of Salisbury, and Sir John Clanvowe' (10).

Bennett admits that 'evidence for a connection between the court of Richard II and the *Gawain*-poet is highly circumstantial' and that 'The lack of documentation of the king's patronage to Chaucer in his capacity as a poet is also a problem' (4), but he has an explanation for this scarcity of documentation, which is that in 'the wake of the Lancastrian usurpation, many items associated with Richard II and his court have disappeared' (15). So Bennett concludes:

> If the deposition and death [of Richard II] were responsible for the breakup of the remarkable coterie of courtiers that had been the primary audience for Chaucer's verse, for the ending of that eccentric flow of patronage that was probably the frame for the finest works of the alliterative revival, it would explain a great deal about the sudden ending of England's first 'golden age' of literature.
>
> (16)

This alleged cultural breakdown will be considered next.

## Views of the 'sudden ending of England's first "golden age" of literature'

It is easy to establish Shakespeare's awareness of that 'first golden age' of English poetry. He was certainly aware of Chaucer's work, which appeared in multiple Tudor editions up to 1602,[37] and he of course also employed John Gower as a source for and as the narrator of *Pericles*. Shakespeare may have felt a special kinship with Gower and Chaucer because both of those Ricardian poets championed civilian ideals over a contrasting militaristic-chivalric ethos. Thus it has been argued that Chaucer's opposition to chivalric fighting infuses Shakespeare's collaborative play *The Two Noble Kinsman* (which takes its plot from Chaucer's 'Knight's Tale'),[38] and this would accord with my view, to be examined in Chapter 4, below, that Shakespeare was averse to a violent cult of masculine 'honour'.

Slightly more problematic is Elizabethan awareness of four anonymous poetic masterpieces that several scholars have argued stood in a peculiarly close relation to Richard II and his court.[39] These four poems, *Sir Gawain and the Green Knight*, *Pearl*, *Cleanness* and *Patience*, are possibly by the same author. They survive in a single manuscript mentioned in a catalogue probably compiled before 1607 by its owner, Henry Savile of Banke.[40] Because Savile moved in circles overlapping with Shakespeare's it is possible that Shakespeare had access to the *Pearl*-poet's works.[41]

In any case, Langland's *Vision of Piers Plowman* was well known to Shakespeare's contemporaries,[42] and it has been claimed that it supplied materials for *Hamlet*.[43] Thus it is evident that Shakespeare appreciated some masterpieces of Ricardian poetry, and indeed adopted materials from some of them.

On the contrary, Shakespeare made very little use of fifteenth-century English poetry.[44] This contrast suggests that he agreed with a number of his contemporaries who held the poetry of the period after Richard's time and before the latter part of the realm of Henry VIII in very low esteem or even unworthy of notice. For instance, the Elizabethan critic usually labelled 'George Puttenham' praises Chaucer highly, then mentions Gower, Lydgate and '*Harding* the Chronicler' with somewhat less enthusiasm, but never mentions any other poet appearing before Sir Thomas Wyatt except 'that nameless who wrote the *Satire* called Piers Plowman and *Skelton*, (I wot not for what great worthines) surnamed the *Poet Laureat*'.[45] Puttenham's enthusiasm soars, however, when describing the Henrician poets '*Henry* Earle of Surrey and Sir *Thomas Wyat*', finding these 'the two chief lanternes of light to all others that haue since employed their pennes vpon English Poesie, their conceits were lofie, their stiles stately, their conueyance cleanely, their termes proper, their meetre sweete and well proportioned, in all imitating very naturally and studiously their Maister *Francis Petrarcha*' (62).

Puttenham's theme is the late emergence, following a long dreary interval, of 'a new company of courtly makers, of whom Sir *Thomas Wyatt* th'elder & *Henry* Earle of Surrey were the two chieftens' (60). He was not alone in finding English poetic excellence in the Ricardian age of Chaucer, and not finding it again before the Tudor period. For instance, Sir Philip Sidney's *Apologie for Poetry* parallels England's '*Gower* and *Chaucer*' with Italy's '*Dante, Boccace*, and *Petrarch*', and then lists other excellent English poets but mentions no writing in the interval between Chaucer's '*Troylus* and *Cresseid*' and 'the Earle of Surries *Lyricks*'.[46] Similarly, in his groundbreaking *Shepheardes Calender* Spenser identifies as his main predecessor 'the olde famous Poete' Chaucer, who had 'excellencie and wonderfull skil in making'.[47] Thus Elizabethan poets and critics alike expressed scant esteem for all the poets between Chaucer and the courtiers of Henry VIII, finding little to praise in 130 years of English poetry.

Numerous modern era literary critics who aim to identify 'literary and aesthetic excellence'[48] agree with the Elizabethans who saw a sharp decline in the quality of English poetry between about 1400 and (in Puttenham's phrase) 'the latter end of [Henry VIII's] raigne'. George Saintsbury, for one, held that there was a 'long dead-season of English poetry, broken chiefly, if not wholly, by poets Scottish rather than English, which lasted through almost the whole of the fifteenth and the first half of the sixteenth centuries'.[49] C. S. Lewis labelled the English poetry written between Chaucer and Wyatt 'bad', 'dull', 'repellent', 'incompetent', 'feeble', even 'rock bottom', and described that interval as a 'real midwinter of our poetry; all smudge, blur, and scribble without a firm line or a clear colour anywhere'.[50] V. de Sola Pinto wrote that 'Poetry as well as learning and the drama awoke as from a long sleep at the court of Henry VIII'.[51] As late as 1980 one critic found 'much that is mechanical and derivative in fifteenth-century lyric verse' because 'verse had become atrophied into mere social gesture, a matter of good form'.[52] So Elizabethan views of Richard's cultural era and its aftermath accorded with more modern critical judgements.

## Bases for imagining Richard II as a poet-king

Robin Headlam Wells argues that Elizabethan England and contemporary Scotland possessed a deeply embedded cultural myth of a poet-sovereign.[53] Wells cites, for example, the 'commendatory sonnets appended to James VI's 1594 *Essayes of a Prentice*' that represent James as 'a poet-prince descended from the gods' (252n33). Certainly, the notion of a poet-monarch would not have seemed outlandish to Shakespeare's contemporaries, for they knew that Queen Elizabeth, her father Henry VIII and her successor-to-be King James VI of Scotland all wrote poetry.[54] Therefore Shakespeare's audiences would have been unsurprised when the King of Navarre in *Love's Labour's Lost* reads out a self-penned sonnet (4.3.25–39), and his courtiers follow suit.

Sonnets by Henry VIII's courtiers initiated the English sonneteering craze and poems by several of them appear in Richard Tottel's tremendously popular anthology *Songs and Sonnets* (which was republished at least ten times between 1557 and 1587). Taking a humorous view of the popularity of this so-called *Tottel's Miscellany*, Shakespeare has idiotic Slender in *The Merry Wives of Windsor* lament not having to hand his 'book of songs and sonnets' when he goes a-wooing (1.1.181–2). Again suggesting the wide impact of the collection, the gravediggers in *Hamlet* sing mangled fragments of a poem by Thomas Lord Vaux also found in *Tottel's Miscellany*.[55] Also, the majority of the lyrics included in Tottel's collection were written by the courtier-poet Sir Thomas Wyatt, and Feste in *Twelfth Night* 4.2.73–80 torments Malvolio by singing snatches of a Wyatt poem (one, however, not collected by Tottel).

Despite such light-hearted gestures, sonneteering was taken very seriously in Shakespeare's era. Thanks to the examples of the stellar courtier-poet Sir Philip Sidney and his followers, Elizabethans could easily accept that an aristocrat would aspire to writing excellent verse. Thus Shakespeare's audiences *could* have imagined Richard II being a poet-king.

In addition, John Bourchier's 1525 English translation of Jean Froissart's eyewitness *Chronicle* has been accounted one of Shakespeare's sources for *Richard II*,[56] and this offers evidence that the historical Richard II took a personal interest in poetry. Thus upon his 1395 return visit to England (where he had spent his 'youthe') Froissart presented of a gift to King Richard in the form of a sumptuous volume containing all the poetry that Froissart had written 'in four and twentie yeres before'.[57] After some misadventures Froissart gained access to the royal presence, whereupon:

Than the kynge desyred to se my booke that I had brought for hym. So he sawe it in his chambre for I had layde it there redy on his bedde. Whanne the Kynge opened it it pleased hym well for it was fayre enlumyned and written and couered with crymson veluet with ten botons of syluer and gylte and Roses of golde in the myddes with two great clapses gylte rychely wrought. Than the kyng demaunded me wherof it treated and I shewed hym howe it treated of maters of loue wherof the kynge was gladde and loked in it and reed it in many places for he coulde speke and rede Frenche very well. And he tooke it to a knyght of his chambre named sir Rycharde Creadon to beare it in to his secrete chambre.

(255v–256r)

Although Froissart's gift fed Richard's famous tastes for ostentatious luxury items,[58] its prompt transportation to a 'secrete chambre' suggests that this book of poems was more valued for its poetic contents than for its display value.[59]

Richard's interest in verse does not prove that he was himself a poet. But neither does the fact that there are no surviving poems definitely written by Richard prove that he did not compose any, because it is known that some Ricardian poetry disappeared during the Lancastrian upheaval.[60] Moreover, scholars comment that Lancastrian supporters expunged or suppressed evidence of Ricardian cultural achievements[61] and evidence exists that Shakespeare would have known of such suppression.[62]

Shakespeare also had access to a text in which Richard II actually compares himself with a great poet. Thus in 1395 Richard designed a magnificent double tomb in Westminster Abbey for himself and his first wife, Anne of Bohemia, which was completed by 1399. Shakespeare reflects awareness that Richard's remains were transferred into it in 1413, for on the eve of Agincourt his King Harry remarks in soliloquy: 'I Richard's body have interred new, / And on it have bestowed more contrite tears / Than from it issued forced drops of blood' (*Henry V* 4.1.292–4). Richard's monument bears an inscription composed by Richard himself (this self-composed epitaph was transcribed and published by William Camden in 1600).[63] Here Richard described himself as: 'tall in body, in his mind he was sage as Homer'. Commenting on Richard likening himself to Homer, Richard Firth Green suggests there is 'even a possibility that Richard II wrote poetry: this at least may be the implication of the epigraph which he commissioned for himself'.[64] In any case it is significant that Richard II compared himself with an arch-poet, rather than say a conquering emperor, and that Shakespeare knew this.

Additionally, Jean Creton's eyewitness chronicle *Histoire du roy d'Angleterre Richard* has been discussed as a source for Shakespeare's *Richard II*,[65] and Rossell Hope Robbins conjectures that in this 'Creton may be reporting the king's actual speech' when he was 'about to be separated from his queen in 1399'.[66] Thus Robbins translates a passage in Creton that he thinks may record or paraphrase French verses made by Richard:

> My mistress and my consort! accursed be the man, little doth he love us, who thus us shamefully separateth two. I am dying of grief because of it. My fair sister, my lady, and my sole desire. Since I am robbed of the pleasure of beholding thee, such pain and affliction oppresseth my whole heart, that oftentimes I am hard upon despair. Alas! Isabel, rightful daughter of France, you were wont to be my joy, my hope, and my consolation; I now see plainly that through the great violence of fortune, which hath slain many a man, I must wrongfully be removed from you. Whereat I often endure at heart so severe a pang that day and night I am in danger of bitter and certain death. And it is no wonder, considering my misfortune, who from such a height have fallen thus low, and lose my joy, my solace, and my consort. I plainly see too that no one maketh a secret of vexing and cheating me; alas! every one attacketh or hateth me; still praised be God in his holy heavens above.
>
> (113–14)

If this passage indeed reflects Richard's own actual verses, then his poetry was exceedingly stiff and formal!

I will return to the question of the style of Ricardian verse, and its connections with the styles of Shakespeare's Richard II, presently. First, however, I need to review some long-running literary-critical debates.

## Debates about Shakespeare's Richard II as poet-king

Debates about Shakespeare's Richard II as a poet-king include William Butler Yeats's angry response in 1901 to what he perceived to be the nineteenth-century Shakespeare criticism's unwarranted disapproval of Shakespeare's aesthetic King Richard. In this riposte Yeats attributes nationalist, militarist, imperialist and racialist motives to commentators on Shakespeare's play who respected only men of action and despised as effete any they found aesthetic or contemplative in orientation.[67] Thus Yeats holds that, 'because every character was to be judged by efficiency in action, [nineteenth-century] Shakespearian criticism became a vulgar worshipper of Success', and in consequence there arose:

> an antithesis, which grew in clearness and violence as the century grew older, between two types, whose representative were Richard II., 'sentimental,' 'weak,' 'selfish,' 'insincere,' and Henry V., 'Shakespeare's only hero.' These books took the same delight in abasing Richard II. that school-boys do in persecuting some boy of fine temperament, who has weak muscles and a distaste for school games. And they had the same admiration for Henry V. that school-boys have for the soldier or sailor hero of a romance in some boy's paper.
> (155–6)

By contrast, Yeats himself greatly prefers Shakespeare's Richard, an aesthetic 'vessel of porcelain',[68] to Shakespeare's victorious King Henry V, a 'vessel of clay' (162–3). Yeats's essay also pours scorn on utilitarian or improving social impulses, suggesting that 'To suppose that Shakespeare preferred the men who deposed his King [Richard II] is to suppose that Shakespeare judged men with the eyes of a Municipal Councillor weighing the merits of a Town Clerk' (159–60). The poet, the dreamer and the saint were for the early Yeats far finer human types than the political animal (although Yeats could be quite political about that).

Yeats's views were more cultural-political than Walter Pater's, for although in 1889 Pater called Shakespeare's Richard II an 'exquisite poet'[69] he did not simply laud aestheticism. Exhibiting his characteristic complexity of attitude, Pater assesses Richard's irenical-poetic temperament rather as analogous to Shakespeare's own: 'With a prescience of the Wars of the Roses, of which his errors were the original cause, it is Richard who best exposes Shakespeare's own constant sentiment concerning war, and especially that sort of civil war which was then recent in English memories' (191). Nevertheless, Pater also refers to Shakespeare's Richard II's 'lax, soft beauty' (193), and takes note of his egoism and carelessness.

Subsequent critical views of Shakespeare's Richard II as an aesthete or poet vary widely. Some tend to see Richard as 'a poet who has unfortunately had kingship thrust upon him',[70] while others harshly condemn his aesthetic leanings. In a striking instance of the latter, one reviewer of Richard Cottrell's 1968–70 production of *Richard II* is pleased that Ian McKellen 'failed to make Richard tragic',[71] because this explodes the 'myth' deriving from an '"exquisite poet" fallacy' that Richard's deposition is a 'tragedy of the sensitive soul'.[72] For this critic Shakespeare's Richard II is not a poetic sensitive soul, but rather an inept, inauthentic and wanton destroyer of order, nation and state. For him, when one of Richard's speeches forms the sestet of a sonnet, this is 'not because Richard is something of a poet but because Shakespeare wishes to point to the artificial stylization Richard adopts in the formulation of his emotions' (41). This continues that Shakespeare's poetic diction in *Richard II* (and also in *Romeo and Juliet*) conveys only the 'deflation of nurtured emotion'. In allied ways other more recent interpretations of Shakespeare's Richard II allow that he indeed has a 'literary temperament with a vengeance',[73] yet despise him because he exercises it despotically 'after the fashion of Nero'.[74]

Commentary on *Richard II* since the 1980s has often been silent or evasive about whether or not Shakespeare meant King Richard to be seen as a poet.[75] Just asking such a question might be felt by some to violate strictures against 'character criticism'. Thankfully, however, resistance to such strictures has prevailed,[76] and critics are once more licensed to regard some Shakespearian characters as if they were rounded figures implying lifelike interiorities and ambiguities. Thus it is possible to imagine Shakespeare's Richard II as a flawed and complex figure who supports, symbolizes and possibly even practices the art of poetry.

## The historical Richard II, Shakespeare's Richard II and Queen Elizabeth I

Shakespeare fictionalized Richard II in a manner that chimes with an Elizabethan perception of analogies between Richard and his time and Elizabeth and hers. Indeed, such analogies are seen as justified by a leading historian of Richard II's age, Nigel Saul. I will therefore survey some of Saul's complex views.

In a 1992 chapter Saul discusses Richard II's new 'civilian' nobility who were also in Chaucer's 'immediate circle' and who 'stood at the center of a vigorous courtly culture'. Saul added that this new civilian, 'service' nobility were literate, administratively competent and 'patrons of art and literature'.[77] Yet in a 1999 chapter Saul holds that 'Though Richard was clearly interested in the imagery and iconography of kingship, he does not on the other hand appear to have been greatly attracted by either literature or learning', and that 'Richard was almost certainly no bibliophile'.[78] In the same chapter Saul makes the debatable claim that Richard II offered 'surprising[ly] little patronage to literature'.[79] Saul's 1997 biography of Richard II seems even more dismissive of the King's literary interests, claiming rather oddly: 'Such evidence as there is suggests that [Richard's] preferred reading was found in the lyrics and romances beloved of the higher nobility; reading, in other words, was for him mainly a recreational pursuit'.[80]

Despite such scepticism, Saul's appraisal of Richard II includes an aspect of great interest here. This is emphasized in Saul's inaugural lecture when he describes Richard's pacifistic ideals and love of ceremony as a 'repackaging of chivalry ... a subtle reordering of chivalric priorities and the placing of greater emphasis than before on display and ritual'.[81] By that means, Saul holds, Richard encouraged 'a more refined and civilized atmosphere at his court: gradually the court's earlier character as a military household was thrown off, and a more prominent role accorded to women and clerks' (19). Thus 'It was now argued that true nobility was to be found less in the practice of arms than in civilized and peaceable pursuits – in learning and manners, and in service to the state' (22).

In his 1997 biography Saul claims that such aspects of Richard's court were not unique to England, and rather matched a broader European 'change in courtly manners and sensibility' in which 'a greater emphasis was placed in court life on the patronage of letters and the arts generally' (346). Saul saw this movement enacted in Richard's court as follows:

> By the middle of the 1380s a new and more lively interest was being taken by the courtiers in letters, and writers like Chaucer and Gower were producing works in a courtly ambience. By Richard's reign the court was shedding the character of a military household; it was evolving into the sophisticated, civilianized, court of the Renaissance.
>
> (334)

Crucially for my purposes, Saul's biography also claims that:

> There can be no doubt that in its main characteristics [Richard II's] court-centred regime differed little from the more lasting one created by the Tudors ... A characteristic of the Tudor, especially the later Tudor, court was its essentially civilian aspect ... there was a cult of good manners; a premium was put on patronage of the arts, and women exercised a civilizing influence on their male colleagues.
>
> (332)

Saul concludes that 'developments in Richard's reign certainly pointed to the shape of things to come' (334).[82]

It will be argued next that Saul's understanding of similarities between the Ricardian and Elizabethan eras matches views also held in Shakespeare's time. Elizabethans were well aware that following Richard II's death without a legitimate heir England suffered the many decades of bloody dynastic struggles that Shakespeare represents in his eight-play *Henriad*. Moreover, in 1595, when *Richard* II first appeared, Queen Elizabeth I neared her grand climacteric or sixty-third year and it became evident that she would die without an heir of her body. For politic reasons Elizabeth refused to nominate a successor, and likewise on account of the 1399 usurpation Richard II could not do so. So late Elizabethans would have perceived analogies in which both the 1390s and the 1590s enjoyed a notable flourishing of civility and the arts, but also both faced the dangers of an unsettled royal succession.[83]

According to an eighteenth-century manuscript, on 4 August 1601 Queen Elizabeth herself expressed anxiety concerning an analogy between her realm and Richard II's. Thus, during a conversation about historical documents with the antiquary William Lambarde, she remarked, 'I am Richard II, know ye not that?'. Lambarde responded, 'Such a wicked imagination was determined and attempted by a most unkind Gent. the most adorned creature that ever your Majesty made', and the Queen replied, 'He that will forget God, will also forget his benefactors; this tragedy was played 40tie times in open streets and houses'.[84] This famous exchange was connected with the legal examination of Augustine Phillips on 18 February 1601 revealing that on 7 February associates of the Earl of Essex had paid the Lord Chamberlain's men (Shakespeare's company) a bonus of 40 shillings in order for a 'play of the deposyng and kyllyng of Kyng Rychard to be played the Saterday next'.[85] That 'Saturday next' was the day before the abortive Essex uprising.

Although it is not certain whether this subsidized performance of Phillips's 'old' and 'long out of use' play was of Shakespeare's *Richard II*, or if it included the deposition scene that is missing from all three editions of Shakespeare's play published before 1608,[86] this anecdote certainly shows that comparisons between Richard II and Elizabeth I were in the air. Indeed, Lily B. Campbell argues at length that 'through the greater part of Elizabeth's reign she was being compared to Richard II'.[87] E. K. Chambers also documents multiple instances illustrating that an 'analogy present to the Elizabethan political imagination' linking King Richard II with Queen Elizabeth was 'Clearly ... familiar'.[88]

That familiar analogy would have brought to mind the deposition of Richard II and ensuing long-lasting civil wars as well as a long lapse in the production of excellent poetry, all of which presented fearful precedents to loyal, peace-loving and culture-loving Elizabethans.

## Shakespeare's Richard II becomes an Elizabethan poet

> ... it is the nature of art, as of human existence, to receive birth, to progress, to become old, and to die. [89]
> 
> Giorgio Vasari, 1555

I will next argue that Shakespeare's Richard II becomes increasingly like an Elizabethan poet throughout his play, and that this would have had a particular impact on Shakespeare's audiences.

A torrent of new writing, reading, manuscript circulation and print publication – as well as the world-beating new achievements in music and drama – indicated the vitality and fruitfulness of Elizabethan culture. However, the Renaissance also recognized cultural mutability as the above fragment from Vasari's Introduction to the first part of his *Lives* indicates. But although artistic movements may have life cycles including birth, growth, maturity and decline, natural senescence differs from assassination. As has already been suggested, Elizabethans knew that the flowering of English poetry in the 'golden age' of Richard II was followed not by growth and then decline, but rather by sudden death, due probably to neglect and devaluation.

As also already mentioned, Shakespeare's contemporaries were aware that the steep decline in the quality of English poetry after 1400 was reversed only long after, in the Tudor period. Tudor poetry generally, however – and even more so the superb poetry of the late Elizabethan age – was unlike the excellent poetry of Richard II's time. Doubly unlike, in fact, because in the late 1590s the Tudor fashion for sonneteering had reached a zenith from which it was about to decline, and at about the same time late Elizabethans developed the remarkable and unprecedented art-song poetics of the English Ayre. Daniel Fischlin writes that the Ayre 'implicitly' cultivates 'the staging of introspection, solitude, and dialogical intimacy', and adds that 'in many ways the ayres embody the notion expressed in Montaigne's essay "Of Solitude" that "you and another are a sufficient theatre one for another, or you to your selfe alone"'.[90] I will next maintain that in a development that is crucial in *Richard II* Shakespeare portrays Richard becoming an Elizabethan-style self-conscious lyricist operating in a theatre of 'himself alone'. In parallel, Richard is increasingly dramatized as searching for a more truthful self-understanding. This quest culminates when, isolated in a prison cell and at last wholly 'alone', Richard consciously strives to become an introspective poet beginning with his workmanlike 'Yet I'll hammer it out' (5.5.5).

Richard clearly exhibits his earlier style when he is informed of a military reversal and he alternates between expressing self-pitying despair and vaunting absurd flourishes such as 'Is not the King's name forty thousand names? / Arm, arm, my name!' (3.2.72–85). This style is somewhat modified, however, when during his forced abdication Richard adopts for his own use Bolingbroke's dismissively intended phrase 'the shadow of your sorrow hath destroyed / The shadow of your face' (referring to an insubstantial image in the mirror Richard has broken). In his reply to this Richard eagerly responds:

> Say that again:
> 'The shadow of my sorrow' – ha, let's see.
> 'Tis very true: my grief lies all within,
> And these external manner of laments
> Are merely shadows to the unseen grief
> That swells with silence in the tortured soul. (4.1.282–8)

Although in this speech, as in much of the play, Richard addresses a public forum from which his egotism takes sustenance, yet here he speaks also of seeking to express that which 'swells' in his interior world.

It might seem otherwise when in both Creton's abovementioned possible recording of an actual poem written by King Richard on parting from his queen and in the corresponding parting speeches in Shakespeare's play (5.1.81–102) the verse is excessively stiff and formal. In both versions it also lacks focus on reality, for neither conveys that Queen Isabelle was only ten years old at the time of the forced separation. Yet Rossell Hope Robbins asserts that there is still a possibility that Creton transcribed or paraphrased Richard's actual speech because Ricardian poets typically:[91]

> resorted to formal poetry in time of extreme gravity; thus Earl Rivers on the eve of his execution in 1483 composed a virelai to Fortune ... George Ashby, a signet clerk, wrote a complaint on being imprisoned in the Fleet in 1463 ... There is nothing improbable in Richard composing a ballade under similar circumstances.

Several other critics also describe Ricardian poets as radically estranged from 'inwardness' by convention when describing personal experiences.[92]

My own contention is that even in the scene of King Richard parting from Queen Isabelle Shakespeare presents Richard's utterances lurching toward becoming more 'Elizabethanized' and therefore less formalized, grandiloquent or attention-seeking than they had been before. I grant that until the last two lines of their final encounter Richard and Isabelle perform a formal duet deploying 'conventional language for publicly expressed grief' (in the words of John Bowers's description of poetic expression in the age of Richard II).[93] However, after pronouncing many frigid parallelisms and overblown hyperboles in chorus with Isabelle Richard finally utters a parting couplet that recants their preceding verbosity: 'We make woe wanton with this fond delay. / Once more, adieu. The rest let sorrow say' (5.1.101–2).

Thus, in common with a gesture concluding several of the best-known Elizabethan sonnets, Richard's couplet at the end of his and Isabelle's long and tedious farewell indicates a sudden reversal of mood.[94] Here also, in accord with a deliberate deployment of plain style that is noted by Richard Strier in a range of late Renaissance English poems,[95] there is a palpable turnaround from overblown gestures to truthful plainness. Moreover, in terms of its topic, Richard's couplet illustrates Inga-Stina Ewbank's remark that 'Most critics agree that *Richard II* is a milestone in Shakespeare's poetic-dramatic development, and that the play – like its poet-hero – is uniquely self-conscious about the power *and* limitations of language'.[96]

Puttenham and Sidney both remark on how the development of intensely self-conscious Tudor poetry was influenced by Petrarch's *Rime Sparse*. That pioneering sonnet sequence was completed in 1374, during Richard II's lifetime, so might Shakespeare's audiences have connected Petrarchan expressiveness with Richard's times? Perhaps not, for Shakespeare's contemporaries knew that English Petrarchanism had to await the latter part of Henry VIII's reign,[97] and was further advanced in Elizabeth's time.[98] Nonetheless Shakespeare's production of Elizabethan-style effects in *Richard II* may have been a gesture intended to link Richard's tragedy with Elizabethan circumstance, for anachronism never seems to deter Shakespeare.

The end of Shakespeare's play shows Richard II self-consciously labouring to forge a style of verse that diverges entirely from conventionalism. Thus Richard is seen straining to find a 'perfited' language, as Puttenham put it, when attempting to describe his grief, beginning with: 'I have been studying how I may compare / This prison where I live unto the world' (5.1.1–66). Here Richard's striving for expressive means diverges from his former modes of expression because he no longer has hopes to alter events or impress others;[99] being sequestered in prison, his 'studying' for expression is driven solely by an internal impetus. Finally the imprisoned Richard comes to a sharp realization of what Ewbank calls language's 'power *and* limitations', for after attempting to encapsulate his situation using a welter of metaphors and images he comes to the stark if belated realization that: 'I wasted time, and now doth time waste me' (5.5.49).[100]

While Shakespeare's Richard II grows into the role of an Elizabethan-like lyric poet, his oppressor Bolingbroke moves in an opposite direction, both emotionally and linguistically. One critic comments that at the start of *Richard II* Bolingbroke's language is enriched rhetorically[101] but, as will next be shown, it is certainly not that near the play's end or in his later Shakespearian appearances. Thus it will next be argued that Bolingbroke's growing taciturnity and bitterness illustrate the destructive impacts on individuals and societies of prejudices against art.

# Decline of language in the second Henriad

Philip Brockbank holds that the diction heard in *The Tragedy of King Richard II* becomes increasingly lifeless and crude after Richard's forced abdication. Thus he compares similar expressions in the two halves of the play, finding that in the earlier portion speeches are richly poetic while when closely parallel circumstances arise in the second portion the language is 'unmusical', we hear only 'laconic ... brevities' and there is a 'poverty of invention'. Hence, according to Brockbank, language use becomes insipid and even 'farcical' under the usurper.[102] In terms of the above suggestions, this decline may be seen to symbolize the cultural decay that afflicts England after the usurpation of King Richard.

The earlier half of Shakespeare's play indeed indicates that high levels of verbal and cultural refinement were prevalent in the court of the actual Richard II. So, upon being exiled, both Mowbray and Bolingbroke lament their losses of a beloved native language and of England's culture, or as Bolingbroke puts it in the quarto text his loss of 'the jewels that I love' (1.3.153–67, A.C. 3–7). Moreover, Bolingbroke's father John of Gaunt counsels his son to imagine himself back in the Ricardian court whilst travelling abroad:

> Suppose the singing birds musicians,
> The grass whereon thou tread'st the presence strewed,
> The flowers fair ladies, and thy steps no more
> Than a delightful measure or a dance.
> (A.C. 21–4, only in the 1597 quarto text)

A supreme irony is that when Bolingbroke returns to England as an invader he initiates a long period of strife that undermines the very culture that he sorely missed when exiled.

In fact, the historical Henry of Derby (Bolingbroke) 'was frequently mentioned as interested in books and music. During the campaign of 1390–91 he had six minstrels in his pay, and in 1392 he also took with him six musicians'.[103] However, the language and gesture in Shakespeare's plays show that *his* Bolingbroke becomes increasingly taciturn and art-resistant as his career progresses. Quantitative observations make this clear. For instance, all of *Richard II* is written in verse while the remainder of the second Henriad, covering a period in which English poetry was in decay, mixes prose with verse. Similarly, Shakespeare's *Richard II* contains 533 rhymes, but the two parts of *Henry IV* contain 39 and 56 and *Henry V* contains 79.[104] References to language also decline in the

Henriad following Richard's death. Correspondingly, the word 'tongue' appears more often in *Richard II* than in any other Shakespeare play, but this frequency is roughly halved in both parts of *Henry IV*, and divided by three in *Henry V*.

Alongside those indicators, Bolingbroke's speech becomes increasingly terse, dull and cautious from the time that he proclaims his kingship in *Richard II* 4.1.103–4. This is not solely because as a king who promises to deliver more efficiency in government than his predecessor he is constrained to practical and business-like speech, but also, I think, Bolingbroke's new brusqueness indicates that he is abashed by and hoping to get away with saying a little as possible about the usurpation.

Bolingbroke's verbal restraint is particularly evident in the scene of Richard's deposition, where his utterances rarely extend beyond flat single lines such as 'I thought you had been willing to resign' or 'Are you contented to resign the crown?'. That factor is pointed out by Richard himself, who scathingly remarks: 'Mark, silent King, the moral of this sport' (4.1.280).

During the same scene Richard performs a virtuoso aria of lament, irony and anger, in that way contrasting himself with the tongue-tied usurper. Thus there is great irony in Richard giving thanks to Bolingbroke for providing him with a new poetic image. This image, based as mentioned above on the breaking of a mirror, prompts Richard to exclaim 'Say that again: / "The shadow of my sorrow – ha, let's see …' and then to append with mock gratitude:

> and I thank thee, King,
> For thy great bounty that not only giv'st
> Me cause to wail, but teachest me the way
> How to lament the cause.
>
> (4.1.283–92)

Here, seizing on the unintended suggestion of what Sidney calls 'invention new' (*Astrophil and Stella*, Sonnet 1), Richard exhibits an avidly inward-looking quest for a way to express himself. Of course, the last thing that Bolingbroke wants to do is to 'teach' Richard 'the way ... to lament'.

This interchange emphasizes that Richard's mode of self-expression is diametrical to Bolingbroke's. Bolingbroke closes the deposition scene with his taut and vicious 'Go some of you, convey him to the Tower', and then adds the laconic 'On Wednesday next we solemnly set down / Our coronation. Lords, prepare yourselves' (4.1.306–10). Bolingbroke's next and final demand concerning Richard is both sinister and gnomic when he says (as reported by Exton): 'Have I no friend will rid me of this living fear?' (5.4.2). Here a paucity of words conveys the murderous innuendo of a tyrant. Thus the contrasting linguistic registers of the two successive sovereigns in *Richard II* imply a decline or decay of civility anticipating the coming civil wars.

The ceremoniousness and pursuit of magnificence characteristic of the court of the historical Richard II also stand in powerful contrast to the depiction by Shakespeare of farcical and indecorous verbal wrangling between a mother, father and a son that breaks out in the presence of the newly crowned Henry IV in *Richard II* (5.3.23–134).

Shakespeare's King Richard II is shown as often self-dramatizing, self-important, loquacious, vacillating and moody.[105] But, although often self-indulgent, he is also capable of condemning the wantonness of his own excesses, as has been noted. He is also depicted as an artistic striver after articulate modes of expression. Thus the King's downfall in *Richard II* may be felt as a dual dishonouring of civilization, which thrives on art, and of art, which requires civilization.

## Scorning art produces suffering.

When met as king in the two parts of Shakespeare's *Henry IV* Bolingbroke is beset by rebellions and nearly overwhelmed by cares. Thus he fretfully issues threats to enemies, and repeatedly pronounces a guilt-ridden wish to go to Jerusalem as a pilgrim. Although *Richard II* 1.4.22–35 indicates that earlier Bolingbroke courted popular esteem, once crowned he admonishes his son Hal to do as he does, which is to make his public appearances infrequent to the point of rarity (*1 Henry IV* 3.2.39–59). Here he denigrates Richard's former 'popularity' (3.2.60–84), exhibiting an aversion rising to the point of prejudice against the civil, ceremonial and magnificent court of his predecessor.

During a long interview with his heir apparent (3.2.1–128), King Henry accuses Prince Hal of being comparable with the 'skipping' Richard II (60–91). Later he reveals that he expects to die knowing that his heir is an unworthy wastrel entirely given over to unruly companions, sports and entertainments (4.3.54–66). Indeed, the fact that the imaginative Hal sets up two playlets in a tavern (2.5.379–485)[106] implies that he might have restored the artistic losses of the Ricardian era had he lived. But Hal does not survive long.

So, the usurping King Henry IV reveals an exhausted and embittered frame of mind when opening *1 Henry IV* with 'So shaken as we are, so wan with care' (1.1.1). On his belated entry in *2 Henry IV* he soliloquizes that he cannot find relief from cares in sleep (3.1.4–31). Thus we see Bolingbroke becoming an aloof, fearful and depressed prig, anxious and joyless. This seems partly the result of both guilt and dangers that arise from his shaky status, but is also connected with how he has set himself up in opposition to Richard II's artistic temperament and his interests in the arts of peace. Thus Shakespeare's Henry IV dies bitterly.

The two parts of Shakespeare's *Henry IV* and all of his first-written tetralogy show the English nation suffering from decades of internecine warfare resulting from the destruction of the refined world of Richard II. The cultural aspects of that loss are emphasized in an interchange in *1 Henry IV* where the war-loving Hotspur expresses prejudicial scorn when responding scathingly to Owen Glendower's boast that in youth he had composed Ricardian poetry. This anti-art outburst follows

Hotspur's mockery of Glendower's Welsh-inflected English, to which 'nationality' bigotry Glendower retorts:

> I can speak English, lord, as well as you;
> For I was trained up in the English court,
> Where, being but young, I frame'd to the harp
> Many an English ditty lovely well,
> And gave the tongue a helpful ornament –
> A virtue that was never seen in you.
>
> (3.1.118–23)

The historical Owain Glyn Dŵr (born *c.* 1359) reportedly did study law in Richard's London, and Shakespeare (for thematic purposes) has his Glendower producing lyrics at Richard's court.[107] Replying scornfully to Glendower's allegation that *he* lacks the 'virtue' of composing poetry, Hotspur sneers at poetry itself and the notion of being a poet:

> Marry, and I am glad of it, with all my heart.
> I had rather be a kitten and cry 'mew'
> Than one of these same metre ballad-mongers.
> I had rather hear a brazen canstick turned,
> Or a dry wheel grate on the axle-tree,
> And that would set my teeth nothing on edge,
> Nothing so much as mincing poetry.
> 'Tis like the forced gait of a shuffling nag.
>
> (3.1.124–31)

It is remarkable that here, while expressing rank prejudice against poetry and poets, Hotspur uses excellent and sinewy blank verse (featuring tight rhythms, alliteration, assonance, spondees, ionic feet). However, 'Whereas Richard's speeches are the poems that Shakespeare puts into his mouth as his own compositions, Hotspur's speeches are Shakespeare's poetry to express the mind of a character who could not himself compose a poem at all'.[108] Hotspur's vivid language thus reveals 'as lustrously as possible'[109] his rashly[110] warlike temperament.

In asserting that he is glad he is *not* a poet the doomed Hotspur represents a militaristic outlook that finds the arts unmanning and degrading. His stance is diametrical to that of Richard II, who is an irenical spirit seeking to advance the civilizing arts. That contrast is underscored when, while admonishing his son, Henry IV compares Hal with Richard II, a weakling aesthete, while at the same time contrastingly lauding war-loving and art-despising Hotspur as 'Mars in his swaddling-clothes' (*1 Henry IV* 3.2.93–128).[111] The complexities of Shakespeare's treatments of similar prejudices denigrating peace and the peaceable will be the topic of a later chapter.

# 3

# Shakespeare on prejudices against 'strangers'

## The topic

This chapter will consider Shakespeare's representations of 'scorns and mislike' directed against the foreign-born or other exotic persons who were called 'strangers' in his time. These prejudices correspond with the sorts of prejudice discussed recently, in which the targets of bigotry are members of minority or disadvantaged segments of society. It will be seen, however, that in many cases Shakespeare's anti-stranger prejudices interlink with underlying prejudices of quite different sorts.

Here I will have to confront views contrary to mine pointed out in Marianne Novy's *Shakespeare's Outsiders* where she notes that since the late 1960s numerous claims have been made that when Shakespeare represented these sorts of prejudices he approved of the bigotry he represented, or even participated in it.[1] Examples include allegations that Shakespeare was a racist, or a chauvinist, as will be seen. However, I find that, on the contrary, Shakespeare's tone is consistently disapproving and admonitory when he portrays anti-stranger prejudices.

Confusions about Shakespeare's own bigotry arise because all his narratives – even the most imaginative or fantastic – link closely with inner and outer realities. These therefore sometimes represent misunderstandings and friction occurring in encounters between diverse sorts of persons (for example, during the interactions between varied nationalities in *King Henry V*). But Shakespeare also portrays responses to unfamiliar 'outsiders' that are untainted by distaste, shunning or stereotyping. For instance, in the Shakespearian portion of the manuscript play *Sir Thomas More* Sheriff More urges on an angry mob the decent treatment of London's refugee 'strangers', insisting in his speech on the kinship of all humanity (*Sir Thomas More* A.2D.81–155).[2] Similarly, Shakespeare responds satirically to denominational restrictions impacting on the religiously dissident 'stranger' resident aliens of his own London.[3] Shakespeare also repeatedly displays French, Spanish, Italian or Danish characters denigrating what they claim to be unworthy *English* national characteristics.[4] These mainly parodic[5] gestures satirize the ubiquity and foolishness of prejudicial derogations of differing nationalities.

# Collective and individual prejudices against 'strangers'

When Shakespeare stages *groups* attacking 'outsiders' such as refugees, an educated minority, educators, a hapless lone poet or a religious pariah, he consistently presents such attacks as deplorable. Shakespearian mobs are thus repeatedly depicted as fickle and unthinking puppets of a contagious, vicious and mundane mindset.

In *The Merchant of Venice* the shameful ordinariness of a jeering mob is indicated when Solonio and Solerio (a dual-act symbolizing a crowd) describe with unholy relish how 'all the boys in Venice' follow the grieving Shylock through the streets of Venice, mocking and taunting him (2.8.12–24). Here an adolescent gang attempts to displace their own well-deserved shame onto their Jewish target. They may not succeed in humiliating Shylock, but their attempt to do just that cannot be doubted. Their taunting is also flaunting and vaunting, as are most such attacks (whether collective or individual) where excited despising deliberately ignores evidence and logic and evidence. The shallow joys of participation in such abusiveness derives from indulging in wilful transgressions of civility.

Although Shakespeare often represents the jejune shallowness of xenophobic bullying or sneering, he treats the mysteries of deeply entrenched xenophobic hatreds in far greater depth and at far greater length. So, for instance, a mention in passing of the shameful-gleeful behaviour (*schadenfreude*) of the Venetian boys taunting Shylock presents far less of an enigma than the Venetian merchant Antonio's unrelenting despising of him. There is likewise a far greater focus in *Othello* on the enigma of Iago's malignant seductions of Othello and Cassio than on Iago's typical misogynistic banter in 2.1 (or on other sometimes vicious ethnicity- or nationality-stereotyping met in the same play). As the psychoanalyst M. Fakhry Davids puts it in relation to 'internal racism': 'Externally one may share one's prejudices with another; internally, the details of what is involved will vary from patient to patient, citizen to citizen'.[6] For that reason, Shakespeare's sophisticated insight into the *internal* forces driving anti-stranger prejudices will be the main topic of this chapter.

The definition of 'a prejudice' in Gordon Allport's massive 1954 *The Nature of Prejudice* provides a useful starting point for an exploration of prejudices against strangers. This carefully considered definition equates a prejudice with 'an avertive or hostile attitude toward a person who belongs to a group, simply because he belongs to that group, and is therefore presumed to have the objectionable qualities ascribed to the group'.[7] In discussions leading up to that definition Allport describes prejudices as 'thinking ill of others *without sufficient warrant*' (my italics), and then quips that 'A wit defined prejudice as "being down on something you're not up on"' (6).

Why does Allport include the tentative terms 'presumed' and 'ascribed' when he defines prejudices? The answer apparently lies in his concern that 'We can never hope to draw a hard and fast line between "sufficient" and "insufficient" warrant' for a negative belief (8). On a trivial level this caveat is fallacious, for under certain circumstances 'sufficient warrant' is certainly available to make a clear distinction between a prejudicial and fact-based belief. For instance, one individual belonging to an actual or imagined category of persons may display genuinely objectionable behaviour (this is always possible unless the category in question is that of angels). If this behaviour is then used as a basis for judging adversely that whole category of persons this would present a clear example of having insufficient warrant for a false generalization, and would be unequivocally prejudicial.

However, faulty logic is not the most usual source, and certainly not the sole source, of negative prejudices. A more serious limitation of Allport's definition of prejudice is that it overlooks the crucial impact on prejudices of obscure mental processes and hidden motivations. Regarding these, the psychoanalyst Roger Money-Kyrle proposes a non-culturally specific difference 'between a normal and a pathological dislike', finding that in the all-too-frequent pathological case malicious and prejudicial dislikes derive from unsound denials, displacements, projections and other psychological aberrations or fantasies.[8] I will next consider a strikingly oblique and convoluted example of Shakespeare's subtle representations of such unconscious mechanisms.

# The Freudian 'uncanny' and psychological projection in *The Comedy of Errors*

... it is precisely the minor differences in people who are otherwise alike that form the basis of feelings of strangeness and hostility between them. It would be tempting to pursue this idea and to derive from this 'narcissism of minor differences' the hostility which in every human relation we see fighting successfully against feelings of fellowship and overpowering the commandment that all men should love one another.

Freud, 'The Taboo of Virginity', 1917[9]

Freud's 1917 observation regarding prejudicial 'strangeness and hostility' in the above quotation met with not untypical-for-him reassessment in his 1930 *Civilization and its Discontents*. There Freud remarked that, formerly, 'I gave this phenomenon the name of "the narcissism of minor differences", a name that does not do much to explain it'.[10] Thus, not discarding his reflection that exaggeration of small differences arises in much bigotry, he asserts that this factor does not explain inter-group prejudices.

Later Freud and his followers uncovered deeper processes underlying prejudices such as unconscious projection of unwanted parts of the self into others. Although unconscious projection is a complex and much-debated topic, it is easy to see why dramatic writers often thematically mirror processes of projection: this is because mirroring of projections may help convey unspoken or even unnameable internal mental states.

A simple but excellent example is seen in the 1939 film *Love Affair*, directed by Leo McCarey.[11] In this a shipboard romance results in a couple falling deeply in love although both are already engaged to marry other wealthy people not present. Just before their ocean liner arrives in New York they agree to meet again in six months, after they have rearranged their lives. Early in the sea crossing, before the love affair flourishes, the hero, who is a celebrity playboy, rescues a young lad whose athletic risk-taking has trapped him in a perilous situation. This heedlessly bold child, on recognizing his helper, says, 'Everybody on the ship's talking about you ... Whenever they start talking about you they make me leave the room'. This comment on his sexual notoriety coming from an unexpected direction is displeasing to the hero, but it does not entail any projection. Projection is evident, however, immediately afterward when the film's heroine, Terry McKay, having overheard this exchange, happens upon the boy again risking injury. She sees the boy once again hanging precariously above a steep drop, and exclaims: 'Oh, be careful there sonny, you'll fall and hurt yourself'. Then she adds, in a tone suggesting a reverie of remembrance, 'When I was little like you I fell and broke my leg'. The boy drags her back to the present by asking impatiently 'How is it now', and she replies in a puzzled way, 'O, it's all right'. The child then responds dismissively, 'Then what are you crabbing about?', Terry looks nonplussed, and the scene ends.

Six months later, rushing to the arranged rendezvous with her lover, Terry McKay is struck down by a motor vehicle because she is looking up toward the top of the high building where he awaits her. She survives but loses the use of her legs. The linkage of these events, one involving a bold child peripheral to the plot and the other an accident central to the film, is multiply resonant. One aspect is that Terry McKay shows a concern for wayward children, especially after her accident. Also, the brief early episode on the ocean liner points the way to larger themes to follow that will involve notoriety overcome and then risk, injury and possible recovery. A third and more important way to appreciate this film's seemingly casual introduction of the reckless boy is to see in Terry's response to him an indication that she warns *herself* that heedlessness in pursuit of grace may result in injury. Thus she expresses a concern lest her excitement and pleasure in her love affair will result in accidental harm (which it does). The construction of the scene with the boy thus indicates that Terry McKay projects out of herself, and into the boy, what she takes to be dangerous tendencies to rash insouciance. In other words, she unconsciously tells herself that 'He is reckless, I am not'.[12]

Next in the film Terry McKay, now disabled and in a wheelchair, exhibits a prejudice against imperfection[13] and so severs all contact with her lover. This prejudice prevents her from even informing him about the accident, so that it seems to him that she has reneged on their agreement to reconnect. However, her formerly rakish lover (now for the first time earning an honest living) does find her at last. Once having rescued the boy in trouble, he later converts her to hope and the film ends with a possibility of their future together.

I next want to link this model, in which a chance encounter is subtly linked with projections and prejudices, with *The Comedy of Errors*. To do so I will need to comment on another of Freud's works, his 1919 essay titled in translation 'The Uncanny'.

This essay begins with a long discussion of its original German title, 'Das Unheimlich'. This notes that the term *unheimlich* is seemingly untranslatable when equivalents are sought Greek, French, Spanish, Arabic and Hebrew.[14] Next Freud cites an important German wordbook which provides as equivalents to the adjective *heimlich* words meaning 'not strange', 'familiar', 'tame', 'intimate', 'homely', 'friendly', 'homelike' or 'arousing a sense of peaceful pleasure and security' (125–7). However, in the second section of the same entry this dictionary supplies equivalents that include 'concealed', 'secret', 'behind someone's back', 'secretive' and 'mischievous' (127–9). Freud then produces more examples, such as Jacob and Willhelm Grimm's definitions of *heimlich* that include on one hand 'free from ghostly influences ... familiar, friendly intimate', and on the other hand 'mystic', 'occult', 'withdrawn from knowledge', 'unconscious' and 'obscure, inaccessible to knowledge' (130–1). He therefore comments that 'among its different shades of meaning the word *heimlich* exhibits one which is identical with its opposite, *unheimlich*' (129). (Freud, in fact, wrote another essay on words with such opposite double meanings.)[15]

Hugh Haughton comments that Freud's 'virtuoso display of lexicographical research' shows that other languages do not convey the strange ambiguity wherein the paired German words *heimlich / unheimlich* overlap in meaning. Thus he points out that the term 'uncanny', although a best fit in English, 'doesn't reproduce the semantic structure which provides the crux of Freud's account of the relation between the *Heimlich* and the *Unheimlich*'.[16]

The remainder of Freud's essay explores this anomaly in depth, offering an explanation that has considerable bearing on a Shakespearian topic. According to Freud, upsetting experiences of the 'uncanny' may arise from encounters with ghosts, sprites, demons or witches (136, 149–50), but equally the same consternation may result from unexpectedly meeting one's 'double' in a mirror, or in the form of a twin (131–3, 156n). The upset arises, Freud claims, because such *heimlich / unheimlich* experiences trigger recognitions of denied or unacknowledged aspects of the self.

Thus, says Freud, encounters seem uncanny when they hint at secrets of one's inner 'home' that have been 'withdrawn from knowledge', and so he explains that the 'uncanny is in reality nothing new or foreign, but something familiar and old established in the mind that has been estranged only by the process of repression' (148). Freud's summary, then, is that in *unheimlich* 'the prefix "un" is a token of repression' (153), and 'that the uncanny proceeds from something familiar that has been repressed' (155).

*The Comedy of Errors* portrays a great many encounters with the familiar/unfamiliar that seem 'uncanny' and therefore produce suspicions, resentments and grievances. From those arise numerous avowals of prejudices targeting foreign places or persons, or targeting seemingly incomprehensible men, women, husbands, wives, servants, merchants and a courtesan.

These uncanny-seeming encounters in *The Comedy of Errors* stem from around fifty misunderstandings occasioned when one or the other of two sets of identical twins are mistaken for one another. These siblings, who do not suspect one another's presence, are premised by Shakespeare to be indistinguishable by sight, speech culture, gesture and even name.[17] Thereby arise multiple *unheimlich* situations of the sort connected with unexpectedly happening upon twins or mirror images, or more specifically with observing a seemingly well-known person behaving in an eerily unfamiliar manner.

From near the play's start much unaccountable bewilderment often leads to expressions of prejudices against 'strangers'. In fact, anti-foreigner prejudice is mooted even before the first of the play's 'errors' occurs – for its opening 'establishing' scene reveals that both Ephesus and Syracuse have enacted statutes condemning to death any citizen of the other city found in the adverse town (1.1.11–21). The Duke of Ephesus launches the play by explaining this legalized anti-stranger prejudice, and so proclaims that the Syracusan 'stranger' merchant Egeon must face the death sentence unless he pays an unobtainable ransom before a five o'clock deadline (1.1.3–25 and 1.1.140–55).[18] Showing some humane concern, however, the Duke urges Egeon to account for himself. Egeon then explains that he had become 'accidentally' bereft of all his family and is searching for a missing son in Ephesus, and adds that he cares little about dying (1.1.28–139). The Duke says that he pities him, but will only delay his sentence for a day (140–55).

A powerful inverse prejudice is exposed in the next scene when Egeon's son Antipholus of Syracuse, newly arrived in Ephesus, erroneously mistakes Dromio of Ephesus for Dromio of Syracuse. In response to that confusion he voices a superstitious distrust and dislike of Ephesus and all its inhabitants, thus:

> *They say* this town is full of cozenage,
> As nimble jugglers that deceive the eye,
> Dark-working sorcerers that change the mind,
> Soul-killing witches that deform the body,
> Disguised cheaters, prating mountebanks,
> And many suchlike libertines of sin.
> (1.2.97–102, my italics)

Antipholus justifies this xenophobic stereotyping of the town and its inhabitants in terms of what *They say*, a locution typical of those sharing anti-stranger prejudices.[19] Here, in two short words, Shakespeare encapsulates the jejune shallowness of collective prejudices.

Prejudicial resentments and even paranoid terrors then mount up throughout the play not in despite of, but *because of* alikeness between 'strangers' in dress, language, speech and gesture – in fact, because the seemingly familiar becomes uncannily unfamiliar. In accord with this Freudian pattern, and in accord with this play's saturation with punning, there is double meaning in Antipholus of Corinth's claims that 'this town is full of cozenage'. For *cozenage*, which signified fraudulence and cheating, was also an old spelling for *cousinage*, a word whose meaning included 'kinship' or 'consanguinity'. Indeed OED2[20] remarks on the word 'cozenage' that it was: 'In form originally identical with cousinage, whence many word-plays'. This encapsulates how unsuspected consanguinity leads to all the manifold dismaying misperceptions of apparent (financial or sexual) cheating (cozenage) in *The Comedy of Errors*.

Shakespeare's representation in this play of the vicissitudes of outwardly indistinguishable twins also suggests the arbitrary nature of nationality distinctions. As was said in Parliament in 1589 in defence of England's strangers, 'the residence of continuance of one nation in one place is not of the law of nature'.[21] However, Antipholus of Ephesus is taken (unseen) to be an intruding outsider (3.1) at the door of his own house. In his outraged account of this he asks, 'And did not she [his wife Adriana] herself revile me there' and 'Did not her kitchen maid rail, taunt and scorn me?' (4.4.73–5), describing typical 'scorns and mislike' of a 'stranger'.

Shakespeare's handling of his 'twins' premise (borrowed from Plautus but doubled up) entails – beyond multiple farcical scrapes – also painful disturbances of mental balance. Antipholus of Syracuse anticipates this in his xenophobic suspicions of 'Dark-working sorcerers that change the mind'. Superstitious fear and alienation soon become evident when the bewildered Domino of Syracuse cries out:

> O, for my beads! I cross me for a sinner.
> This is the fairy land. O spite of spites,
> We talk with goblins, oafs, and sprites.

If we obey them not, this will ensue:
They'll suck our breath or pinch us black and blue.
(2.2.191–5)

His master Antipholus of Syracuse expresses a parallel view of Ephesus in 'There's none but witches do inhabit here' (3.2.162) and 'Lapland sorcerers inhabit here' (4.3.11). Finally, feeling untethered to reality, Antipholus laments, 'here we wander in illusions. / Some blessed power deliver us from hence' (4.3.43–4). Superstition then links with misogyny when he conjures the Ephesian courtesan with 'Satan, avoid' and 'Avoid, thou fiend! (4.3.48, 65) and in the next scene he claims his sister-in-law and his probable future wife are 'witches' (4.4.148).

These prejudices, occasioned when illusive sameness collides with eerie-seeming difference, cause numerous characters to find themselves 'estranged from [themself]' (2.2.123), 'transformed ... in mind' (2.2.198-9), 'to myself disguised' (2.2.217). One even asks 'Am I myself?' (3.2.74). Confronted with cascading contradictions, the Duke of Ephesus concludes at last 'I think you all have drunk of Circe's cup ... I think you are all mated or stark mad' (5.1.271, 282). All in the play are indeed 'mated' by misapprehensions so unsettling that they provoke mental aberrations.

This pattern of psychic upsets within *The Comedy of Errors* is reminiscent of Freud's account of disturbing encounters with the unfamiliar-familiar 'uncanny'. But to establish this analogy I must next explain just what, as Freud put it, has 'been repressed' at the heart of this play.

This repressed material relates to a prejudicial fault revealed at the play's start when Egeon of Corinth tells his history to the Duke of Ephesus. What is revealed there implies an unexpected deep linkage between the Egeon plot and the 'twins' plot of the play. Before addressing that, I want to indicate its plausibility by pointing out some shallower but more evident links. One lies in the coincidence that the sum of money that Egeon requires and cannot obtain for his ransom (a thousand marks) precisely matches Antipholus's thousand marks that is misdirected from the start of the errors plot. Other parallels are that both Egeon and the Corinthian Antipholus come to Ephesus to search for missing family members, and that both Egeon and the Ephesian Antipholus are arrested.

A more profound link involves first an asymmetry in the play's 'errors' plot wherein the two pairs of outwardly identical twins are actually opposed in situational and temperamental ways. Thus Antipholus and Dromio of Ephesus are married or engaged household members firmly settled in their community while their doubles from Corinth are contrastingly unsettled itinerants presently lacking homes and community links (as is Egeon). All find families (and most find wives) at the end of *The Comedy of Errors*. In this Shakespeare's play diverges from its partial source, Plautus' *Menaechmi*, which concludes with the citizen twin leaving his marriage and restrictive home[22] to become 'a natural man' who 'gleefully repudiates social institutions by ridding himself of his nameless and shrewish wife and burdensome property, and leaves the city and all its troublesome parasites'.[23]

All these circumstances have bearing on the theory offered by Barbara Freedman that expounds a vital link between Egeon's account of his personal history in 1.1 and the ensuing twins plot and its many uncanny encounters. Freedman's core perception is that when the merchant Egeon recounts his misfortunes he lets slip that he was personally responsible for his family's tragic losses (although he tells his story in a way that half-obscures this). Thus, Freedman explains,

> Egeon admits that he was responsible for his separation from his wife, led on by the call of business. He appears to have desired to maintain that divorce, despite his protests to the contrary. He is careful to note that it was his wife, not he, who made provisions for her to follow him ... and finally admits that he was unwilling to return home with her: 'My wife ... / Made daily motions for our home return. / Unwilling I agreed'. That unwillingness may explain Egeon's curiously passive acceptance of obstacles to his return home. When confronted with 'A doubtful warrant of immediate

death' in the form of a ship-tossing tempest, Egeon tells us it was a fate that he 'would gladly have embraced', were it not for his family's pleas for rescue. Yet rescue of a different sort is provided, for the storm not only prevents Egeon's return home, but serves to separate husband and wife once again. Fate functions here as a disowned aspect of Egeon's will, undoing his wife's efforts to retrieve her husband and remain with him, and restoring the prior marital separation which Egeon had enforced. The woeful tale of a 'helpful ship ... splitted in the midst', of fortune's 'unjust divorce' of a family, of a man 'severed from my bliss', is a highly elaborated and very well disguised fantasy of a man's desire to cut himself off from his previous life.[24]

Attention to the long interchange in question (1.1.35-120) sustains this view of Egeon's half-admitted neglect of his pregnant wife. Egeon's narration conveys his sharp despondency over his losses yet does not convey an equally vividly acceptance of his contribution to the disaster, so an impression arises that he has repressed awareness of his fault and that it still preys on him in the form of unconscious guilt. Thus we see, as Freedman puts it, 'Egeon's curiously passive acceptance of harsh Ephesian punishment' (374).

Denials or neglect of family ties are also multiply imaged in the confusions in the twins plot of the play. Thus, as Freedman puts it,

> Egeon's story is the missing link which turns an arbitrary plot into a meaningfully directed fantasy. His denial of his marital identity and obligations explains ... the use of twin sons, divided selves, to represent him.
>
> (374)

Although Freedman identifies other patterns as significant,[25] from the point of view of this study the originating fault in *The Comedy of Errors* is best described as Egeon's initial prejudicial rejection of what will be called in my last chapter 'Anterotic love'.

Leaving aside until then a fuller consideration of prejudices against mutual and committed love, I want to raise two points concerning this alleged reflection of Egeon's matrimonial fault in the twins' 'errors'. The first is that prejudices of one sort (here, prejudices against a settled married life) may be expressed in terms of other sorts of prejudices. For instance, when describing his own flight from a possible marriage (which exaggerates Egeon's youthful behaviour) Dromio of Corinth exhibits a strong prejudice against one particular Ephesean woman. Thus, following the Ephesean servant Luce/Nell's reported erotic advances based on her mistaking him for his twin who has been 'assured to her' (3.2.77-161; 146), the Corinthian Dromio directs a string of jibes against her physical attributes.

Interestingly, this Dromio's derogatory comparisons between Nell's anatomy and geographical regions invert the ecstatic geographical imaging of a desired female body in John Donne's *Elegy: To his Mistress Going to Bed*.[26] But finally Dromio overgoes his misogyny and concludes his rant with an animal comparison: 'As from a bear a man would run for life, / So fly I from her that would be my wife'. This imaging of the 'kitchen wench' Nell as sub-human signals the worst sort of anti-'stranger' prejudice, and instances how antipathetic reactions to someone *other* may stand in for rejections of *something else*.

A second point concerns the nature of the connection between the prejudicial and the 'uncanny' elements in *The Comedy of Errors*. In my view this connection, which as Friedman puts it 'turns an arbitrary plot into a meaningfully directed fantasy', represent a psychic projection at work. That would explain how seemingly mechanical or 'revolving-door' farcical permutations of mistaken identity are played out in portrayals of real-seeming pain. For instance, the nearly catastrophic falling out between Antipholus of Ephesus and his wife Adriana is only partly attributable to confusions of identity. Rather, confusion is propelled toward crisis by genuine flaws in their marriage involving jealous suspiciousness, excessive possessiveness, highhandedness, irascibility, shrewishness and vengeful reactions to frustration.

Thanks to psychological verisimilitude accompanying fantastic plotting, the 'happy ending' of Shakespeare's *Comedy of Errors* suggests the repair of broken connections between dramatic characters who are not simply marionettes for farce. So, when damaged relations between married partners, parents, children, and siblings are restored at the end of this play, a mood briefly emerges resembling that seen at large when recognition, reconciliation and forgiveness conclude each of Shakespeare's four late Romances.

To conclude, the risk-taking acrobatic boy seen in the film *Love Affair* embodies a projection of the heedlessness disowned by this film's heroine. Patterns of projection are likewise *embedded into the structure* of *The Comedy of Errors* when the play's twins re-enact the love-resisting propensities of Egeon. In both cases the structure of the narrative mirrors a displacement into others of that which is close to home but remains unrecognized. However, a deeper than allegorical *psychomachia* is at work when the terrors and vicissitudes of the twin sons and twin servants in *The Comedy of Errors* express father Egeon's repressed guilty self-knowledge. The mirroring of parallel motifs in *The Comedy of Errors* (as in many other Shakespeare contexts) goes beyond structural patterning, and suggests as well a representation of plausibly genuine human relations. Thus a representation of projection in the play becomes so lively as to depict unconscious psychic forces at work.

Before considering several similar Shakespearian depictions of displacement as a source of prejudice, I will next consider the causes of a pattern of implacability in prejudices against strangers.

# The obduracy of prejudices against strangers

When prejudicial judgments are pronounced and attempts are made to refute them these refutations often fall on deaf ears or else provoke further rationalizations. Such a process proclaims in effect 'it doesn't matter what you say'. Disregard of all refutations is of course inevitable where an ostensible target of a prejudice stands-in for a projected *something other*, for in such cases no reply to the surface bigotry can address the underlying prejudice.

The mechanism of projection in its simplest form involves getting rid of something unwanted, as when Terry McKay in *Love Affair* half-recognizes her own potential for recklessness and projects it away into the athletic boy (the thought being 'he is reckless, not I'). Hence she denies tendencies in herself that she considers dangerous and discreditable.

Similarly, during the tense and stormy scene in which those on shore await Othello's arrival in Cyprus, Iago projects onto others his own discreditable characteristics of furtive resentfulness and deceitful disloyalty. Thus Iago says of his wife Emilia 'She puts her tongue a little in her heart, / And chides with thinking' (*Othello* 2.1.110-11), actually describing, in fact, himself. He next accuses women at large (including Desdemona) of sly deceit:

> You are pictures out of door,
> Bells in your parlours; wildcats in your kitchens,
> Saints in your injuries; devils being offended,
> Players in your housewifery, and hussies in your beds
> (2.1.112-15).

I will have more to say in the final chapter about Iago's shallow and brittle parading of misogyny, and here will consider only why his supposedly 'humorous' bantering against 'you' women is treated with less complexity by Shakespeare than his hatred of Othello. A probable cause is that prejudices are relatively more straightforward when they are based on projections onto others of disliked and disowned parts of the self. Greater complications arise when prejudices are based on projections onto others of good or desirable qualities felt to be lost to the self or lacking there. Those sorts of prejudices typically involve not only denigration of others, but also powerful resentment arising from feelings of being weakened, deprived or bereft. Thus, following God's declaration that Christ in whom 'Love hath abounded more then Glory abounds' is 'anointed' his Son 'by Merit', Milton's envious Satan 'thought himself impair'd'.[27]

Anti-'stranger' prejudices that stem from envious resentments of good qualities in others are more than ordinarily resistant to contrary evidence. Such resistance features centrally in the 'common mental device' that Gordon Allport labels 're-fencing'. In this, Allport writes, prejudiced persons suppress truths so that when a commendatory 'fact cannot fit into [their] mental field, the exception is acknowledged, but the field is hastily fenced in again and not allowed to remain dangerously open' (23). Allport illustrates this with an imaginary dialogue:

MR. X: The trouble with the Jews is that they only take care of their own group.

MR. Y: But the record of the Community Chest campaign shows that they give more generously, in proportion to their numbers, to the general charities of the community, than do non-Jews.

MR. X: That shows they are always trying to buy favor and intrude into Christian affairs. They think of nothing but money; that is why there are so many Jewish bankers.

MR. Y: But a recent study shows that the percentage of Jews in the banking business is negligible, far smaller than the percentage of non-Jews.

MR. X: That's just it; they don't go in for respectable business; they are only in the movie business or run night clubs.[28]

This stream of accusations, confutations and replacements might run on forever because that that which is really resented is hidden and lies outside the re-fencer's litany of complaints. Re-fencers promptly erect new fences enlarging an imagined paddock of demerit because they project a despised or feared *something else* into *someone other*. Thus in Allport's imaginary dialogue repeated rebuttals asserting good qualities fail to deflect or cancel an unshakable prejudice.

A similar pattern – in which rebuttals of alleged reasons for prejudicial dislikes are overwritten or ignored – appears in numerous Shakespearian plays where negatively stereotyped characters go unheard when speaking in their own defense. These members of discriminated against and oppressed groups insist that they are similar to, and certainly not inferior to, their mainstream detractors, but their claims are ignored by others or society at large.

The most famous among such allegations of parity or normality in Shakespeare plays is Shylock's claim in *The Merchant of Venice* beginning 'Hath not a Jew eyes?' (3.1.54-68). Here the protestation is as usual wholly disregarded, but is also 'undercut' in a way that Marianne Novy finds typical.[29] This is because Shylock concludes by claiming that Jews equal Christians in vengefulness, disregarding the biblical verse beginning 'Vengeance and recompence are mine' (Deuteronomy 32:35).[30]

Shakespeare likewise represents the desperate pleas of Malvolio, an outsider to the festive cabal in *Twelfth Night*, that 'I am no more mad than you are', that 'I am as well in my wits, fool, as thou art', and that 'I am as well in my wits as any man in Illyria' (4.2.48-9, 4.2.90, 4.2.109-10). This plea of normality is again undercut, for Malvolio has been exposed as being 'sick of self-love' (1.5.86). However in his case he is not wholly unheard and Olivia's sympathy is evoked by his immoderate punishment (5.1.375).

Antipholus of Ephesus in *The Comedy of Errors* is similarly falsely stigmatized as insane, and also makes a desperate unheard plea that 'I am not mad' (4.4.59).[31] In another instance of a Shakespearian 'outsider' denying that he is inferior to others the bastard Edmund's asserts that his qualities are equal to his legitimate brother's. He begins:

> Why 'bastard'? Wherefore 'base',
> When my dimensions are as well compact,

My mind as generous, and my shape as true
As honest madam's issue?'

(Folio *King Lear* 1.2.7–9)

Edmund, however, goes on to rationalize ill doing, so like Shylock he undercuts the sympathy his protest may have evoked.

Shakespeare also highlights gender discrimination when some of his women claim parity with men.[32]

In all these instances Shakespeare's strangers or outsiders fail to access fair treatment despite their refutations of claims that they are inferior to their despisers. The reason is that their logic does not address the source of the abuse.

The remainder of this chapter will mainly focus on two Shakespeare plays, *The Merchant of Venice* and *Othello*, in which prejudices against outsiders are immovable because they represent displaced resentments. To frame these discussions I will next outline some useful observations concerning differing kinds of prejudice.

# A helpful framework

In her *The Anatomy of Prejudices*, a study of biases directed against groups of persons, the psychoanalyst Elisabeth Young-Bruehl holds that Gordon Allport and his social scientific followers were mistaken in thinking that 'prejudice' is a single entity. She proposes on the contrary that there are three different sorts of prejudices having distinct psychic roots. Her categorization of differing prejudicial tendencies accords with a threefold 'character typology' derived from Freud's structural theories of the mind, as follows:[33]

| *erotics* | *obsessionals* | *narcissists* |
|---|---|---|
| hysterical traits predominate | obsessional traits predominate | narcissistic traits predominate |
| = id dominated | = superego dominated | = ego dominated |

In ensuing discussions (202–38) Young-Bruehl describes the typical 'silencing' of the 'other' by obsessionals, the splitting off and denigration of the 'other' by erotics, and the objectification and exclusion of the 'other' by narcissists. In Young-Bruehl's estimation anti-Semites are likely to be obsessionals, snobs and racists are likely to be hystericals and sexists and xenophobes are likely to be narcissistic.

Young-Bruehl does not clearly identify her source, which is Freud's 1931 essay 'Libidinal Types'. Here Freud stresses that his threefold division of character types is empirical rather than essential, and that 'It may at once be admitted that these libidinal types need not be the only possible ones even in the psychical field, and that, if we proceeded from other qualities, we might perhaps establish a whole set of other psychological types'.[34] Freud also observes that most people's characters display a mixture of his three types (218–19), and Young-Bruehl also acknowledges that her three categories may be mixed or merged in practice (209, 238–52).

That is indeed true, but nonetheless some of Young-Bruehl's distinctions will be useful here. For instance, her notion that obsessionals such as anti-Semites often resort to *silencing* will prove valuable here with regard to the non-hearing in *The Merchant of Venice* of Shylock's protestations concerning a Jew's humanity. These fail to penetrate deaf ears and so are effectively silenced; I will next investigate *silencing*, amounting to tacit re-fencing, in the interactions of Shylock and Antonio.

# Animosity and silencing in *The Merchant of Venice*

In one real sense Shylock is very obviously 'silenced', for he is the only major Shakespearian figure who suffers defeat and withdrawal and is entirely absent from the fifth act of his play. Before that, however, Shylock is certainly *not silent*. Rather (and despite his claims to patience or 'suffrance' in the face of abuse and discrimination),[35] he is remarkably outspoken in his complaints.

Indeed, Shylock's very distinctive modes of speech account for him looming so large in his play. Thus a highly individual 'Shylock music' (radically different from G. Wilson Knight's 'Othello music') is unmistakably recognizable, even though it is heard in only five of the play's fifteen scenes. I, among other critics,[36] have elsewhere described how that music sounds, whence it derives and whereby it is silenced, and will briefly reiterate here some points that are particularly relevant to questions about prejudice.

These include the fact that Shylock's verbal music is raucous, skilful, challenging and obliquely highly expressive, yet seems wholly disregarded onstage. I have proposed that in portraying that rejection of a virtuoso performance Shakespeare alluded to a classical myth (very well known in his period) in which the satyr Marsyas, a talented upstart or 'underdog' figure, challenges the god Apollo to a competitive musical contest. Although he is certain to prevail on the strength of his talent, Marsyas is unfairly defeated and then destroyed. Multiple symbolic and formal details in *The Merchant of Venice* correspond with elements in that myth. Among these, Marsyas' contest with Apollo has multiple aspects in common with Shylock's lawsuit against Antonio.[37] For one, in Natalie Conti's Renaissance retelling of the story and in some classical versions, Apollo suddenly alters the rules of the contest midstream in order to negate Marsyas' winning performance.[38] Similarly, Shakespeare's Portia disrupts upstart Shylock's legal claims – which as will be seen were unimpeachable in Elizabethan law – by suddenly bringing in an unanticipated Venetian anti-alien criminal statute. Thanks to this and other parallel ruses[39] the challenges of the underdog Marsyas and the Jew Shylock are both reined in. The initiative and talents of these outsiders are thereby ignored or silenced, their originality overwritten by means of rule changing, or in effect re-fencing.

The outcomes are that virtuosic Marsyas is utterly destroyed while Shylock is financially and civilly disenfranchised, then driven to mumbling plainness and lastly wholly silenced. Hence at his final exit the verbally agile Shylock is reduced to the dullness of: 'I pray you give me leave to go from hence. / I am not well' (4.393–4).

Why this reversal occurs has often been associated with adverse attitudes to Shylock's Jewish religion,[40] but I cannot agree with those who argue that Shakespeare or many in his original audiences would have considered Antonio and his cohort's anti-Semitic views in accord with their own. On the contrary, some scholars have claimed that Shylock would have been recognized by Shakespeare's audiences as a bad Jew, rather than bad because he was a Jew.[41] This would have been mainly because Shylock is bent on revenge, while biblically literate Elizabethan Christians would have known that his religion, as did their own, counselled forgiveness and 'turning the other cheek'.[42] Elizabethans might also have noticed that several of Shylock's remarks defied Jewish religious injunctions to behave humanely towards 'strangers', servants and domestic animals.[43]

Moreover, Shakespeare's original audiences would have been acutely aware of an ongoing European history of bloody confessional conflict. Although zealots on either side of the divides between Protestants and Catholics, or between moderate and more reformed Protestants, often accused their opposites of 'Jewish' blindness to the light of revelation,[44] such zealotry was not to Shakespeare's taste. On the contrary, Shakespeare's work repeatedly alludes to officially sanctioned and widespread Elizabethan impatience with dogmatic religious divisiveness.[45] Correspondingly, scholars have shown that many of Shakespeare's plays merge elements of Catholic and Protestant doctrine in order to indicate a theological mid-course.[46] Additionally, as I have shown,[47] comic figures in a number of Shakespeare's plays travesty doctrinal oppositions of the sort that divided 'young Chairbonne the puritan and old Poisson the papist' (*All's Well* 1.3.61–2).

The hatred of Antonio in *The Merchant of Venice* seems focused on only one theological issue, the supposed sin of usury.

So, when Shylock justifies taking interest on loans (1.3.59–101), Antonio vehemently denounces what he calls taking 'a breed of barren metal' (1.3.132). However, as Martin Yaffe points out,[48] Antonio seems to be the only person in mercantile Venice adopting such a position. Such a stand would also have seemed very odd in mercantile Elizabethan England where raising capital on interest was both commonplace and socially acceptable. Not at all atypically, Shakespeare himself borrowed in order to fund his several investments.[49] Moreover, an authoritative study of documents relating to legal action taken against Shakespeare's father for alleged 'usury' comments that 'To be convicted of usury in the 1570s was to fall victim to an anachronistic law which amounted to a random tax on trade. Trade in the sixteenth century was heavily reliant on credit'.[50]

Although hypocritical Polonius includes in his long-winded advice to Laertes 'Neither a borrower nor a lender be' (*Hamlet*, 1.3.75), borrowing and lending with a 10 per cent interest premium was legal in England by Shakespeare's time.[51] Shakespeare moreover repeatedly specifically alluded to several English case law developments that eased the process of borrowing on credit, indicating that many in his audiences would have recognized and been amused by references to detailed modes of financial transaction.[52]

Shakespeare's Antonio causes Shylock to complain bitterly that 'He hath disgraced me, and hindered me half a million; laughed at my losses, mocked at my gains, scorned my nation, thwarted my bargains, cooled my friends, heated mine enemies' (3.1.50–3). He says also that Antonio 'lends out money gratis, and brings down / The rate of usance here with us in Venice ... He hates our sacred nation, and he rails, / Even there where merchants most do congregate, / On me, my bargains, and my well-won thrift – / Which he calls interest' (1.3.42–9). The play indicates that as a result of such insults and harms Shylock has long hoped to catch Antonio 'on the hip'.[53]

Shylock makes no secret of his anger when he complains, 'You call me misbeliever, cut-throat, dog, / And spit upon my Jewish gaberdine / And all for use of that which is mine own', and to this Antonio responds with redoubled rancour, 'I am as like to call thee so again, / To spit on thee again, to spurn thee too' ((1.3.110–12, 128–9). The terms 'use', 'usance', 'bargains' and 'thrift' here and in the above point to commercial practices equally familiar in Shakespeare's mercantile London as in his imaginary Venice. Shakespeare's London was also increasingly a centre for legal disputation, often in relation to economic disputes, and the resemblance continues in that *The Merchant of Venice* features a lawsuit over an unpaid debt.

As Mary Sokol and I have shown (Sokol and Sokol, 1999), the trial of Antonio in *The Merchant of Venice* instigated by Shylock has often been wrongly understood from linked legal-historical and religious perspectives. Thus numerous critics have connected the conduct of this lawsuit with a prejudice Martin Yaffe calls the 'Christian repudiation of Jewish law ... the millennial antagonism between Christian and Jew, New Law and Old, with the unfortunate Jew as the loser'.[54] On the contrary, Portia/Balthazar apparently understands that Jewish law did not mandate rigidity as opposed to forgivingness, for she exclaims: 'Then must the Jew be merciful' (4.1.179). Despite that, over several decades many critics of *The Merchant of Venice* subscribed to a mistaken association of the Jewish Old Law with the English common law courts and the Christian New Law with the English Equity jurisdictions. They further confounded that error by muddling supersessionist theological theories with the strained relations of those jurisdictions resulting from constitutional and political conflicts that emerged after *The Merchant of Venice* was written.

In brief, the Elizabethan courts of Equity were bound in their operations by definite maxims and procedures, and certainly did not dispense 'mercy', 'leniency' or 'pardons' ad hoc according to 'conscience'.[55] Pardon, for instance, was in the hands of the queen or parliament alone.[56] Moreover, in the latter part of Elizabeth's reign relations between the officers of the common law jurisdictions and of the equity jurisdictions were mainly cordial and cooperative. This is dramatized in the (c. 1606[57]) quarto version of *King Lear*, which sees the heads of English equity and law 'bench[ing]' side by side as 'yokefellow[s]' during the mock trial of Goneril (S13.32–4), a joint sitting that reflects actual practice in Elizabethan state trials, and images jurisdictional cooperation.[58]

Consequently, audiences would not have responded to notions of opposing courts of 'equity' and 'law' when *The Merchant of Venice* first appeared, around 1597. Nonetheless, in the wake of the 1965 publication of a fanciful college essay written by Mark Edwin Andrews decades earlier, a myth that the play reflects historical oppositions between courts of 'law' and 'equity' widely took hold in Shakespeare studies. As often, some misapplied facts lie in the vicinity of an unwarranted theory. Thus early modern England, becoming ever more litigious, saw a mounting competition for business between its multiple and sometimes overlapping legal jurisdictions.[59] More than professional fees were at issue when, from about 1610, the common law courts championed by Parliament and headed by Sir Edward Coke increasingly employed legal devices to attack the powers of the ecclesiastical courts and the newer prerogative courts. Eventually Coke attempted to restrict the increasing sway, under the chancellor Ellesmere, of the top equity court of Chancery. These moves have been interpreted as an attack by Parliament and the common lawyers on King James's royal prerogative. Political tracts appeared and passions flared, and in 1616 the King's intervention resulted in the dismissal and disgrace of Coke.[60] Critically, however, those crucial events occurred over a decade after *The Merchant of Venice* appeared. Therefore connecting the political explosion of 1616 (or the build up towards it from 1610) with the trial in *The Merchant of Venice*, as Andrews and his many followers do, is unwarranted.

However, other early modern jurisdictional issues actually do impact on *The Merchant of Venice* in a significant manner that would have been sharply apparent to many among Shakespeare's amazingly litigious contemporaries.[61] The first of these concerns the instrument of debt at issue in *Shylock v Antonio*. Shylock's lawsuit concerns the non-redemption of a sealed and notarized 'bond' (1.3.143–76), a type of legal instrument that by the time of the play's composition was widely used by lenders to ensure repayment.[62] Its popularity was due to the fact that if a borrower had not retrieved his actual paper or parchment bond from the lender by payment of their debt on time then the creditor's mere physical possession of that bond constituted a legal claim to the penalty written on its outward face that was unanswerable in civil law. Hence Shylock believes himself enabled to 'silence', as-it-were, objections to his demand for the specified penalty, and proclaims, 'I'll have my bond. I will not hear thee speak' (3.3.12) or 'I'll not answer that' (4.1.39). Here Shylock triumphs in silencing those who have silenced him, so instead of 'turning the cheek' as his religion demands,[63] he 'turns the tables'.

During the trial Shylock offers a rationale for his stark insistence on his bond that matches a widely accepted view held in Shakespeare's England. Thus in the King's Bench case Waberley v Cockrel (1571) the plaintiff claimed that he had paid his debt but foolishly did not destroy the bond, which was then allegedly snatched back by the creditor Cockrel. The court decided that Waberley had to pay the debt again because 'Even if it is truth that the plaintiff was paid his money, it is nevertheless better to suffer a mischief to one man than an inconvenience to many, which would subvert the law'.[64] Shakespeare's Portia/Balthazar echoes the identical position that individual mitigation is best overlooked in order to protect a principle lest 'many an error by the same example / Will rush into the state' (4.1. 216–19). The despondent Antonio himself earlier acknowledged the pragmatic reason for this:

> The duke cannot deny the course of law:
> For the commodity that strangers have
> With us in Venice, if it be denied,
> Will much impeach the justice of the state,
> Since that the trade and profit of the city
> Consisteth of all nations.
>
> (3.3.26–31)

Shylock echoes the same reasoning during the trial, declaring that if he is denied the 'forfeit of my bond ... let the danger light / Upon your charter and the city's freedom' (4.1.36–8). That danger would be Venice's commercial ruin following a loss of alien traders' confidence. Notably, Shylock who had been spurned like a '*stranger* cur' (1.2.117), speaks of '*your* charter' (4.1.38, my italics).[65]

Another legal-historical aspect of the same trial is its swerve at 3.1.343–60 from a hearing concerning an unpaid debt to the criminal trial of the resident alien Shylock. No *English* jurisdiction could combine such actions in a single tribunal, but one particular kind of international tribunal that was periodically convened in England could do so. As I have argued in detail elsewhere, only the courts of the international Law Merchant could offer the combination of civil and criminal judgments depicted in Shakespeare's play.[66]

In England and throughout Europe tribunals of that traditional Law Merchant were set up by markets, fairs, ports and boroughs in order to allow swift resolution of mercantile disputes. Law Merchant tribunals often adjudicated disputes between merchants of differing nationalities, and so it was sometimes stipulated that a proportion of foreigners sat in judgment. Correspondingly, in Shakespeare's Venice a young lawyer purportedly from Rome, and recommended from Padua, comes to judge a case brought against a citizen by a plaintiff who is identified as 'alien' (4.1.346). An important aspect of the tribunals of Law Merchant was the rapidity and finality of their operations, a feature valued because commercial life cannot abide expensive delays. Likewise, the trial in *The Merchant of Venice* features swift summary justice. Also, the Law Merchant helped build confidence in international economic transactions because it was understood and applied equally across nations. Legal certainty and transparency are likewise noted to be economically valuable by both Antonio and Shylock (in 3.3.26–31 and 4.1.37–8). Moreover, Law Merchant tribunals were often presided over by mayors of trading towns, and the Duke oversees the court in *The Merchant of Venice* (where great Venice shrinks when warned against risks to 'the city's freedom'). Finally, as in *The Merchant of Venice*, Law Merchant tribunals could address both criminal and civil matters. This is dramatized in Ben Jonson's 1614 *Bartholomew Fair*: 2.1.1–48 where Adam Overdo, Justice of a 'Pie-poudres' (Law Merchant) court, hunts for criminal 'enormities of the Fair'.[67]

The introduction of a criminal anti-alien statute during the civil trial in *The Merchant of Venice* may correspond to the operation of such courts, but it also alludes to Elizabethan ethical and political debates concerning singling out aliens for special treatment under the law. So, during Shakespeare's lifetime several attempts were made to push economically restrictive anti-alien laws through parliament, but all of these were successfully opposed.[68] Here again Shakespeare's play may be glancing toward matters involving prejudices and resistances to them.

Other readings of Shakespeare's Venice find it mainly a venue of nascent capitalism, but I think these inadequate. Thus, at the start of *The Merchant of Venice* Antonio vehemently denies that fears of economic loss are the cause of his wearisome 'sadness' (1.1.1–7, 45). Shylock also seems un-mercenary when he lends 3,000 ducats to Antonio for three months without demanding interest (1.3.135–9). Antonio seems likewise free-handed when later dispensing Shylock's sequestered funds to others (4.1.377–87).

Nonetheless, Martin Yaffe claims that 'Profit-and-loss calculation have replaced pious contemplation' in Shakespeare's Venice.[69] His evidence for alleging that secularism has overtaken Venice includes Solanio's sacrilegious quip that the stones in the 'holy edifice' of a church will remind Antonio of the 'dangerous rocks' that threaten his profitable merchant ventures (1.1.29–36).[70] However, the jabbering Solanio's random remark indicating secularism is atypical in Shakespeare's Venice. Rather, in 1.3.97 Antonio complains about a claimed misuse of 'scripture', and in 4.1.384 he demands Shylock's forced baptism. Yaffe's allegation about rampant materialism is more justified, for Portia's inherited wealth greatly interests would-be 'Jasons' in mercantile Venice as well as more widely (1.1.172). The monetary nexus is, however, not of a dour Puritanical sort either in Venice or Belmont, for both venues particularly feature festivities involving the musical arts.

The importance of commentary on music in the play may connect with the above discussion of Shylock as a Marsyas-like figure, although I would not go so far as Kenneth Gross when he asserts that Shylock-the-unrestrained-artist is an alter ego to Shakespeare-the-artist.[71] Rather, I think that Shylock is Marsyas-like in so far as he is silenced and unable to prevail despite his uniquely piquant style of ironic self-expression. For instance, Shylock operates in a characteristically ironic mode when in conversation with Antonio in 1.3.69–89 he alleges parallels between certain biblical and commercial matters. Here Shylock replies to Antonio's boast that *he* never takes interest on loans (1.3.59–62) by first recalling the biblical patriarch Jacob's stratagem to acquire Esau's birthright. He next delivers an extended account of how Jacob obtained a cunning advantage from his uncle Laban's seemingly ungenerous offer of payment for years of his labour in the form of all newly born 'parti-coloured' lambs. Shylock concludes that Jacob's tricking of Laban was 'a way to thrive; and he was blest; / And thrift is blessing, if men steal it not'. Hearing this account of Genesis 30–1, but deaf to what Shylock subtly conveys by telling it,[72] Antonio remarks dismissively, 'The devil can cite Scripture for his purpose' (1.3.97).

Here Antonio's inattention to the import of Shylock's words displays the effective silencing a despised *someone else* who substitutes for *something else* that Antonio has unconsciously projected onto him because he does not wish to acknowledge it (or its lack) in himself. That something else connects with Antonio's inability to allow space in his mind for thinking about the care-taking and consequent thriving that Shylock associates with 'thrift'.

Most in Shakespeare's Elizabethan audiences would not have been as scornful of 'thriving' or as deaf to praises of 'thrift' as Shakespeare's self-denying Antonio. Many would have remembered that God ordains Jacob's thriving, and so sends an angel to show him how to achieve it (Genesis 31:4–13). Thus Jacob is recompensed for longstanding ill treatment when by the use of special breeding techniques he acquires Laban's best cattle. In the Geneva Bible (often used by Shakespeare) this passage is marginally glossed, 'This declareth that the thing, which *Jackob* did before, was by Gods commandement, and not through deceite', and 'This Angell was Christ'.[73]

In citing this passage Shylock warns Antonio that offering 3,000 ducats on his 'merry bond' may resemble oppressed Jacob's sly contract, or justified stratagem. This warning goes unheard because Shylock is, as usual, unheeded and effectively silenced.

The mode of warning given here closely resembles many of Shylock's utterances in being at once brash and sophisticated, strident and unheeded, indirect in tonality when most declarative in content.[74] A striking example of the same arises when, in reply to the Duke's request that he explain his 'lodged hate' and 'certain loathing' of Antonio, Shylock replies by naming a range of phobias against a rat, pig, cat and a bagpipe. Blaring bagpipes are associated with Marsyas (as is the penetrating 'wry-necked fife' decried by Shylock in 2.5.30), but aside from those Shylock's animal imagery may well suggest retaliation for repeatedly being called a cur or wolf.

Shakespeare frequently represents bigotry in which an outsider or 'stranger' is equated with some animal. This chapter has noted one instance of this in *The Comedy of Errors* and the next chapter will note multiple examples in *Coriolanus*. Such imaging is especially prominent in *The Merchant of Venice*, which contains nearly eighty contemptuous animal references. The most egregiously prejudicial of these is Lancelot Gobbo's 'jest' that his pregnant mistress – identified only as a nameless 'Negro' or 'Moor' – is less than a fully human being (3.5.35–40).[75] This is almost topped by Shylock when he counters a plea for mercy by alleging that the Christians of Venice who ill treat their 'purchased' human 'slaves' as well as their 'asses', 'dogs' and 'mules' might equally well 'marry them to your heirs' (4.1.88–97). This complex passage, which also alludes to biblical materials, thus contains Shylock's oblique innuendo that Christians might marry their heirs to vile animals.[76]

Here a typical mordant pseudo-logic characterizes a 'Shylock music' laced with irony and ambiguity. Yet, I would claim, Shylock's ambiguities are more penetrable than are Antonio's. As in life, so in artistic representations, ambiguity, verbal slippage and contradiction may attest to hidden psychic configurations. Accordingly, I will next attempt to address the paradoxical and secret repressed motives of Antonio's prejudicial opposition to Shylock.

# Why Antonio hates Shylock (and Portia)

To anticipate, the conclusion drawn here will be that self-idealizing Antonio resembles what has been called a 'libidinal narcissist', which is to say someone desperately needing yet incapable of forging genuine bonds with others.[77] The source of that might be an inadequately worked through initial maternal bond.

Useful preliminary observations include that when referring to the patriarch Jacob's 'wise mother' Rebecca (1.3.72), and equally when speaking sorrowfully about his late wife's precious squandered ring (3.1.112–14), Shylock is unique in *The Merchant of Venice* in expressing positive attitudes to motherhood. All of the ten or so other allusions to motherhood in *The Merchant of Venice* refer to cuckoldry, bastardy or the child-murdering Medea.

Additionally, and very oddly, the play at one critical juncture vitiates its own pervasive castration motif. That motif is seen when Portia's unsuccessful suitors must swear to lifelong celibacy (2.1.41–2, 2.7.75), when Shylock laments his loss of 'two sealed bags' and two precious 'stones' (2.8.18–24), when Antonio compares himself with 'a tainted wether' (4.1.113) and when Gratiano threatens to 'mar the young clerk's pen' (5.1.237). A threat of castration might also seem implicit where Shylock sets the penalty on his 'merry bond' to be 'an equal pound / Of your fair flesh to be cut off and taken / In what part of your body pleaseth me' (1.3.147–50). Indeed, one of Shakespeare's likely source texts specifically identifies the endangered body part as the merchant's 'priuie members'.[78] Therefore a strange transformation is seen in the play's court scene when Portia/Balthazar reads out the penalty clause of Antonio's forfeited bond, that states 'the Jew may claim / A pound of flesh, to be by him cut off / Nearest the merchant's heart' (4.1.228–9). Confirming this, she then commands Antonio to 'lay bare your bosom', and Shylock echoes his 'Ay, his breast. / So says the bond, doth it not, noble judge? / "Nearest his heart" – those are the very words' (4.1.249–51). This tacit alteration between Acts 1 and 4 of the text of Antonio's bond reveals something other than a classical Freudian 'displacement upwards' intended to allay fears of castration.[79] It signals rather a hidden source of Antonio's fierce prejudices that are directed at least as much against marriageable Portia as against thrift-admiring Shylock.

An explanation of this lies in Lyn Stephens's insight that Shylock's intended sadistic attack on his adversary's breast links with Antonio's 'unconscious maternal phantasies'. Stephens adds that in the play only 'Portia and Shylock do not collude' with those phantasies.[80] Thus, all but those two allow Antonio to image himself as an infinitely all-giving and always nothing-receiving mother. For instance, when granting Shylock's confiscated wealth to Jessica and her feckless Lorenzo (4.1.379–82), Antonio effectively proclaims himself possessed of an infinitely generous breast.

In reality, however, Antonio is the worst of mothers to Bassanio, for he demands in recompense for providing necessary nurture an exclusive gratitude that precludes all other relationships. This demand for exclusivity is especially evident when Antonio declares himself happy to die in order to prove to Portia that 'Bassanio had ... once a love' – that love being not hers at all, just his (4.1.261–74).

Antonio's salvation in the trial occasions only his further importuning. So, promptly after the lawsuit concludes he insists that Bassanio give the 'civil doctor' a marriage ring that he had promised Portia he would never 'give away' (3.1.171–4, 3.1.182–4, 4.1.424–51). Antonio's exact demand is: 'let him have the ring. / Let his deservings and *my love* withal / Be valued 'gainst your wife's *commandement*' (4.1.446–8, my italics). Then, thus having engineered a rift between husband and wife, the self-obsessed love-extorting Antonio again places himself in the midst of their marriage, averring '*I* am th' unhappy subject of these quarrels' (5.1.238, again my italics). Finally, he overtops his former aggressive self-sacrifices by pledging his very *soul* for Bassanio's benefit, telling Portia:

I once did lend my body for his wealth
Which, but for him that had your husband's ring,
Had quite miscarried. I dare be bound again,
My soul upon the forfeit, that your lord
Will never more break faith advisedly.

(5.1.249–53)

Lyn Stephens comments that 'In Antonio's "I once did lend my body ..." we hear the tones of a mother over her child', and adds, 'I think this is supported by use of "miscarried"' (100).[81] Here Stephens alludes to the obstetric meaning of the term. This seems correct, but additionally, in Shakespeare's time, the meanings of 'miscarry' included 'to mislead, delude, or seduce' (OED3 3), while the adverb 'advisedly' (besides meaning 'deliberately, intentionally') may poignantly allude to Antonio having misled or seduced Bassanio with coercive *advice* to override his commitment to his wife.

Antonio is finally defeated in his love contest with Portia when she forces him to deliver her wedding ring to

Bassanio (5.1.254–6). Nevertheless, the denigration of the married state implicit when Antonio sarcastically commends Bassanio to 'your honourable wife' (4.1.270) persists. This animus derives from the *'something else'* that Antonio has displaced into Jewish Shylock, his hated *'someone other'*.

The major 'projective identification'[82] represented in *The Merchant of Venice* is Antonio's unconscious relocation into both Shylock and Portia of certain tendencies or qualities that he fiercely denies possessing. These are qualities having to do with 'thrift' (meaning being careful and in consequence thriving[83]). Having dispensed with these valuable qualities, having unconsciously projected them away from himself and into Portia and Shylock, Antonio feels himself impoverished, or even a 'tainted' castrated 'wether' (4.1.113).

Most interestingly, Shylock's word 'thrift' and allied words are associated with procreation in Shakespeare's *Sonnets*.[84] We may note that (uniquely in this play) Shylock is a living father, albeit a disappointed one, and he was a loving husband to his Leah. Thriving is also made possible by the procreative mutual love between Bassanio and Portia, and that love is also a target of Antonio's intended malice.

For Shylock, 'thrift' and 'thriving' are literally the divine blessings that allow, and reward, justified self-interest. His admiration for such thrift immediately sets him at odds with an Antonio who begins the play vehemently disowning suggestions that he cares about mundane pecuniary matters. Such a disavowal by a merchant would have seemed very strange to Elizabethans – even one twice identified as a 'royal merchant' (3.2.237 and 4.1.28).[85] However, Antonio's anti-acquisitive obsessions are not only driven by a thin-skinned pride, but also have more complex roots to be examined next.

In the light of his fastidious scorning of mere lucre it may seem surprising that Antonio supplies Bassanio with 'the means' (1.1.173) to enter into an international contest to gain control of the fabulous wealth of the heiress Portia. Yet he readily borrows from Shylock in order to fund Bassanio's attempt to profit from Portia's subjection to 'the will of [her] dead father' (which she laments in 1.2.20–6). As odd as that profit-seeking enterprise may now seem, borrowing to fund a marital venture with potentially huge rewards was not unknown in Shakespeare's age.[86] But still, how does his giving the means and lamenting the outcome fit with the image of the self-denying Antonio?

Martin Yaffe proposes that Antonio purposely encourages the spendthrift lifestyles of his friends in order to encourage dependency and thus feed his compulsion to be their all-provider.[87] This seems correct, but leaves unexplained Antonio's 'want-wit' sadness when Bassanio goes off to Belmont to seek marriage. Whether interpretations of his homoerotic impulses are accepted or not, the play subsequently reveals that the 'generous' Antonio does not respect Bassanio's marriage, or any marriage. This is because he despises human relationships based on reciprocity, negotiation and agreed-upon realistic limits. That is to say, Antonio's aim to be all-giving opposes *thrifty* arrangements that allow for the *thriving* of mutual and mature (as opposed to asymmetrical and infantile) exchanges of affection and dependency.

My final chapter will focus on Shakespearian representations of challenges to committed mutual erotic linkages, but it should be mentioned in anticipation of that that similar issues arise in *The Merchant of Venice* when Bassanio and Lorenzo are taught that they cannot 'generously' dispose of the symbols of marital exclusivity (their marriage rings) without risking the fidelity of their wives.

In *The Merchant of Venice* Shylock's vengeful grievance derives from external ill treatment and his daughter's abandonment of her home and heritage,[88] while Antonio's urge to destroy has to do with arrested development and internal rigidities. All the female leads in the play declare they have been oppressed by patriarchal domination (1.2.21–6, 2.3.1–3) but, unlike the men, all of these women circumvent impulses to infantile acting out and vengeance. Instead, all of them ameliorate adverse situations by acquiring agency through cross-dressing. I wonder if it is implied that, once undisguised, they will be thrust back into subordinate roles? Perhaps so, for once she is undisguised Jessica seems forced to comply with her new husband's squandering of her mother's emotionally valued turquoise ring.[89] Are Portia and Nerissa likewise fated to adapt to 'the way things are'?

In any case, *The Merchant of Venice* draws attention to societal and psychic arrangements that produce deeply felt exclusions of gender. Elsewhere I have given detailed attention to psychological resonances in this play of gender issues,[90] and will further explore related matters in the last chapter of this book.

# Was Shakespeare's age much concerned about 'racial' outsiders?

Together with many others I have pointed out that racist notions that possessing a particular skin colour per se will limit a human being's capacities did not figure largely in Western culture before the eighteenth or nineteenth century.[91] Perhaps a precursor theory of inherited inferiority lay in the earlier notion that a lack of 'purity of blood' discredited Jewish *conversos*. This belief is brilliantly satirized in an interlude written by Shakespeare's contemporary Cervantes,[92] and is also contradicted when Jessica in *The Merchant of Venice*, although only newly converted to Christianity, is said by bigoted Salerio to have entirely different 'blood' than her Jewish father Shylock (3.1.36–7).[93] Her purification by baptism is thus accepted by many, if not all, in Shakespeare's play.[94]

According to Mary Floyd-Wilson, an ancient theory that held that a person's propensities and abilities may be delimited or enhanced by the climatic conditions of their place of birth (because the weather determines their balance of their 'humours') found 'new currency' in Shakespeare's age.[95] These 'climate' or 'geohumoural' theories align well with

Shakespearian depictions of some of his foreign characters (for instance, the low libido of Aaron the Moor and the high libido of the Goth Queen Tamora in *Titus Andronicus*). However, the Prince of Morocco denies them flatly in *The Merchant of Venice* when he insists on the parity of his 'blood' with 'the fairest creature northward born' (2.1.1–12).[96] Geohumoural theories are also revealed to be only misleading when Desdemona applies them to deny the possibility of Othello's jealousy:

EMILIA
                Is he not jealous?
DESDEMONA
  Who, he? I think the sun where he was born
  Drew all such humours from him.
                                    (3.4.29–31)

Another contradiction is that geohumouralism holds that southern origin results in weak erotic drives such as those of Shakespeare's Aaron the Moor, but this is unlikely to apply to Othello. Geohumouralism also holds that southern origin fosters greater mental agility and subtlety than northern, yet cunning Iago is subtler than his southern-born general.[97]

These points of dissention from received theories bear witness to Shakespeare's untrammelled thinking. That, in turn, gives grounds for what some may think a shocking claim. This claim is that, despite some appearances to the contrary, Iago's hatred of Othello has little to do with his skin colour. Although many may disagree with this proposition, some critics have supported it vehemently.[98] I myself will offer support for it by demonstrating comparability between Iago's 'malignity' towards the two 'strangers', 'black' Moorish Othello and 'white' Florentine Michael Cassio.[99]

It is interesting to note that although Stanley Edgar Hyman's book-length attempt to delineate Iago's motivations ranges widely – importantly claiming that no single critical perspective can do justice to Shakespeare's play[100] – it never once mentions 'race', 'blackness' or 'ethnicity'. This is, of course, despite

Iago's racialist provocations of Brabantio at the play's start featuring vile animalistic slurs.[101] Questioning why Hyman (who was a close friend of Ralph Ellison) discounts these slurs leads me to suppose that, had he considered them, Hyman would have categorized them alongside Iago's rumination on having been cuckolded by Othello, which he calls an altogether 'unconvincing explanation' of Iago's motivation. Thus, Hyman categorizes Iago's 'charge' that 'it is thought abroad that "twixt my sheets / [the Moor"] has done my office' (1.3.379–80), as something that 'is patently untrue, is flatly contradicted by other things that Iago says about Othello, and after one more repetition in Act II, scene 1, is entirely forgotten' (104).

Iago being blasé about Emelia's suspected adultery results from the crucial fact that his extreme egotism makes him immune to suffering on account of others' actions. Such immunity characterizes what psychoanalysts call 'thick-skinned destructive narcissism', a narcissism that discounts all human connectedness while admitting an 'enormous idealization of the destructive parts of the self which [are] felt to be attractive because they made the [narcissistic] patient feel so omnipotent'.[102] Enjoying that idealization is, I think, Iago's only source of pleasure, leaving no space for genuine feelings about Emilia's fidelity, or Emilia herself. Thus in the only scene in which pair are alone together Emilia delivers Desdemona's stolen handkerchief in a miserably unsuccessful attempt to win her husband's affections (3.3.304–15). Moreover, even when musing on the possibility of her infidelity Iago reacts as though Emilia's true behaviour is insignificant, his own mental processes being all-important: 'I know not if 't be true; But I, *for mere suspicion* in that kind, / Will do as if for surety' (1.3.380–2, italics mine).

I have said that Iago resembles a 'thick skinned narcissist', and can back that up by citing his unperturbed reaction when Cassio insinuates that he lacks the 'breeding' and 'courtesy' to understand the 'manners' of the well-bred (2.1.100–2), and also when the drunken Cassio asserts that precedence of rank applies soteriologically so that 'The lieutenant is to be saved before the ensign' (2.3. 102–3).[103]

The reason I doubt that Iago is similar to the 'thin-skinned narcissists' described by Herbert Rosenfeld as 'hypersensitive and easily hurt'[104] is his manifestation of typical 'thick-skinned' patterns of pseudo-rationality and hyper-objectivity.[105] These emerge when he pretends at being an 'honest' and 'plain' Diogenes-like vice-detecting figure.[106]

Returning briefly to the question of 'racism', it is notable that scholars have determined that the word 'Moor', which is heard about sixty times in *Othello*, was not necessarily a derogatory 'racial epithet' in Shakespeare's age.[107] Also, very few in the *Othello* play-world deploy adverse epithets against *any* exotic outsiders, any of whom might have been called 'moors'.[108] The exceptions to this include, as mentioned, Iago and Roderigo when they set out to bait Brabantio, but also Othello himself when he compares his despairing self-slaughter to his overcoming of 'a malignant and a turbaned Turk' (5.2.361–5). Othello's denigration of this Turk reveals how splitting off bad parts of the self and projecting them into an exotic stranger may beget prejudicial 'racial' epithets.[109] (Interestingly, this remark is the sole place in the entire play where Venice's Turkish adversaries are referred to with anything but respect.)

In fact, the loyal, brave, vigorous and effective Othello consistently elicits the opposite of denigration from almost all the play's Venetians, who repeatedly call him a 'noble Moor', 'valiant Moor', 'brave Moor', 'the Moor my lord', etc. Even the Duke of Venice, upon hearing from Othello that the patrician Brabantio 'loved me, oft invited me, / Still questioned me the story of my life' (1.3.127–8), asserts that knowledge of Othello's brave exploits 'would win my daughter too' (1.3.170).

Therefore mere prejudice against the 'race' of 'someone other' does not appear to be a prime driver in *Othello*, and this raises the question of what projected 'something else' provokes Iago's prejudicial hatred.

# Iago's prejudices: where despising *someone other* is a projection of *something else*

Iago recognizes that 'The Moor is of a free and open nature' (1.3.191–4), albeit only because he thinks these qualities make him ripe for exploitation. The positive nature of such qualities becomes evident when as acting as governor of Cyprus Othello wields authority with grace and ease. Later on, when patrician Lodovico visiting from Venice witnesses Othello abusing his wife, he is shocked and amazed. So Lodovico exclaims 'this would not be believed in Venice / Though I should swear I saw't' (4.1.242–3), and he can only posit the mental breakdown of this erstwhile 'noble Moor' (4.1.266–71).

Before his downfall Othello seems free of bigotry, but after his seduction by Iago he stereotypes Desdemona as 'that cunning whore of Venice' (4.2.93) and labels the 'turbaned Turk' who 'Beat a Venetian and traduced the state' a 'circumcised dog' (5.2.361–4). Among the half-dozen derogatory mentions of dogs in *Othello* Lodovico labels Venetian Iago a 'Spartan Dog', but only one of these refers to an ethnic outsider. That one, Othello's, may rank among the worst of all the dehumanizing animal metaphors heard in Shakespeare.[110]

A crucial phrase spoken by Iago is 'I follow but myself' (1.1.58). A thoroughgoing narcissist, he considers Roderigo, his wife and Desdemona as conveniences to be steered and exploited at will. In the same passage (to be considered more fully presently) Iago speaks of a 'peculiar end' that he will pursue through dissimulation, for 'I am not what I am' (1.1.60, 65). As will be seen, Iago's 'peculiar end' is not to seek to 'thrive' materially (as he alleges in 1.1.53), but rather to provoke chaos and destruction.

That destruction takes two forms. The deaths of Roderigo, Desdemona and Emilia serve only as means to Iago's ends, while the disgracing of Cassio and the complete unmaking of Othello are more purposeful. When Iago speculates, beginning

'Were I the Moor' in 1.1.57, he adumbrates his purposes, for his modal subjunctive shadows the unstated question, 'why am I *not* the Moor, the one who is loved, respected and renowned for his courtesy and grace?'. Iago similarly half-reveals himself and half-lies to himself when he posits a contingent reason (safety) for inciting a fight in which Cassio 'must die'. The true root of his scheming is admitted in his immediately preceding remark that Cassio 'hath a daily beauty in his life / That makes me ugly' (5.1.19–22).[111] Thus Iago betrays destructive envy that has nothing in common with emulative jealousy or acquisitive desire.

In fact, Shakespeare's Iago never seriously seeks to obtain anything that he values or covets, which is possessed by another, for himself. For instance, his cunning ploys are never directed toward getting the lovely Desdemona into his bed[112] and I would maintain that he has no designs on her at all except to use her as a means to bring Othello down.[113] My basis for alleging this (in the face of contrary readings)[114] is that whereas brilliantly manipulative Iago manoeuvres both Othello and Cassio into appallingly discreditable behaviours that they sorely regret,[115] Desdemona's mental suffering is only incidental to his schemes. Therefore he allows her to exhibit an unsullied nobility of spirit until she dies.

Seemingly contrary to these propositions, Iago rationalizes that he has certain acquisitive or vengeful motives in his soliloquy at 1.3.375–96. However, I believe that he reveals at the same time that he is lying to himself. Thus he states that in gulling Roderigo he follows his longstanding policy of filling his 'purse' at the expense of a contemptuously viewed 'fool' or 'snipe', adding that he does this 'But for my sport and profit'. This locution suggests that wealth obtained by trickery is useful, but feeling superior to its snipe-like possessors has a stronger draw.[116] Next Iago half-heartedly rationalizes his hatred of 'the Moor' by musing that Othello may have cuckolded him (a claim soon dropped, as noted above). Another rationalization then appears, that Iago aims to 'get [Cassio's] place'. This new claim to an acquisitive motive is bracketed, however, by Iago's sneering remarks that 'Cassio is a proper man' and that by displacing Cassio he will 'plume up my will'.

Thus, as opposed to *getting* anything, bringing low a 'proper man' and pluming up his self-esteem seem crucial for Iago. This is confirmed toward the end of the same soliloquy when Iago resolves to cast doubts on Desdemona's fidelity. For surely his sharp intelligence knows that destroying Othello's marriage will not gain him promotion or any other external benefit. It will, however, yield the satisfaction he remarks on of proving that Othello may be 'as tenderly led by th' nose / As asses are' (1.3.393–4). The soliloquy then concludes with Iago invoking 'Hell and night'. The context shows that this is the hell of envy rather than the mundane locale of acquisitive 'mimetic desire'.[117]

Iago's drive toward destruction differs from anything accountable for in terms of emulative jealousy. This is confirmed when Iago opens the play with remarks addressed to Roderigo, but mainly spoken to himself, concerning Cassio's recent promotion. The promotion was unwarranted, he claims, because Cassio is only a theoretical soldier skilled in 'Mere prattle without practice' while he is a battle-tested veteran (1.1.18–32). Iago's venom proceeds not from being thwarted in his desire for recognition, but rather from his sense that he is too good to have been denied it. Thus when he recalls how his supporters, three 'great ones of the city', met only Othello's peremptory reply 'I have already chose my officer', Iago states he should not have had to ask for help, for 'I know my price, I am worth no worse a place' (1.1.7–11).

The question of 'place' is a crucial one in the play. For instance, a fine discrimination concerning 'place' is seen when Brabantio initially treats Othello with benign curiosity and even affection, but later claims that only witchcraft could have induced his daughter to marry this elderly soldier having a 'sooty bosom' (1.2,64–76). Despite these remarks on skin-colour and age, patrician Brabantio's objection to the runaway marriage is more 'class' based than 'racially' based (to use two convenient anachronisms). This is because, as Shakespeare could have known, the military chiefs of Venice were not drawn from its patrician classes, but were rather *condottieri* often hired from far afield, giving the Venetian forces a 'Noah's ark quality'.[118] Thus Brabantio can socially entertain the bought-in General Othello, but cannot abide him, for dynastic reasons, as a family member.

Iago's animus against Othello and also against Cassio may appear to come conversely 'from below', based on 'class antagonism'. But, in addition to that, Iago's particular outrage arises because neither Othello and Cassio are native to Venice and yet both have acquired more esteem and risen to higher positions that the intelligent and capable native son that he is. Feeling marginalized in comparison with upstart 'strangers', in a familiar pattern Iago finds them worthy of prejudicial contempt.[119]

The concept of an egotist with a weak ego may seem paradoxical, but this is seen at work when, via his deliberate self-presentation as an unrefined, blunt, straight-speaking soldier lacking any sophistication, Iago deliberately feigns the characteristics of debased social and cultural levels. This is among other complex reasons why he provokes others to call him 'honest Iago' – when, according to Weston Babcock, calling someone 'honest' implied social condescension.[120] Just as the play begins Iago alleges that his lowly 'honesty' is a ruse or sham, and his pretence at being a humble and plain-dealing subordinate a deliberate contrivance. However, I imagine that one way an actor might play this feigning accords with George Orwell's description: 'He wears a mask, and his face grows to fit it'.[121]

Thus Iago tacitly (but boastfully) associates himself with clever but fawning 'Others' in his description to Roderigo of:

> Others there are
> Who, trimmed in forms and visages of duty,
> Keep yet their hearts attending on themselves,
> And, throwing but shows of service on their lords,
> Do well thrive by 'em, and when they have lined their coats,

> Do themselves homage. These fellows have some soul,
> And such a one do I profess myself – for, sir,
> It is as sure as you are Roderigo,
> Were I the Moor I would not be Iago.
> In following him I follow but myself.
> Heaven is my judge, not I for love and duty,
> But seeming so for my peculiar end.
>
> (1.1.49–58)

The play indicates that Iago's chosen 'peculiar end' is first to sully, then to break and bury, all positive human connections. Such an attack resembles the indiscriminate attacks on inner and outer objects that the psychoanalyst Ronald Fairbairn ascribes to an anti-libidinal 'internal saboteur'.[122]

A belief that he can never attain Othello or Cassio's positive qualities, their 'beauty' or innate nobility, infuriates Iago. Envy thus drives his murderous attacks on two greatly esteemed 'strangers', one of whom is coincidentally what we call 'white' and the other 'black'.

The 'peculiar end' that Iago pursues indeed has nothing to do 'love and duty', as he says himself. It is equally opposed to desire, truth and beauty. His aim is death and destruction because Iago's prejudicial despising of the 'others' Iago and Cassio is a cover for his dismissals of positive qualities that he believes are unattainable by himself. Here projecting 'something else' into 'someone other' shows itself at its worst.

# 4

# Prejudices against peace

*And peace proclaims olives of endless age.*
*Now with the drops of this most balmy time*
*My love looks fresh, and death to me subscribes*
    SHAKESPEARE'S SONNETS 107

                                        *peace,*
*Dear nurse of arts, plenties, and joyful births*
    HENRY V 5.2.34–5

*Sword, pike, knife, gun, or need of any engine,*
*Would I not have ...*
    GONZALO'S UTOPIA, THE TEMPEST 2.1.187–8

*Why, I in this weak piping time of peace*
*Have no delight to pass away the time,*
*Unless to spy my shadow in the sun*
*And descant on mine own deformity.*
    KING RICHARD III 1.1.24–7

# The possibility of this topic despite an alleged 'instinct' for violence

For the speaker in Sonnet 107 a time of peace is a 'balmy time' occasioning love and plenty. Reflecting debates of his age, varied characters in Shakespeare's plays and poems sometimes yearn for and sometimes despair of fighting or warfare. Many critics agree that bellicose Shakespearian voices are usually presented as flawed or unsympathetic, and that Shakespeare characteristically suggests that peace is valuable and violent conflict harmful.[1] Of particular interest here is that Shakespearian figures' preferences for violence over peace often bear the hallmarks of the misguided thoughtlessness that characterizes prejudice.

This investigation might seem to lie athwart certain views in which human aggression is seen as inevitable and inherent. Yet I am not convinced that R. A. Foakes insists on this when his study of *Shakespeare and Violence* focuses attention on propensities to violence that 'may be related to the deepest instincts in human beings, especially in males'.[2] Rather, Foakes adopts a point of view from which the whole of our literary tradition suggests 'there is such a thing as human nature, giving us instincts and modes of behaviour that are still affected by the deep-rooted urges to claim territory, defend the tribe, protect women and children, and use violence to fight for and maintain possessions' (2). For Foakes, then, an inherent 'human aggressiveness' underlies 'the force of impulses and instincts we have to learn to manage' (21). Taking this perspective, however, does not preclude the possibility that desires for peaceable and kindly human relations may also advance human survival and the thriving of human families and societies – and does not prevent noting that Shakespeare may attest to just such tendencies and desires.

A propos 'instincts', it may be noted the word 'instinct' never appears in this book (other than in quotations). That omission is partly to avoid suggesting that certain propensities in the realms of emotions or behaviour are so monolithic and static as to be unopposed by contrary ones. This term is also avoided because there has been great confusion over its uses, and because there have been well-argued complaints that notions of 'instinct' have been unscientifically reified.[3] Such caution, however, does not prevent discussion of Shakespeare's representations of contrasting and sometimes contradictory human drives.

The following chapter will therefore focus on a propensity for conflict resolution and the avoidance of violence that is exhibited by some Shakespearian characters and is prejudicially opposed or shunned by some others. A few examples might clarify this. Seduced by Iago, Othello self-pityingly mourns his loss of the 'Pride, pomp, and circumstance of glorious war!' and laments that 'Othello's occupation's gone' (3.3.359–62). He then abuses, assaults and murders his wife. Yet earlier Othello was his play's 'noble Moor' who quelled impending violence by a sheer display of his own authoritative better disposition: simply by intoning 'Keep up your bright swords, for the dew will rust 'em' (1.2.60). This portrayal of a shining character type presents a no less authentic example of what Foakes calls the 'human condition' (21) than does the play's subsequent portrayal of murderous Othello.

Likewise, when Romeo attempts to dispel mindless hot-headed aggression in 3.1.67–71 (to be discussed presently) he is not presented as less genuinely human than are the combatant factions of Verona. As early in his career as the *Henry VI* plays Shakespeare depicts the horrors of conflict and warfare in which sons kill fathers and fathers sons; the tone of abnormality there also indicates that Hobbsean civil war or dissention is far from the only human possibility. I will thus call certain rejections of peaceable outlooks and behaviours 'prejudicial', because they are unwarranted attacks on human potentialities that are good in themselves.

The first three sections below will discuss Shakespeare's portrayals of violent personal feuds and duels based on prejudice-inducing notions of 'honour'. The remaining sections will consider how prejudices may inspire preferences for war over peace.

# One-to-one combat in law, legend and Shakespeare

> And sometimes [in duelling] men ... suffer themselves to bee carried awaie and overmastered too much with choler and rage ... take heede that you suffer not your selfe to bee blinded and carried awaje with rage and furie.
> 
> Vincentio Saviolo, 1595[4]

> these Italianated, weake, fantasticall, and most divellish and imperfect fights ...
> 
> George Silver, 1599[5]

At the extremely dishonourable end of a wide spectrum of fighting portrayed by Shakespeare, thuggish brawling in *2 Henry IV* results in the arrest of Mistress Quickly and Doll Tearsheet as accomplices to murder: 'for the man is dead that you and Pistol beat amongst you' (5.4.16–17). Near the opposite end, a chivalric challenge to one-to-one combat is generously deferred, with honour kept intact, in *Henry V* 4.8.40–72 when the common soldier Williams challenges the disguised Henry V and is pardoned and given compensation. This section will consider Shakespeare's widely varied representations of 'honour'-based personal fighting, and ask to what extent those varieties present reprehensible prejudices against peace.

Some one-to-one combats portrayed by Shakespeare are legally sanctioned trials by combat authorized by medieval law. Others are bouts between national champions that accord with (perhaps mythical) ancient laws of war.[6] In these cases victory was supposed to yield justice and truth via divine intervention. Some also believed that winning would reveal contested truth (or who truly 'lied') in the 'honour'-led private duelling that was illegal but still prevalent in Shakespeare's England.

I will be arguing that Shakespeare always presents legally or traditionally sanctioned one-to-one fights as problematic, and that he represents private duelling as particularly irrational, absurd and dangerous. However, he is sometimes more sanguine when presenting ceremonial tournaments or swordplay intended for sport and display, as for instance when impoverished Prince Pericles' personal merit outweighs wealth and station and he wins a royal bride in an artistically performed ceremonial display of arms. Shakespeare himself apparently countenanced a contemporary revival of ceremonial chivalric displays, and indeed was very well paid, when he composed the text of an *impressa* that was painted on the shield of a contestant entering the ceremonial royal lists in 1613.[7] On the other hand, in *The Two Noble Kinsmen* contention for a bride results in a less peaceable tilt; there the winning competitor dies when thrown from his horse (which hardly seems a sign of divine sanction). Worse still, the courtly demonstration of skilled swordplay ending *Hamlet* is subverted with murderous intent when the trappings of courtly ritual become 'a mere scutcheon' covering a covert scheme to supply a poisoned rapier (agreed to in 3.7.112–21) and Claudius's aim to bypass legal due processes (admitted to in 4.7.9–24).

The highly questionable legality and morality of all private duelling will be a main topic in this section. That must be distinguished from the allowed legality of certain other modes of single combat. For instance, in the English Middle Ages an 'appellant' was allowed to seek a *trial by battle* when making a legal *appeal of felony* or *wager of law*.[8] Such trials by battle were not officially abolished in England until 1819 – however, such a challenge issued in 1571 'caused contemporary astonishment and much antiquarian interest', the outcome being arbitration and a 'token fight' between champions in the lists.[9]

Interestingly, each time Shakespeare represents even such sanctioned trials by battle they are either aborted (as in Bolingbroke v Mowbray in *Richard II*), portrayed as absurd (as in Thump v Horner in *2 Henry VI*), or else are doubly legally illegitimate (as in *King Lear* where Edgar is disguised and Edmund is a bastard).[10] Thus Shakespeare consistently portrays judicial battles as failing or flawed, suggesting that he did not consider legalized violence a means to truthful or just outcomes.[11]

Shakespeare also consistently represents as ineffective or inconclusive fights that accord with a (probably mythical) convention whereby outcomes of warfare are decided by which of the champions of two armies defeats the other in single combat. Susan Snyder also explains that, 'where single combat is offered in place of massed battle', then Shakespeare makes 'it clear enough that such gestures have little to do with the realities of warfare'.[12] Snyder's examples are *1 Henry IV* 5.1.96–103 where Prince Hal is denied his wish to challenge Hotspur to single combat, *Antony and Cleopatra* where Antony's challenge to single combat with Caesar (conveyed in 3.13.24–36) is rejected and ridiculed (4.1.3–6), and *Troilus and Cressida* where the duel 'between Hector and Ajax, is ludicrously brief and indecisive' (201–2). To these examples may be added *1 Henry VI* 1.7.1–15 where Joan seems to prevail over Talbot in single combat but then breaks off her fight without resolution.

Onstage single combats between national champions may sometimes belong to a *theatrical* convention in which results of a battle between armies is signalled by the outcomes of a symbolic fight between leading figures; Susan Snyder calls this a 'synecdoche, made necessary by limited theater space and personnel' (210). However, more than that is at stake in *1 Henry IV* when Prince Hal encounters Hotspur on the battlefield and single-handedly vanquishes him. Before that unplanned chance meeting Hal expresses his wish for an arranged single combat 'to save the blood on either side' (5.1.99). Hotspur similarly wishes 'O, would the quarrel lay upon our heads, / And that no man might draw short breath today / But I and Harry Monmouth!' (5.2.47–9). However, the verbal exchange leading up to their fight (5.4.69–79) conveys a contrary impression that both combatants hold their reputations and honour more precious than others' or their own lives, so their humanitarian concerns for others seem subordinated to their personal vaunting. In yet another reversal, Hal takes no personal credit for having defeated Hotspur and instead allows the reputation for this victory to pass to Falstaff, who is not only rankly dishonourable in battle but also the avowed enemy of honour (5.1.127–40).

Is Hal's motive for doing this solely to save Hotspur's reputation from 'ignominy', as he suggests in 5.4.98–100? Another possibility, which I think correct, is that Hal accepts that the outcome of his single combat with Hotspur represents the judgement of higher powers, and not his own prowess.[13] That would mean he is not honour-led, but rather justice-led.

Ancient instances of national champions vanquishing or being vanquished vary all the way from the providential nature of the Israelite David defeating the Philistine champion Goliath (1 Samuel 17) to the squalid mob killing of Trojan Hector depicted in Shakespeare's *Troilus and Cressida*. That latter instance, which will be examined in detail presently, is particularly dishonourable, for Hector allows the bested Achilles to live after their one-to-one bout in 5.6.13–19 only to be slaughtered when caught unarmed by Achilles and his Myrmidon henchmen (5.9.9–15). Very similarly, Shakespeare's Aufidius shirks conclusive single combat with Coriolanus (1.9.14–15), and later ignobly slays him.

Although the term 'honour' appears in every one of Shakespeare's plays and poems, totalling almost 300 instances, Shakespeare consistently undermines the concept of military honour. That was perhaps because by his time chivalric honour on the battlefield was often seen as meaningless or unwarranted, as for example when Sir Philip Sidney's heroic but foolish eschewing of leg armour resulted in a slow, agonizing death following a gunshot wound. Thus Susan Snyder emphasizes that by Shakespeare and Sidney's time siege tactics and massed armies were decisive in warfare, and personal valour counted for little. Grace Tiffany similarly maintains that Shakespeare's two historical tetralogies indicate that gunpowder made the rules of chivalric warfare increasingly nonsensical.[14]

In counterpoint to these developments in attitudes regarding warfare, a penchant for violently defending personal honour was an increasing trend in Elizabethan England and contemporary Europe. Training for private duelling had become so fashionable that even Shakespeare's idiotic wooer Slender in *The Merry Wives of Windsor* attempts to impress middling-class Anne Page by alluding to how he had 'bruised my shin th' other day, with playing at sword and dagger with a master of fence' (1.1.263–5). The fashion for duelling shared some of the presumptions of other forms of one-to-one fighting (especially that a victor is *morally* vindicated). Yet it also differed in significant ways. For one, duelling was not ceremonial in essence, in that its combatants did not wield the bated swords used in training or in fencing competitions, and rather used weapons capable of inflicting severe harm. Also the deadly belligerence in duelling was not sanctioned by law or by martial customs.

Nevertheless, many in Shakespeare's society regarded duelling as required when affront was taken. Other Elizabethans, however, held that the cult of duelling posed a serious threat not only to individual lives, but also to the stability of civil life. It will be argued that Shakespeare's works lean toward the latter view, and also often expose prejudicial elements in the culture of duelling.

The historical background to this is that, despite several royal proclamations prohibiting duelling and several treatises decrying its vogue,[15] English private duels occurred with mounting frequency from the 1580s through the 1610s, often attracting much publicity.[16] Hence Shakespeare's audiences would have recognized cowardly Pistol's ranting parody of a challenge to a duel '*solus*' in *Henry V* 2.1.44–51, Touchstone's parodic disquisition on the approved basis for a formal *duello* in *As You Like It* 5.4.46–101, and foppish Osric's bombast about fencing in *Hamlet* 5.2.107–41. Likewise, the social pressures that compelled unwilling combatants to accept duelling challenges are travestied in *Twelfth Night* 3.4.141–96 and 215–301 and *The Merry Wives of Windsor* 1.4.103–15, 2.1.189–215, 2.3 and 3.1.

Elizabethans adopted not only the conventions of honour, courtesy, reputation, insult and challenge that underwrote the endemic cult of duelling in France, Italy and Spain, but also the foreign weapons used there in connection with it. Thus, despite voices raised against this, many Elizabethans abandoned traditional English broadswords and learned the use of flexible, pointed continental rapiers. Their effective use required more in the way of practised skill than of raw strength and those duelling weapons, intended for thrusting, were particularly lethal in comparison to heavy military swords.[17] So Osric in *Hamlet* reports that Laertes has come home to Elsinore from Paris having acquired 'excellence ... at his weapon' (5.2.106–8), and Hamlet retorts, 'Since he went into France, I have been in continual practice. I shall win at the odds' (5.2.156–7). The wagers laid on their contest include 'six French rapiers and poniards' (5.2.113–14) – a 'rapier' is mentioned five times in the text and once more in a stage direction (tln 3777) in the Folio *Hamlet*. Overall, 'rapiers' are named thirty-one times in sixteen Shakespeare plays.[18]

These instances align with the everyday Elizabethan practice of carrying bladed weapons.[19] The frequent use of these by hot-headed young men too often led to deadly outcomes; one source claims that 'many "distinguished" families in England had lost at least one member in a duel'.[20] Another estimate is 'that England, especially after 1603, probably resembled France with regard to mortality rates from duels; in France between 1590 and 1610, despite the illegality of duelling there, "one-third of the nobility – around 4,000 men – were killed in private combats"'.[21] The main question here is whether Shakespeare's representations of the dangers of such private fighting expose prejudices against peace.

# Violence in *Romeo and Juliet* and a vogue for murder à la mode

Shakespeare's treatments in *Romeo and Juliet* of endemic fighting in Verona, and of opposition to fighting there, imply important insights into prejudices against peace. To begin explorations of those insights the present section will investigate Elizabethan legal-contextual matters alongside likely Elizabethan audience reactions to the fights that result in the deaths of Mercutio and Tybalt and the exile of Romeo.

Shakespeare's representations of fighting must have been inflected by the late Elizabethan situation in which increasingly destructive but increasingly rife 'honour'-based interpersonal violence was accepted or approved of by many, but not all. According to Michael Ovens, Shakespeare himself expressed an 'opposition to the fashionable institution of duelling'.[22] In this regard he would have resembled Francis Bacon, who was particularly notable among those holding anti-duelling positions.[23] In 1614 Bacon published a speech he had made in Star Chamber that argued for the punishment of a two men who had arranged a duel. In this speech Bacon asserted a hope to establish a strong legal precedent that would prohibit duels in England,[24] and laid out several reasons for doing so. These include that duelling 'gives the law an affront' when 'the year books and statute books must give place to some French and Italian pamphlets, which handle the doctrine of *Duells*' (10), and that duelling is 'a desperate evil … it troubleth peace, it disfurnisheth war, it bringeth calamity upon private men, perill upon the state, and contempt upon the lawe' (11). 'Touching the causes' of duelling, Bacon approves of a 1613 proclamation of King James that deplores '*bewitching Duells*', and then elaborates 'that we have not to doe, in this case, so much with perticuler persons, as with unsound and depraved opinions, like the dominations and spirits of the ayre, which the Scripture speaketh of' (11–13).

Bacon thus refers to a social-psychological obsession that may overlay the free will of 'perticular persons'. However, Bacon (and Shakespeare as well, as will be seen) did not believe that the bewitchment of duelling was inescapable. On the contrary, in his two essays, 'Of Revenge' and 'Of Anger', Bacon expounds reasons to believe individuals capable of resisting 'unsound and depraved' impetuses to fight with one another. Bacon's first essay (11–12) famously begins 'Revenge is a kind of wild justice' and then contrasts revenge with forgiveness and with true justice, noting that 'the more man's nature runs to [revenge], the more ought law to weed it out'. The law may weed out revenge killing, but Bacon's essay also stresses that nobility of spirit alone dictates pardoning of injuries, and thus cites Solomon's *'It is the glory of a man to pass by an offence'*. Bacon's second essay, 'Of Anger' (145–6), denies the possibility of extinguishing anger but insists that acting rashly as a result of it may be restrained. So Bacon acknowledges dangerous aspects of human nature, but claims wisdom, willpower and good intentions may overcome folly.

Alongside a growing prominence of the practice of duelling, and also of opposition to it, another historical factor bears on how original audiences may have perceived the sword fight in *Romeo and Juliet* in which Romeo kills Tybalt. Some details will be needed to explain this.

Romeo's love for Juliet makes him hope for the cession of the violently expressed mutual scorns and mislike between their families. So, even in the face of strong verbal provocations, he initially addresses Tybalt as 'good Capulet' (3.1.67–71). He also pleads that angry Tybalt and Mercutio heed the Prince's forbidding of 'bandying in Verona streets' (3.1.86–7). Why, then, does the just-married Romeo, who wises to promote peace and defuse conflict, soon after give way to a violent impulse?

At first Romeo refuses to take the bait when Tybalt tauntingly calls him 'a villain' and addresses him as 'Boy' (3.1.60, 65–6). He concludes his response, rather, with 'good Capulet – which name I tender / As dearly as mine own – be satisfied' (67–71).

However, his friend Mercutio, being present, perceives this as 'calm, dishonourable, vile submission' (72). So Mercutio challenges Tybalt to fight, which is gladly accepted. Next Romeo solicits Benvolio's help to 'Beat down their weapons' (84), but this intervention enables Tybalt's rapier thrust 'under [Romeo's] arm' (103) that mortally wounds Mercutio.

Several studies indicate that a typical Elizabethan awareness of fencing styles would have strongly affected audience perceptions of these events. Because of its knowledgeable audiences, according to Charles Edelman, Elizabethan theatre staged sword fighting 'with the most convincing sort of realism'.[25] Lois Potter (concerning court performances) and Evelyn Tribble (more generally) agree, and Jay P. Anglin adds that 'Shakespeare's patrons at the Globe ... would surely have distinguished in minute detail the differences between foreign and domestic codes of swordsmanship'.[26] Adolph L. Soens further claims that in England 'by the 1590s Italian technique had replaced the Spanish technique' of fencing,[27] and this is backed by in other studies.[28] Soens then makes a suggestion, well supported by contemporary fencing treatises and details of Benvolio's description of the fight, that Shakespeare's Elizabethan audiences would have recognized a stark contrast between the 'efficient and popular Italian fencing [style] of Mercutio' and 'the formal, deadly and pedantic Spanish fencing of Princox ... Tybalt'.[29] Thus, Soens explains, the upright posture in the Spanish fencing style used by Tybalt gains him a distinct advantage over Mercutio 'crouched in stoccata' when both their rapiers were 'beaten down from the side'. Soens adds further that Renaissance fencing masters warned of the likelihood of an unfair outcome if a third party attempted to part active fencers, and that for fear of this danger Italian authorities prohibited anyone interposing between fencers (126–7 and 127n22).

Soens claims, moreover, that this contrast of fencing styles involves not only easily recognizable differences in 'posture and motion', but also has 'implications' (126). For present purposes, the most significant implication bears on Romeo's reaction to Tybalt's killing of Mercutio. Several possibilities arise (and may overlap), including that Romeo is infuriated by Tybalt's opportunistic and literally underhanded taking of an unfair advantage when he delivered the death blow. Romeo is possibly also overwhelmed by guilt and chagrin because he had carelessly ignored the warnings of experts about the dangers of interposing between fencers.

Also Romeo – likely in common with many in Shakespeare's audiences – may mislike the image presented by Tybalt's Spanish manner of fencing. Thus Evelyn Tribble asserts that 'Mercutio fences Italian style, which at this point had become appropriated as a native English style ... In contrast, Tybalt fights by "the book of arithmetic" ... the "Spanish style"'.[30] For late Elizabethan audiences this Spanish style of fencing might have seemed outdated and outlandish, and its old-fashioned upright posture and dance-like footwork might even have appeared ridiculous. Such responses might have paralleled explicitly articulated prejudicial ridicule of the absurd Spaniard Don Adriano de Armado in *Love's Labour's Lost*. In that play, written close in time to *Romeo and Juliet*, Armado is identified as 'A man of fire-new words, fashion's own knight' (1.1.176). This refers to the wild excesses of Don Armado's euphuistic speech, which parodied a literary fashion outdated by 1594–5. Another possibility is that, thanks to Elizabethan England's discordant relations with Spain (reflected in Don Armado's name echoing 'Armada'), anything Spanish might have seemed repugnant then and excited nationalistic prejudices. A third possibility is that Tybalt's Spanish style of fencing, involving fiddly rapier jabs rather than wholehearted lunges, might have seemed unfair and inelegant equally to Shakespeare's audience and to Romeo.

When the dying Mercutio says 'A plague o' both your houses. / They have made worms' meat of me' (3.1.106–7) Romeo promptly flies into exactly the rage that Vincentio Saviolo warned against in his treatise on duelling (see Figure 4.1).[31] However, nationalistic prejudices or repugnance against unsportsmanlike behaviour cannot fully explain why Romeo enacts Francis Bacon's 'wild justice' rather than allowing the state to punish Mercutio's killing in accord with its edict against public fighting. Rather, I think, another and deeper prejudice, to be explored in the next section, also surfaces in the lead-up to Romeo's fatal fight with Tybalt.

Figure 4.1 *'O WORMES MEATE: O FROATH O VANITIE: WHY ART THOV SO INSOLENT'*, in *Vincentio Saviolo his practise: in two bookes: the first intreating of the vse of the rapier and dagger, the second, of honor and honorable quarrels* (London: Iohn VVolfe, 1595), 2 vols, book 1 sig. k3. © Senate House Library University of London ([S.L.] I [Saviolo – 1595]).

# Prejudice and violence in *Romeo and Juliet*: the internal dimension

*Romeo and Juliet* shows that *personal* predilections are involved, and not just communal ones, when prejudices in favour of violence are acquired, succumbed to or overcome. This reflects a general principle with wide application that may be illustrated, first of all, with reference to another text.

That text, Saint Augustine's *Confessions*, vividly portrays that peer pressure plus the weakness of his own will results in Augustine's student and friend Alypius participating in the socially sanctioned relishing of Rome's 'cruel and deadly' gladiator fights. Previously, when living in Carthage, and with Augustine's help, Alypius overcame a time-wasting obsession with less 'despicable' races and games. Then Alypius became a student in Rome, and thanks to the 'forceful horseplay of friends' is 'pulled' into the gladiatorial Amphitheatre, all the while objecting strongly. Once there, despite his prior experience, deliberate intentions and better nature, Alypius is swept into participation with the audience's frenzied 'blood lust'.[32]

Crucially, Augustine never suggests that this sinful behaviour is automatic, inevitable or irreversible.[33] Likewise, *Romeo and Juliet* shows that compliance with group savagery may be overcome. For instance, Benvolio resists Mercutio's horseplay-like urgings to join violence-admiring youths keenly set on disrupting Verona's civic peace (3.1.1–52). As noted, Romeo also attempts to deflect aggression and prevent fighting.

For the sake of contrast, I will next consider an interpretation of the penchant for violence in *Romeo and Juliet* that is precisely opposite to my own. In this Susan Snyder claims that the Capulet–Montague vendetta is a timeless 'given' in Shakespeare's Verona, having the 'always already' quality specified in theories of ideology derived from Louis Althusser and his followers.[34] Thus, regarding the play's first scene, Snyder alleges that:

> the feud, like ideology, flattens out personal differences, slotting individuals into predetermined roles; after some actual Montagues arrive on the scene, [the formerly-not-physically-aggressive] Gregory quickly falls into line with Sampson's pugnacity – just as Benvolio, whose natural bent is to peacemaking and who a few minutes later tries to stop the servants' scrap, must nevertheless slide into his appointed slot to cross swords with Tybalt.
>
> (89)

Snyder then asserts that the cause of Benvolio's inevitable 'sliding', and indeed of the actions of all the other participants in this first scene, is the 'dominance of an "assigned form of subjectivity"' (89).

However, the play does not set up its theme of violence in this manner. For instance, even before its first scene its Chorus states (in sonnet form) that an old enmity between two of Verona's households has flared up 'From ancient grudge ... to new mutiny', thus alluding to a variability of any supposedly 'always already' forces in Verona. The action then begins with the servants of the two households that the chorus has just called (in ironic double entendre) 'alike in dignity' swaggering thuggishly and boasting intended violence. These two liveried groups then collide, insult one another, 'give the lie' and draw swords. Next Romeo's cousin Benvolio (whose name reveals his constitutional make-up) attempts to part these ruffians, drawing his sword. The hot-headed Capulet Tybalt next enters, armed, and Benvolio explains to him, 'I do but keep the peace. Put up thy sword, / Or manage it to part these men with me' (1.1.65–6). Tybalt's prompt response is to attack Benvolio. Hence Benvolio's response to Tybalt's assault is a matter of self-defence, and not one of sliding into an Althusserian 'assigned subjectivity'.

Next the town watch arrives, and attempts to subdue the riot. These are followed by the doddering seniors of the two households, each threatening violence and each restrained by their wives. The mêlée ends when Duke Escalus enters to chide all sternly. The overall impression given by the play's bloodless first brawl is that a misunderstanding of Benvolio's pacifistic motives contributes to a new outbreak of armed antagonism based on clannish mindlessness.

However, the play soon demonstrates that this combativeness is not consistently acted upon, and indeed may be suppressed voluntarily. So, old Capulet enters that first scene crying out for 'my long sword' (72), which, as noted above, was an outdated weapon. Although Capulet's wife promptly amends this with her caustic 'A crutch, a crutch – why call you for a sword?' (73), and old Montague's wife likewise holds him back physically (76–7), it is clear that at this excited moment both are inclined to do violence. However, soon after, Tybalt claims that Romeo has come to 'scorn at' the masked ball, and would attack him, but old Capulet restrains his nephew's violent impulse, even rebuking him as 'a saucy boy' (1.5.60–86). An ongoing battle begets violent emotions in the old man, but peaceable enjoyment begets the opposite.

Of course, the most crucial instance in *Romeo and Juliet* of behaviour contradicting a theory that unshakable ideology mandates the scorns and mislike between Shakespeare's Capulets and Montagues is the behaviour of Romeo and Juliet themselves. Precisely contrary to the proposal in Snyder's article that, 'Ideology is what constructs our consciousness and makes sense of our world' (30), Shakespeare's play instead illustrates that love may give birth to a new kind of consciousness and a new sense of the world free from ideological constraints.

In fact, for Romeo and Juliet love creates a new *mental* space – mirrored in a uniquely new *verbal* space – contrasting with the other realities and conceptions reigning in their households and culture. Thus Romeo and Juliet's love gives rise to verse language wholly differing from the Petrarchan moonshine parodied earlier in the play.[35] Nor does it accord with the reductive account of sexual allure with which Mercutio mocks Romeo's desires for Rosaline in 2.1.6–21, and even less with the salacious boasting of Samson in 1.1.10–28. It also bears no comparison with the elder Capulets' upwardly mobile marriage ambitions for Juliet. It connects with Friar Lawrence's civil peace-making agenda only functionally, and soars over Juliet's Nurse's notion that procreation is the only sound use for a male human animal, which motivates her initial complicity with Romeo and her subsequent shift to championing 'lovely' County Paris in 3.5.212–25.

Thus everyone in Shakespeare's Verona misconstrues Romeo and Juliet's experience. In consequence young Juliet ends her life wholly isolated, having become unknowable to all others. This tragic situation constitutes a precise opposite to Susan Snyder's repeated claims that everyone in Verona is formed by 'interpellation', is socially 'constructed', is enclosed by 'social formations' and is 'constituted' as a subject by ideology, that all are 'predetermined' by ideology, are made 'mechanical' by it, are 'assigned' subjectivity by it, are 'prescribed' roles by it, are deeply 'conditioned' by it, are 'inscribed' upon by it. The play's tragedy occurs precisely because none of those things are true about its lovers.

Instead, Romeo and Juliet are shown attuned to one another's beings and to their own beings in ways that separate and liberate them from all prevailing discourses, even the one that Snyder labels 'The discourse of romantic courtship'.[36] Hence, a certain pessimistic generalization often heard now[37] and certainly not unknown in Shakespeare's age[38] is shown by these lovers to be precisely untrue. The way Snyder puts that generalization is 'That which is necessary to give us a stable identity and a consistent view of the world [e.g. ideology] is by the same token what limits and distorts us'.[39] The lovers' tragedy in *Romeo and Juliet* is felt so strongly by audiences or readers precisely because love activates psychic forces and human capabilities that are *not* subsumed by ideologies that limit and distort.

However, when Romeo decides to attack Tybalt after the mortal wounding of Mercutio he does falls prey to a prejudice indicating a false ideology. Lamenting that his 'friend' Mercutio received a 'mortal hurt / In my behalf', he then repudiates his pacifistic wish to overlook verbal insults and comes to believe that his 'reputation' is 'stained / With Tybalt's slander' (3.1.110–12). At that moment Romeo fatally and crucially denounces, and betrays, his newly-founded love, saying:

> O sweet Juliet,
> Thy beauty hath made me effeminate,
> And in my temper softened valour's steel.
>
> (3.1.113–15)

Here Romeo adopts a prejudice against the love of a woman that parrots the stereotypical language of sex-shy misogynistic masculinity. Shakespeare therefore merges a possible anti-foreigner (anti-Spanish) prejudice and a definite anti-love prejudice into the anti-peace decision that leads to the destruction of both Romeo and Juliet.

Such anti-love prejudices are the topic of the next chapter, so I will leave them for the moment and next consider prejudices against peace on the part of several over-committed fictional warriors shown by Shakespeare to be prejudicially unwilling to think carefully about what they say or do.

## Shakespeare's warlike war-likers

FIRST VOLSCIAN SERVINGMAN
> Let me have war, say I. It exceeds peace as far as day does night. It's sprightly walking, audible and full of vent. Peace is a very apoplexy, lethargy; mulled, deaf, sleepy, insensible; a getter of more bastard children than war's a destroyer of men.
>
> *Coriolanus* 3.5.226–30

What is the cause, why States, that war and win,
Have honour, and breed men of better fame,

> Than States in peace, since war and conquest sin
> In blood, wrong liberty, all trades of shame?
> Force-framing instruments, which it must use,
> Proud in excesse, and glory to abuse.
> The reason is; *Peace is a quiet Nurse*
> *Of Idlenesse*, and Idlenesse the field,
> Where wit and Power change all seedes to worse,
> By narrow self-will upon which they build,
> And thence bring forth captiv'd inconstant ends,
> Neither to Princes, nor to People friends.
>
> Fulke Greville, *Caelica* CVIII[40]

The eminent international lawyer Theodore Meron has argued persuasively that Shakespeare displayed 'pacifist sympathies throughout the length of his career'.[41] Others detail how Shakespeare shared the irenic views of earlier humanists and religious thinkers,[42] and some allege that Shakespeare implicitly supported the peace-seeking policies of King James,[43] or even that Shakespeare's 'visions of universal peace and religious unity probably went much beyond what James would ever have been prepared to accept'.[44] It has also been shown that Shakespeare was exceptionally sensitive to the waste and ruinous horrors of warfare, and especially to its impact on women, the poor and the vanquished.[45] This last may help explain why Shakespeare was not wholly averse to the chivalric ideals of honour and service that, according to Meron, 'helped to humanize the conduct of war in some ways'.[46]

The observation made by Susan Snyder and others that single combat often serves as a convenient 'synecdoche'[47] to allow the theatrical presentation of battles on Shakespeare's limited stages may be combined with the also above-noted circumstance that almost all Shakespearian representations of single combat fail to produce outcomes in accord with justice, to produce the suggestion that Shakespeare was generally dubious concerning warfare. Yet, despite that, varied sorts of warriors appear with great regularity in Shakespeare's Histories, Tragedies and Comedies. These range all the way from Miles Gloriosus figures to seasoned professional soldiers to reluctant recruits, and they display widely varying aims, including seeking to advance national interests, or to purse glory, power, profit or personal vengeance (as when Shakespeare's Troilus hunts for Diomed on a battlefield, or his Achilles hunts for Hector). In addition, some of Shakespeare's soldiers are unthinking proponents of warfare pursued for its own sake. Among these are Shakespeare's fanatical militarist Hotspur, met in Chapter 2 as a poetry-derider, who also displays prejudicial 'scorns and mislike' of all peaceable persons or activities.

The volatile and aggressive Mercutio in *Romeo and Juliet* likewise mocks lovers and love poetry, and peace. Indeed, Shakespeare repeatedly depicts the anti-erotic biases of young men inclined to war, such as those of the wife-scorning Count Bertram in *All's Well* and of the love-scorning Benedick in *Much Ado*. Those last two figures are redeemable, and indeed are finally redeemed by women. Also the martially inclined young princes in *Cymbeline* who are not yet inclined to erotic love might overcome that limitation after they pass through a developmental phase in which they cannot bring themselves to sing a lovely song. In their case adolescent callowness linked with physical bravery is treated with wry indulgence by Shakespeare,[48] as if half admirable and half comical.

There is, however, no corresponding humorousness in the portrayal of Shakespeare's fanatical militarist Martius Caius Coriolanus. Until near his play's end Coriolanus also consistently heaps scorns and mislike on all persons who are not dedicated to extreme belligerence. His despising of all but valour extends to peace-making as well as to peace, so that he associates acceding to a peace treaty with emasculation and with a mother soothing an infant:

> My throat of war be turned,
> Which choired with my drum, into a pipe
> Small as an eunuch or the virgin voice
> That babies lull asleep!

(3.2.112–15)

A lullaby is no music for this rough, tough soldier-man. The themes here of an opposition between nurturing an infant and enacting ruthless violence is prominent in *Macbeth* as well. There Lady Macbeth imagines dashing out an infant's brains (1.7.54–8), Macbeth twice employs thugs to murder children, and their prejudices against the 'procreant cradle' named in 1.6.8 induces this childless couple to disown 'pity, like a naked new-born babe, / Striding the blast' (1.7.21–2).[49]

Like Coriolanus as well, Shakespeare's Richard of York opposes weak music-making to supposedly virile warfare when lamenting 'this weak piping time of peace' (*Richard III* 1.1.24). A contrasting of supposedly unmanly art with supposedly manly warfare persisted through centuries, as seen in Ezra Pound's 1909 poem 'Sestina: Altaforte', beginning 'Damn it all! all this our South stinks peace'. Thus Sir Philip Sidney had to insist defensively in his *Apologie for Poetrie* that poetic and warlike temperaments are compatible, claiming 'Poetrie is the companion of the [military] Campes'.[50]

Despite Sidney's claim, throughout most of *Coriolanus* Shakespeare's hero vehemently rejects and scorns all softness or emollient ways of being, thereby exposing the prejudices that will be the topic of the rest of this chapter.

# Preliminaries to a discussion of *Coriolanus* and prejudice

One practical matter is that Shakespeare's warrior initially called 'Martius Caius' only gains his additional title 'Coriolanus' in the tenth scene of his play (at 1.10.64). This produces a problem of nomenclature that I will resolve by calling Shakespeare's hero 'Coriolanus', even in some places where the name 'Martius' should properly be used.

Another issue that needs to be noted is that Thomas North's translation of Plutarch's 'The Life of Caius Martius Coriolanus' provided the main source for Shakespeare's

*Coriolanus*,⁵¹ but for the purposes of the current investigation what Shakespeare alters or omits from Plutarch's life may be more telling than what he adopts from it.⁵² The divergences of greatest importance here are between Shakespeare and Plutarch's modes of accounting for the behaviour of this hero. In particular, Plutarch's biographical essay tends to *tell us about* its subject didactically, and so repeatedly attempts to explain or generalize about or moralize upon Coriolanus's characteristics and actions. On the contrary, Shakespeare's play only *shows* us the peculiar actions of its chief figure, and thus invites wonderment and speculation. Correlative to that, Shakespeare's hero is dramatized as often behaving in very extreme ways and as performing astounding feats (such as subduing an armed city single-handedly) that are impossible in any conceivable real world. The purpose of this is to supply images of Coriolanus's psychic or internal world. This psychological rendering of the hero in *Coriolanus* is only one facet of Shakespeare's play,⁵³ but it is the facet of crucial importance for a discussion of Shakespeare's treatments of prejudice.

A third general point is that not only are the spectators or readers of Shakespeare's *Coriolanus* challenged when confronting the peculiar actions of this play's central figure, but so too are many of the other characters in that play whose often heard assessments of the hero range all the way from the dismissive 'he did [all] to please his mother, and to be partly proud' (1.1.36–7), to the lukewarm 'He hath deserved worthily of his country' (2.2.24), to the extolling 'His nature is too noble for the world' (3.1.255).

Actions alone must imply the nature of this Shakespearian hero, for unlike all other Shakespearian tragedies, *Coriolanus* contains almost none of its protagonist's self-revealing soliloquies or asides. Therefore this play receives no mention at all in Peter Milward's study that sets out to 'offer a fairly complete anthology of Shakespeare's tragic soliloquies … with a commentary to bring out their context and significance'.⁵⁴ For instance, Coriolanus's solo passage, at 4.4.12–26, contains only a string of platitudes about the 'slippery' fickleness of human affairs and the irony of friends becoming enemies and enemies becoming friends. Likewise, when he is possibly alone or unheard in 2.3,112–24,[55] Coriolanus expresses distain when required to obtain Rome's citizens' consent to his Consulship, but thus exposes only his already evident extreme despising of the citizens. He is also uncommunicative as to motive at 4.4.1–6 and 4.5.5–6 where he states that he intends to enter the Volscian enemy city incognito but expresses no reason for taking such a risk.

In general Shakespeare's Coriolanus gives us access to his impulses and obsessions only through displaying repetitive patterns of behaviour and uses of language. This lack of self-explanation has led Katherine Stockholder to suggest that the absence of what she calls the 'missing scene' in which Coriolanus explains his reasons for joining forces with the Volsces 'might be taken to symbolize Coriolanus' denial of his own interior depths'.[56] However, any purported lack of interior depths is something that I will contest. On the contrary, I will argue that Shakespeare's hero seeming to act through much of the play without regard for any long-term plans or aims does not represent such an absence, but results rather from Coriolanus being in the grip of a complex inner life. To begin pursuit of that I will start with questions concerning *virtus* and 'honour'.

# 'Vertical honour', Roman *virtus* and Coriolanus's hidden drives

Shakespeare's Coriolanus's silence about having any plan or motive when joining forces with the Volces is characteristic of him in a way that is typically challenging to his beholders on stage and offstage. Within the play, therefore, some attribute cunning strategies to Coriolanus that fail to match up with his actions. For instance, the tribunes Brutus and Sicinius misattribute complex schemes to him at 1.1.261–76. On the contrary, Plutarch represents his less mysterious Coriolanus as an effective strategist (349, 350).

Plutarch moreover explains Coriolanus's violent rashness and prejudicial opinions in terms of deprivation, and in particular by the fact that he was 'left an orphan by his father' (313), and so 'for lacke of education' grew up so 'chollericke and impacient, that he would yeld to no living creature' (314). Thus Plutarch deploys Coriolanus's character faults as fodder for illustrating generalities, such as that education 'teacheth men ... to be civill & curteous' (314). But Shakespeare contrastingly makes no mention of Coriolanus's education or lack of it, and leaves unremarked his lack of a father, and instead gives him a father figure in Menenius (explicitly in 5.1.3, 5.2.71 and 5.3.10).

In another divergence Plutarch attributes Coriolanus's prejudices against those less heroic than himself solely to the ethos of pre-imperial Rome, claiming: 'Nowe in those dayes, valliantnes was honoured in ROME above all other virtues: which they called *Virtus*'. Shakespeare partly concurs, but once again where Plutarch states generalities Shakespeare dramatizes complexities concerning early Rome's inculcation of ideals of hardiness, showing the adoption of these to be less mechanical and more subject to choice.

Thus in *Coriolanus* Volumnia recounts how she applauded her son's propensities to aggression (1.3.5–25), and soon after the Roman matron Valeria reports finding it charming when Coriolanus's young son torments and then dismembers a small living creature (1.3.55–89). That incident may seem to imply Roman society's approbation of violent cruelty (something Shakespeare always detested), but Shakespeare's play also indicates that Coriolanus's wife Virgilia vehemently disagrees with Volumnia's happiness in expecting that Coriolanus will return home with new wounds (1.3.36–40).

A social value that Shakespeare's hero and Plutarch's with the same name evidently share is valorousness. That partly accounts for his aspiring to the exclusion of all else for the militaristic 'honour' incessantly mentioned in Shakespeare's *Coriolanus*.[57] However, this honour is of a different sort than that which is contested by the duelling or feuding antagonists represented, for instance, in Shakespeare's *Romeo and Juliet*. Thus Markku Peltonen divides the Renaissance concept of 'honour' into the varieties 'horizontal honour', 'reflexive honour' and 'vertical honour', where only horizontal and reflexive honour relate to personal fights or duelling. 'Horizontal honour' is obtained only by being born into a particular a social position and 'reflexive honour' requires the issuing a challenge to fight if a person possessing horizontal honour is insulted and their reputation sullied. Peltonen therefore explains that horizontal honour can 'be preserved, lost, or diminished' but can 'never be increased'.[58] On the contrary, 'vertical honour' is acquired through deeds performed, and so can be gained or enlarged as well as diminished or lost.

Through most of Shakespeare's play Coriolanus lives only to enlarge his *vertical* honour. In pursuit of such honour he exhibits overwhelming prejudices of a sort that today would be labelled those of an 'extremist'. This extremism has several very peculiar aspects. One is that Coriolanus regards his honour solely in terms of the heroic deeds he performs, and not at all in terms of the service he renders, the reputation he gains or any rewards produced by his deeds. In this way his idealization goes far beyond the norm in a heroic-valour idealizing culture. For instance, although his commander gives him the additional name 'Coriolanus' as a reward for what his mother calls his 'deed-achieving honour' (2.1.170), a more accurate description of Coriolanus's own view of the matter would be that his honour has the purity of being wholly 'deed-achieved', and is definitely not acquisitively 'deed-achieving'. In doing heroic deeds Coriolanus seeks nothing – not pleasure not treasure, not even fame[59] – aside from the confirmation within himself, and for his own sake alone, that his essential selfhood is one and the same as the vertical honour that he has attained through active fortitude and valour. Until very late in the play Coriolanus's desire to surpass all in 'honour' dominates every aspect of his existence. This is, and is seen as, exceptional: even Coriolanus's mother finds his radical all-else-ignoring pursuit of vertical honour excessively 'absolute' (3.2.40–52).

Coriolanus's extraordinary drive to heroic 'doing' without prior planning or thinking about consequences matches a pathological condition that the psychoanalyst Ronald Britton identifies as 'libidinal narcissism'. In this 'the judgmental authority of the superego is invested in the narcissistic object whose approval then becomes a matter of life and death'.[60] Thus to fail to rush into heroic action would call down on Coriolanus the worse-than-deadly disapproval of a powerfully idealized inner voice or split-off 'object'.

On the other hand, the psychoanalyst Herbert Rosenfeld describes a differing condition called 'destructive narcissism' in which to 'receive help is experienced as weakness and failure by the destructive narcissistic organization which provides the patient with his sense of superiority'.[61] This too matches Corliolanus' propensities, for throughout almost all of the play he refuses to accept help from any quarter. These two sorts of narcissism are typically found mixed in pathologically narcissistic individuals,[62] but it will be argued that in Coriolanus the predominant type is the libidinal. To begin exploration of this I will next consider Coriolanus's consistently strange reactions to being offered praise.

## Coriolanus's reactions to praise

Attempting to goad the petulant warrior Achilles into action, Shakespeare's Ulysses in *Troilus and Cressida* reads aloud to him from an author who writes that

... man, how dearly ever parted,
How much in having, or without or in,
Cannot make boast to have that which he hath,

> Nor feels not what he owes, but by reflection –
> As when his virtues, shining upon others,
> Heat them, and they retort that heat again

and that

>                       no man is the lord of anything,
> Though in and of him there be much consisting,
> Till he communicate his parts to others.
> Nor doth he of himself know them for aught
> Till he behold them formed in th' applause
> Where they're extended.
>
> (3.3.91–6, 110–15)

This ploy succeeds and the talented Achilles is persuaded to return to the battlefield in order to gain the applause and esteem of others.

Shakespeare's Coriolanus enters into battle with entirely different aims.[63] His powerful internal belief that he possesses surpassingly great valour requires no confirmation in the opinions of others and, on the contrary, his language and behaviour consistently convey pained aversion to being offered praise. This is because, as Anne Barton puts it, Coriolanus 'deludes himself that he, a single individual, constitutes Rome's best and only self'.[64] For that reason, he believes that none other than himself has standing high enough to praise him.

In one extended example of this, upon his victorious return from Corioles Coriolanus is greeted by Cominius with plaudits beginning:

> If I should tell thee o'er this thy day's work
> Thou'lt not believe thy deeds. But I'll report it
> Where senators shall mingle tears with smiles,
> Where great patricians shall attend and shrug,
> I' th' end admire …
>
> (1.10.1–5)

Then another officer begins to report more of Coriolanus's astounding deeds, but is interrupted by the hero's:

> Pray now, no more. My mother,
> Who has a charter to extol her blood,
> When she does praise me grieves me.
>
> (1.10.13–15)

His claim here to being grieved is, I think, entirely unfeigned. Cominius then insists on heaping even more praise on a Coriolanus who continues to balk, saying, 'I have some wounds upon me, and they smart / To hear themselves remembered' (1.10.28–9). I believe that this remark should be taken literally when it indicates that Coriolanus actually suffers pain when being praised, even by a patrician of high military standing. Coriolanus next refuses to accept reward for his exceptional service, and insists that all share booty equally. 'A long flourish' is then sounded accompanied by cheering (tln 794–6), to which Coriolanus objects, saying:

> May these same instruments which you profane
> Never sound more. When drums and trumpets shall
> I' th' field prove flatterers, let courts and cities be
> Made all of false-faced soothing. When steel grows
> Soft as the parasite's silk, let him be made
> An overture for th' wars. No more, I say.
> For that I have not washed my nose that bled,
> Or foiled some debile wretch, which without note
> Here's many else have done, you shout me forth
> In acclamations hyperbolical.
>
> (1.10.41–50)

Is this an instance of modesty 'hyperbolical', or an expression of genuine distress at being applauded? I believe the latter is the case, and would draw attention to the imaging of being soiled and needing to wash.

Next, while still battle bloodied, Coriolanus reacts with reluctance to being given the additional name 'Coriolanus'. An image of being soiled recurrs when Coriolanus flushes not on account of modesty or pleasure, but rather of discomfort:

> I will go wash,
> And when my face is fair you shall perceive
> Whether I blush or no.

(1.10.67–9)

Tones of distress here, together with the repeated images of soiling, suggest that Shakespeare's Coriolanus is averse to approbation because he feels himself sullied by praise. As I have proposed, the prejudice underlying these responses is that Coriolanus believes that *no one stands high enough to give him* praise – indeed, that any offer of praise (or reward) for his services constitutes a detraction from, a besmirching of, his self-assumed unmatched superiority.

If this is so, it puts a different light on Coriolanus later balking at the necessity of seeking the plebeians' approval in order to confirm his election as consul. His impolitic rudeness to the citizens when faced with the ritual of showing his battle scars in the marketplace (not duplicated in Plutarch's 'Life', 332) would then be not merely another instance of his despising the plebeian 'rabble', but would accord with a deeply rooted pattern of not being able to endure acclaim.

Thus Coriolanus rejects all praise for his heroic exploits, even from his mother or general, because in his extreme arrogance he experiences vexation when lesser mortals applaud his deeds. Lesser mortals can be anyone, so he says to Rome's august Senators, 'Your honours' pardon, / I had rather have my wounds to heal again / Than hear say how I got them' (2.2.68–70). Here again the only acknowledgement of his valour that he can accept without pain is his own self-acknowledgement.

I will next examine an allied pattern in which Coriolanus's belief in his *absolute* difference from others results in a prejudicial despising of almost everyone other than himself.

# Coriolanus's despising of plebeians and others

Shakespeare's Coriolanus denounces Rome's plebeian citizens as cowards and repeatedly likens them to lower animals, thus expressing contempt in a manner wholly characteristic of prejudices against reviled 'outsider' groups (as was mentioned in the previous chapter). Hence he calls the citizens 'curs', 'hares ... geese' and 'rats' (1.1.166, 169–70, 249), 'minnows' (3.1.92), 'crows' (3.1.142) or 'curs' again (3.3.124). He adds that they constitute a 'herd' (1.5.2 and 3.1.35) or 'a beast with many heads' (4.1.1–2), or have the 'souls of geese' (1.5.5). Scabrous images of animal parturition are added when he asserts that the citizens have been 'littered' or 'calved i' th' porch o' th' Capitol' (3.1.238–9).

However, Coriolanus's uses of derogatory imagery hardly make him unique among his fellow Romans. For instance, in 1.10.7 the consul Cominius speaks of 'the fusty plebeians', almost matching Coriolanus labelling them 'Our musty superfluity' in 1.1.226. Cominius also calls the tribunes 'the herdsmen of the beastly plebeians' (2.1.93), paralleling Coriolanus's animal imagery. Coriolanus's mentor Menenius likewise identifies the plebeians with 'rats' (1.1.160), while Coriolanus's mother Volumnia calls the tribune Sicinius 'thou foxship' and denominates the plebeian 'rabble' as 'Cats' (4.2.20, 35–6).

On the other hand, one of the plebeians calls Coriolanus 'a very dog to the commonality' (1.1.27) and the tribune Sicinius compares him with a 'dog' ready to worry 'sheep' (2.1.254). However, this two-sided Roman 'class hatred' lacks the unique breadth and depth of Coriolanus's prejudicial outlook, for he alone believes he possesses an unbridgeable superiority over *all* others. I will spell that out next.

The plebeian citizens of Rome are shown capable of holding a variety of opinions on other topics, but all concur in a wish for peaceful plenty. Thus their tribune Sicinius describes them happiest when 'Our tradesmen singing in their shops' are 'going / About their functions friendly' (4.6.8–9). That makes them perfect opposites to Coriolanus, who relishes the privations, risks and pains of combat, and in turn sets them up as perfect foils for his self-idealization. However, Coriolanus reveals scorn as well for his fellow patricians when he refuses, under the guise of modesty, to accept praises, rewards or offers of help from them. Later, in exile he explicitly denounces Rome's patricians as 'dastard nobles' (4.5.76). Thus his fulminations against the lower orders match his almost universal 'scorns and mislike'.

An exception lies in Coriolanus's admiration for the Voslcian general Aufidius. I will next argue that his encounters with that figure indicate that his narcissism is primarily libidinal.

# Coriolanus's unsupported sally into Corioles and its aftermath

The first of Coriolanus's three entries into a Volscian city contrasts with the episode in *1 Henry VI* 2.3 in which the great English warrior Lord Talbot responds to a social invitation from an enemy, the Countess of Auvergne. The Countess is at first surprised by Talbot's moderate physical stature, thereby becoming sure that she will succeed in her plot to take him prisoner. However, she is soon disabused of a belief that Talbot's power resides in the mere man himself, for, as he tells her, his physical being is 'but Talbot's shadow ... but a shadow of myself' (2.3.45–50). Talbot then winds his horn to summon in his numerous troops who are his real puissance, his 'substance, sinews, arms, and strength' (63). This accords with Talbot's earlier realism when remarking 'Where is my strength, my valour, and my force? / Our English troops retire; I cannot stay them' (1.7.1–2).

On the contrary, realism gives way to the mythic when in 1.5.1–17 Coriolanus's troops refuse to advance from their trenches but Coriolanus nonetheless thrusts himself into an armed enemy city that should be a far more lethal trap than the Countess of Auvergne's castle. Shakespeare modified Plutarch's account in which Coriolanus enters 'the cittie [Corioles] with very few men' (322) – and rather specifies he enters with none at all – in order to illustrate that for *his* Coriolanus the less help he has the better. Thus he presents an actual 'impossibility' of the sort that Aristotle found preferable and more telling in artistic representations than an 'implausibility'.[65] This impossibility is emphasized when Coriolanus is presumed dead by all observers after pursing the retreating Volscian enemy army into Corioles. But then he exits the gates covered in blood, having miraculously 'himself alone' made the city ready for conquest (1.5.14–33).

In a register that is actually not boastful (to be discussed presently), Coriolanus acknowledges this when taunting Aufidius with 'Alone I fought in your Corioles' walls, / And made what work I pleased' (1.9.8–9). Yet in 1.10.81–90 Coriolanus mentions that 'a poor man' had been his host and 'used me kindly' in Corioles. When recalling this Coriolanus admits that during the battle 'wrath o'erwhelmed my pity' so that he ignored the pleas for help of his 'poor host' who had been taken prisoner. After the victory he attempts to have his host released, but fails because he forgets the name of this man who had aided him. This forgetfulness is not paralleled in Plutarch, where Coriolanus does obtain relief for 'an olde friend and hoste of mine, an honest wealthie man' (326). Does Shakespeare's variation indicate snobbery, ingratitude, selfishness or mere fallibility?[66] I think, rather, that Shakespeare's Coriolanus cannot recall the name of his helper because he cannot, as usual, bear to acknowledge having been helped.

In line with that, Coriolanus's superhuman unaided deed of valour inside Corioles follows a Folio stage direction (tln 524) that has Coriolanus entering 'Cursing' his outnumbered followers who hesitate at the walls of Corioles. He then harangues his troops with the likes of 'All the contagion of the south light on you, / You shames of Rome!' (1.5.1–2). This is hardly persuasive, and contradicts both Plutarch's claim that Coriolanus is 'no lesse eloquent in tongue, then warlike in showe' (349–50) and also Coriolanus's mother's recollection in Shakespeare's play that he has been capable of using 'gentle words' as a means to and end in warfare (3.2.47–69). On the contrary, Coriolanus's exceedingly ungentle language here includes calling his reluctant troops a 'herd', saying he hopes they may be plastered with 'boils and plagues', and proclaiming they are 'geese', worse than 'apes' (1.5.2–7). So, again contrary to Plutarch's account of Coriolanus (322), here Shakespeare's hero shows no ability to inspire allegiance and rally his men effectively. His abuse having failed to gain any support, Shakespeare's Coriolanus thus enters the gates of Corioles 'alone' and is seemingly fatally 'shut in' (1.5.18, 22, tln 538).

The refusal of Coriolanus's troops to sacrifice their lives futilely is unsurprising, but Shakespeare's depiction of their reluctance to follow him into Coriolis may have another thrust as well. This is that, by insulting them, Coriolanus may unconsciously deter these others from assisting him and thus diluting his attainment of self-gratifying glory. This is to say that he engineers a precious opportunity to perform his most heroic feat single-handedly and unsupported, thus proving his total lack of dependency on others. A side benefit is that this gives him an opportunity later to deride the proletarians' cowardice by claiming that they 'would not thread the gates' of Corioles with him (3.1.125–7).

Thus at the mere cost of insane indifference to his own survival, joined with a rank denial of reality, Coriolanus pursues self-glorification. This is not, however, a consciously planned strategy, but rather the recklessness of a man keen to manufacture mad risks in order to confirm his inordinate self-esteem. In other word, it represents a prejudicial scorning of all prudence.

Quite on the contrary, Shakespeare's Achilles in *Troilus and Cressida* both schemes and lies his way to increased fame.

Thus, once roused from his sulking, he enacts a stratagem whereby his henchmen surround the unarmed Hector and do him to death. Achilles' plans for this sordid ambush are laid in 5.7.1–8. Its enactment is depicted via couplets in which Hector calls out 'I am unarmed. Forgo this vantage, Greek', but Achilles commands, 'Strike, fellows, strike! This is the man I seek' (5.9.9–10). Even more diametrically to Coriolanus, Achilles then seeks acclaim, commanding, 'On, Myrmidons, and cry you all amain, / "Achilles hath the mighty Hector slain!"' (5.9.13–14). Finally Achilles' self-advertising desecration of Hector's corpse (5.9.21–2) completes a process wherein Hector's chivalric challenge to single combat (1.3.257–80) is overwritten by Achilles' self-display and dishonourable cynicism.

In one more example of an opposite behaviour, on his victorious return to Rome Coriolanus is heralded with:

> Know, Rome, that all alone Coriolanus did fight
> Within Corioles' gates, where he hath won
> With fame a name to 'Coriolanus Caius'; these
> In honour follows 'Coriolanus'.
> Welcome to Rome, renowned Coriolanus!
>
> (2.1.159–63)

Characteristically pained by praise, Coriolanus promptly rejects this flourish with 'No more of this, it does offend my heart. / Pray now, no more' (2.1.165–6).

However, the notion that Coriolanus always refuses to claim credit for his deeds may seem contradicted when soon after his conquest of Corioles he encounters his enemy Tullus Aufidius and taunts him with:

> Within these three hours, Tullus,
> Alone I fought in your Corioles' walls,
> And made what work I pleased. 'Tis not my blood
> Wherein thou seest me masked.
>
> (1.9.7–10)

However, despite appearances, this is not actually boastful, for it constitutes rather a 'flyting' or deliberate soldierly insult intended to provoke single combat. Here and elsewhere Shakespeare portrays Coriolanus's misconception that Aufidius is his only worthy opponent, his one-and-only dearly-behated.[67]

In his reply to this 'flyting' Aufidius ominously compares Coriolanus with the Roman people's 'bragged' ancestor 'Hector' (1.9.11–13). This is ominous because in alluding to Hector Aufidius places himself in the position of Hector's adversary Achilles, and (as just noted) Shakespeare's Achilles is entirely dishonourable when he kills Hector.

When Coriolanus conceives the illusion that Aufidius is his sole equal he mirrors a psychic mechanism whereby parts of the self are relocated elsewhere. Although such projection may enable empathic understanding, it may also be highly misleading. Thus Janet Adelman claims:

> Shakespeare takes pains to emphasize the distance between the Aufidius we see and the Aufidius of Coriolanus' imagination. The Aufidius invented by Coriolanus seems designed to reassure Coriolanus of the reality of his own male grandeur by giving him an image of himself; his need to create a man who is his equal is in fact one of the most poignant elements in the play and helps to account for his tragic blindness to his rival's true nature as opportunist and schemer.[68]

Crucially, Coriolanus ignores actual experience that proves that his location of self-admired parts of himself in Aufidius is unfounded. For instance, just following the above-noted flyting a Folio stage direction to 1.9.13 reads 'Heere they fight, and certaine Volsces come in the ayde of Auffi. Martius fights til they be driuen in breathles' (tln 740–1). Coriolanus surely notices that, for he ends the scene with the remark 'Officious and not valiant, you have shamed me / In your condemned seconds' (1.9.14–15), and yet he subsequently wholly overlooks this.

Ignoring such clear evidence, Coriolanus later judges Aufidius to be a suitable potential ally. Aufidius dissembles that he will be such a one (4.5.102–36). However, he long before decided that since he cannot beat Coriolanus in a fair fight he will destroy him by dishonest means: 'I'll potch at him some way / Or wrath or craft may get him' (1.11.15–16). Therefore scheming Aufidius, who also becomes consumed by envy of Coriolanus's successes against Rome, concocts a plan to destroy him once Rome is defeated: 'When, Caius, Rome is thine, / Thou art poor'st of all; then shortly art thou mine' (4.7.56–7). Finally, by finding a 'pretext to strike at him [that] admits / A good construction' (5.6.19–20), Aufidius enacts his murderous plan. This opportunity arises from an accumulation of meaningful contradictions that I will explore next.

## Coriolanus's partial transformation

A combination of his own arrogance and his enemies' machinations result in Coriolanus's exile from Rome. Coriolanus thereafter undertakes a second highly dangerous, and then a third fatal, entry into a Volscian city. That city is confusingly identified in Shakespeare's play, because Aufidius is said to reside in 'Antium' in 3.1.11–19 and 4.4.1–8, but returns with Coriolanus to 'Corioles' in 5.6.92. Plausible explanations of this anomaly have been offered,[69] but a nice symmetry emerges if we suppose that Coriolanus symbolically thrice enters into the same dangerous place.

In his first solo sally Coriolanus invades walled Coriolis as an armed conqueror, but on the second occasion he enters a Volscian stronghold not only alone, but also stateless, unarmed and seeking alliance with another. He is aware that his former enemies there might seek 'revenge' (4.5.96), and remarks several times that he anticipates the possibility of his death (4.4.4–6 and 24–5, 4.5.80–102). What would be his motive for taking such a desperate step?

Plutarch's simplifying view is that Coriolanus seeks to ally himself with Aufidius solely in order to pursue revenge for his banishment (345), but I would add that Shakespeare's Coriolanus is also keenly in pursuit of an opportunity to engage once again as a warrior.[70] Anne Barton observes that 'Shakespeare ignored' accounts in both Plutarch and Livy that the Volscian Lords and Commons were reluctant to continue their war with Rome, and that Shakespeare instead represented Volscian society as one in which 'everyone seems to regard war as a natural and even desirable condition of existence'.[71] In such a society, Barton asserts, Shakespeare's Coriolanus does indeed 'find a "world elsewhere"', that 'world' being a society more primitive than Rome which is (like Coriolanus himself) unthinkingly opposed to peace (122). Because he assumes such a society will foster the militaristic idealization that he conflates with himself, Coriolanus attempts to join the Volces, and is delighted when they accept him as an ally.

I further believe that Shakespeare implies that in joining forces with the Volscians Coriolanus's motives of revenge are secondary to his need to live the life of a peerless warrior. Evidence for this accumulates when he retorts to Rome's citizens, 'I banish you' (3.3.127), and on his departure proclaims that when exiled he will be a 'lonely dragon' (4.1.31–2). We may be misled here by a Romantic era and later usage in which 'lonely' indicates 'Dejected because of want of company or society' (OED3 4.a),[72] for in Shakespeare's time 'lonely' signalled only a state of separateness (OED3 'lonely' 1). Thus, Coriolanus imaging himself a 'lonely dragon' who has banished his countrymen need not suggest a sorrowful exile, but rather a dangerous, independent, self-idealizing monad of militarism.

The nuances of a word may similarly inflect Coriolanus's self-explanation when he offers his services to the Volsces acting 'in full spite / To be full quit of those my banishers' (4.5.83–4). Here to 'be *quit*' may signify to be 'free, clear, rid *of* (OED3 'quit' 1.b) rather than standing as a contraction of 'be *quits*' meaning to be 'Even or equal with, esp. by means of repayment or retaliation' (OED3 'quits' 2.a). If this is correct, it again indicates that Coriolanus aims to sever his former ties in order to become a totally self-sufficient warrior. That would support a notion that Coriolanus's chief reason for offering to serve the Volscian armies is to fulfil his burning desire to exercise prowess in a society that he believes to be single-mindedly dedicated to military glory.

## Coriolanus's radical second transformation

In support of his fanatical belief in his own *virtus*, Shakespeare's Coriolanus maintains a massively prejudicial belief in his own incommensurable superiority to others, a belief underscored by his certainty that he has no need for anyone's help. For instance, immediately after comparing himself with a 'lonely dragon', the exiled Coriolanus refuses Cominius' offer to accompany him when he leaves Rome and specifically rejects a plan for Cominius to then 'devise with thee' in order to 'determine on some course' (4.1.39–48). Accepting help and forming a deliberate strategy are equally contrary to Coriolanus's inclinations, and again Shakespeare diverges from Plutarch's text in which *his* Coriolanus exits from Rome not alone, but accompanied by 'three or foure of his friends' (343).

However, these inclinations are totally overturned before the play ends. An intriguing analogy to that arises in the one other place where Shakespeare uses the word 'lonely'.[73] This is in *The Winter's Tale* 5.3.18 where Paulina says that she has kept Hermione's supposed statue 'Lonely, apart'. Both here and in *Coriolanus* 'lonely' does not reference a state of dejection, but rather a condition of unyielding separation. In both cases this separation entails a stony hardness arising in response to ill-treatment. Both of these Shakespeare plays portray a conversion of a hard 'lonely' thing to surprising warmth, softness and connectedness. In both, as well, a transformative emergence of human relatedness follows the taking of a hand and an embrace. Thus when husband and wife are finally reunited in *The Winter's Tale* Leontes is first urged to 'present your hand' and an onlooker reports 'She embraces him' (5.3.107, 112). Coriolanus likewise signals a reunion with his wife in his 'O, a kiss / Long as my exile, sweet as my revenge!' (5.3.44–5), and then a Folio stage direction indicates that before speaking with his mother he 'Holds her by the hand silent' (tln 3539).

Coriolanus's radical transformation follows a meeting with his wife, child and mother who come to plead with him not to destroy Rome. Although he allows this visit, Coriolanus insists that 'Aufidius and you Volsces' witness it (5.3.93–4), his evident purpose being to enhance his glorious vertical honour by demonstrating his steadfastness against their appeals. However, in the face of 'Great nature' Coriolanus cannot fulfil his aim to 'stand / As if a man were author of himself' (5.3.33–6), and thus he discovers his deep relatedness to others, exposing unseen and unexplored humane elements in his being.

Coriolanus's change is signalled by his unprecedented handholding, his tears and his expressions of regret (5.3.183–90), and yet he still obeys an urge to preserve horizontal honour by returning to confront his erstwhile Volscian allies. So he says to Aufidus, 'I'll not to Rome; I'll back with you and pray you / Stand me in this cause ' (199–200). Here he expresses his first ever sincere request for assistance, and indeed assistance with arguing for the acceptance of a 'convenient peace' (192).

Thus, unprecedently, Coriolanus all at once requests help, plans his future action and promotes a compromise supporting peace and prosperity. He also imagines that Aufidius will empathize with his plight, and so he says, with good hope:

> Now, good Aufidius,
> Were you in my stead would you have heard
> A mother less, or granted less, Aufidius?

To this Aufidius slyly replies, 'I was moved withal'. Coriolanus responds, 'I dare be sworn you were. / And, sir, it is no little thing to make / Mine eyes to sweat compassion' (5.2.192–7).

This use of a comical euphemism for tears does not undermine the extraordinary nature of Coriolanus's sudden change in outlook and mental status. In accord with the entire reversal of his former absolutist scornfulness, Coriolanus then urges the Volsces to consider the benefits that he has brought them in terms both of honourable victories and substantial spoils, and pleads with them to accept a treaty of peace. He even goes so far as to mention the 'full third part' in profit he has brought them in booty above the costs of 'the action' (5.6.71–84). Here, breaking away from his former despising of all compromise and all remuneration, Coriolanus manifests what Jonathan Lear calls a 'break' with a former 'psychic structure'.[74]

A mystery arises, however. Given that Coriolanus (mistakenly) believes that he has gained Aufidius's sympathy, and given that he believes the Volscian assembly will agree that he has rendered good service and accept his proposed compromise,[75] why does he anticipate grave danger when he agrees to spare Rome, saying:

> O my mother, mother, O!
> You have won a happy victory to Rome;
> But for your son, believe it, O believe it,
> Most dangerously you have with him prevailed,
> If not most mortal to him. But let it come.
>
> (5.3.186–90)

The next section will propose a reply to that question.

## The terror of change

Through most of Shakespeare's play Coriolanus's bizarre words and gestures indicate that he has over-idealized valour and excellence in warfare and then self-identified with that split-off ideal. It has been remarked that such kinds of self-idealization involve 'denial of both material and psychic reality', and that such '[o]mnipotent introjection and identification with an ideally good or ideally bad object may offer protection from envy and persecution but it prevents development'.[76] When Coriolanus relinquishes such 'protection' by acknowledging dependency on others he immediately experiences fear, seemingly for the first time ever. That fear, I believe, results from his realization that he himself cannot fulfil all of his own needs, bringing a new sense of vulnerability. This, I think, accounts for his remark that his new stance may be 'most mortal to him'.

Prior to that Coriolanus held the 'depressive position' at bay by means of what are known as 'manic defences'. In her foundational paper on 'Manic-Depressive States', Melanie Klein writes that a '*sense of omnipotence* ... first and foremost characterizes mania'. She adds that in mania 'The ego is unwilling and unable to renounce its good internal objects and yet endeavours to escape from the perils of dependence on them', while at the same time the ego 'endeavours ceaselessly to master and control all its objects, and the evidence of this effort is its hyperactivity'.[77] I believe that just such a pattern of denial and defence is signalled by the hyperactive striving, the self-adulation and the all-others disparaging at first manifested by Shakespeare's Coriolanus.

Moreover, these characteristics suggest that Coriolanus's narcissism is predominantly of the libidinal rather than of the destructive variety. Ronald Britton explains that in the libidinal form 'a narcissistic object relationship can be motivated by the wish to preserve the capacity for love by making the love-object seem like the self', while in the destructive form 'it can be aimed at annihilating the object as the representative of otherness'.[78] Destructively narcissistic Iago, for example, does not project a vision of goodness onto anyone, but rather seeks to annihilate all. Libidinal Coriolanus, conversely, does project an idea of goodness onto the unworthy Aufidius.

Thereafter Coriolanus accepts the pains and imperfections of a more genuine love, and so weeps and admits to his terror in the presence of his wife, son and mother. Following this he returns to urge the Volscian public to accept an honourable truce (5.6.71–84). In doing this Coriolanus acknowledges pain, seeks empathy, pursues negotiation, pleads for compromise, claims due credit for his achievements, allows realistic goals to trump abstractions about 'honour' and thinks about means toward a desired outcome. On top of those revolutionary reversals warrior Coriolanus also advocates for peace – while any truce earlier seemed to him tantamount to an unmanning.

Previously, as Aufidius puts it, Coriolanus's character prevented him from 'moving / From th' casque to th' cushion ... commanding peace / Even with the same austerity and garb / As he controlled the war' (4.7.42–5). But even after Coriolanus begins his transformation, cunning Aufidius detects a remaining 'spice' of his old self-defeating weakness, which is 'a defect of judgement / To fail in the disposing of those chances / Which he was lord of' (4.7.39–41). Relying on that, Aufidius baits Coriolanus by first calling him a dishonourable 'traitor', and then announcing publicly that Coriolanus wept when holding his mother's hand. Aufidius misrepresents the encounter in terms of lost profits and lost 'honour', thus: 'But at his nurse's tears / He whined and roared away your victory, / That pages blushed at him, and men of heart / Looked wond'ring each at others' (5.6.99–102).

Following this accusation of unmanliness, Aufidius addresses Coriolanus as 'thou boy of tears' (5.6.103). This taunt provokes Coriolanus's infuriated reply that he had bested Aufidius several times in combat and that 'like an eagle in a dove-cote, I / Fluttered your Volscians in Corioles' (109–10, 115–16). Quite rightly Coriolanus identifies this as 'the first time that ever / I was forced to scold' (106–7, and quite rightly Aufidius labels this response as one of a 'braggart' (119).

Coriolanus then loses his temper, giving Aufidius his sought-for opportunity to direct his gang to murder him as planned. Next Aufidius dishonours Coriolanus's dead body[79] (as Achilles does Hector's), and finally he cants about his 'sorrow' over the loss of Coriolanus's 'noble memory' (5.6.148,154).

## Who or what is responsible for Coriolanus's ruin?

Playing a 'blame game' is foreign to psychoanalytic thinking, but is prevalent among several critics of *Coriolanus*. Some lay the blame for Coriolanus's sad fate on Rome and its values, overlooking the hero's churlishness and unsociability named by Plutarch and displayed by Shakespeare. They instead allege that Coriolanus shows exceptional integrity and authenticity in the face of bogus Roman values that are contaminated by self-interest.[80] Such readings overlook as well that until near his end Shakespeare's Coriolanus never troubles himself with consideration of others, of himself or indeed for reality, but on the contrary adheres obstinately to rigidly held unexamined beliefs. That those beliefs make him cruel to himself as well as to others does not make Coriolanus noble or truthful.

Other critics lay the blame for Coriolanus's downfall on his mother Volumnia. Several note that when Volumnia lauds martial valour she evokes nearly the precise 'phantasy' images of a damaged maternal breast that Klein describes as characteristic of a primitive 'splitting' process in the infantile 'paranoid-schizoid position':

> The breasts of Hecuba
> When she did suckle Hector looked not lovelier
> Than Hector's forehead when it spit forth blood
> At Grecian sword, contemning.
>
> (1.3.42–5)

These critics further allude to Klein's formulation of the oral basis of infantile aggression when noting Volumnia's assertion to her son that 'Thy valiantness was mine, thou sucked'st it from me' (3.2.129).[81] As interesting as this is, the play itself indicates that, although Volumnia is ambitious for her son and proud of him, she is not the sole author of his character. She asserts this herself in her limited claim that 'Thou art my warrior / I *holp* to frame thee' (5.2.62–3, my italics). Moreover, Coriolanus resists Volumnia's advice to use his fame to become consul although she proclaims

> I have lived
> To see inherited my very wishes,
> And the buildings of my fancy. Only
> There's one thing wanting, which I doubt not but
> Our Rome will cast upon thee.
>
> (2.1.196–9)

Rather, despite her wishes, Coriolanus consistently scorns all outwardly profitable outcomes. Such strong divergences of Coriolanus's aims from those of his mother show that she did not entirely form him.

In summary, Coriolanus's initial anger-saturated outlook is not the mere outcome of an ill upbringing, or of a perverse social setting. Rather than arising from external distortions of value, his rigid prejudices arise from internal distortions of love. More prejudices focused in that way will be the topic of my next and final chapter.

# 5

# Prejudices against 'Anteros' or mutual erotic love

## 'What is this thing called love?'

This question posed in Cole Porter's 1929 lyric is better rephrased in relation to Shakespeare as: 'What is this actively-lived thing called love', for Shakespeare's work is mainly concerned with love in action. Nonetheless, Shakespeare's many astute observations of varied sorts of erotic configurations do reveal several important distinctions germane to a 'definition of love'.

The Renaissance understood that there are two opposite ways to define an entity. One is by seeking the essences that give Reality to that thing (e.g. deciding what Platonic Forms that thing partakes of). The other is by pursuing a chain of distinctions between contrasting categories so that 'the substance of [the] thing and its definition' is the '*last* differentia' (Aristotle, *Meta*. 1038a 19).[1]

In line with an Aristotelian method of 'division', 'this thing called love' was distinct for Shakespeare from the distress that afflicted many fashionable youths in his age who subscribed to a cultural mode that may be labelled 'Petrarchanism'.[2] So 'love' is not equated for Shakespeare with the anguish of unrequited desire – it is not, as Andrew Marvell somewhat later suggested (echoing Plato), 'begotten by Despair / upon Impossibility'.[3] On the contrary, Shakespeare's young men afflicted by unobtainable erotic yearnings are repeatedly presented as ludicrous (although this mockery is often gentle). Shakespeare often underscores this by satirizing the flaccid and derivative versifying of such would-be amorists.[4]

Another distinction made by Shakespeare is between a sudden attraction and long-lasting mutual love relations. Some modern theory that has been offered on this difference is well worth examining because it very usefully contrasts with Shakespeare's different perceptions and helps to point these up.

Thus Robert J. Stoller differentiates between briefly enthralled lovers and lovers forming a lasting bond by first holding that in mere 'romance', as he calls it, 'altruism is spectacular and superficial' and that 'romance' is both 'likely to fade' and is 'heavy with scripts'.[5] Immediately after, Stoller asks:

> What differentiates the love we admire from romance? This above all: minimal fetishizing. Which implies, in varying amounts, empathy; identification; the need to need and the need to be needed; high-pleasure altruism; reduced inventing of the other to fit our primordial fantasies; not too much ego ideal or other idealizations; the capacity to survive one's own and the other's rage and fear (stoically, with good spirits, even with humor); curiosity: the unending antidote to boredom; respect: admiring and unmalicious envy (that is, pride in the other's qualities); capacity to keep one's boundaries in the midst of merging; constructive guilt; happy vulnerability. Mutuality, obviously.

This undoubtedly insightful description of lasting love has, however, some peculiar limitations.

Indeed, near the end of this same article Stoller admits to certain deficiencies in his description of 'love', which are that there is 'hardly a nod here to joy, fun, reparation, gratitude, quietude, laughter, curiosity engaged and satisfied, tenderness, care, commitment, good humor, rest, safety' (436). But this apology does not relate to his article's major contentions that 'love and romance [equally] ... inhibit erotic potency', that 'hostility and anxiety ... energize erotic excitement' (435). Stoller explains those strange contentions by alleging that in all cultures most human males have an innate 'fear of intimacy with women' deriving from infant dependency.

In this claim Stoller clearly borrows (but I think with significant distortion) from a constellation of ideas that are summarized in Melanie Klein's *Envy and Gratitude* thus:

> The stifling of love, which I have described as a manic defence against the depressive position, is rooted in the danger threatening from destructive impulses and persecutory anxiety. In an adult, dependence on loved person revives the helplessness of the infant and is felt to be humiliating ... There is also the fear that love will lead to too much responsibility and will make too many demands.[6]

What Klein additionally propounds, however, which Stoller omits, is that defences that stifle love may be overcome so that the 'depressive position' can emerge, and that in turn can allow love to flourish, albeit not in a painless or idealized form. On the contrary, Stoller's article is focused only on an idealized vision of love and lovers. A vision of perfectibility probably accounts for the fact that just after his above-quoted description of love Stoller inserts the additional remark: 'And it is rare' (416).

By contrast, in his assessment of the non-ideal locale of love represented by Shakespeare's Forest of Arden in *As You Like It*, Jonathan Lear finds this to be 'a field of irony'.[7] I similarly believe that visions of perfectibility resembling Stoller's do not correspond with any Shakespearian depictions of love.

A basis for Stoller's dubiety is summarized in his article's abstract where he claims that there are universal love-adverse 'forces that, transcending cultures, create gender identity in males and females', and that these 'give us hints as to why love is often so unloving' (413). This theorization of universal anti-love forces is important for the present discussion because it has been adopted by an influential Shakespeare critic who holds that when Shakespeare begins to portray mutual erotic love he is always compelled to reverse himself. Presently I will return to such claims.

This chapter will argue that Shakespeare's representations do not support Stoller's two assertions that 'hostility and anxiety ... energize erotic excitement' and that lasting mutual love is nearly impossible or very 'rare'. On the contrary, although Shakespeare depicts love as subject to instabilities and vulnerable to vicissitudes, he still finds mutual love possible, and not even rare, in an un-ideal world. Thus Shakespeare shows that attainable degrees of courage and strength may underwrite genuine love's development, continuance or (when needed) restoration.

If, as alleged by Stoller and his followers, universal psychic forces oppose lasting love, then the aversions to love seen in several Shakespeare characters would be realistic and justified behaviours. Against this I will argue that for Shakespeare love-disrupting tendencies are not natural or universal, but express rather pathological *prejudices*.

# Shakespeare is not autobiographical when portraying prejudices against love

Some critics suggest that Shakespeare's portrayals of aversions to love mirror aspects of his own emotional life. I believe, however, that this sort of 'autobiographical' reading aims to *explain away* Shakespeare's achievements rather than appreciating that imaginative poets 'imitate' nature in order 'to teach and delight', as Sir Philip Sidney put it.[8]

Readings of his works based on speculations about Shakespeare's personal erotic dilemmas not only tend to straitjacket and desiccate artistic productions, but also produce a conundrum. That is that Shakespeare portrayed such an extraordinarily wide range of erotic configurations and predicaments as to make it impossible that he could have experienced all that variety within a single lifespan.[9]

An extreme example of a narrowing of the range of Shakespeare's treatments of the erotic is seen when one critic proposes that for Shakespeare, always, 'Desire *is* death' (quoting the speaker in Sonnet 147).[10] This is no more true of Shakespeare's work on the whole than is the anguished assertion by the speaker in Sonnet 129 that all sexual intercourse (called by him 'lust in action') is wasteful and shameful. On the contrary, Shakespearian figures voicing desperate unhappiness about love or sex, such as are seen here, disclose uniquely distressed mental states occupying only an extreme end of the wide spectrum of responses to Eros portrayed by Shakespeare.

Other critics narrow the range of Shakespeare's views on love and sex by alleging his private misogyny;[11] others maintain that his misogyny matches pervasive attitudes of his time and culture;[12] others claim that Shakespeare's own 'ambiguous sexuality' explains why he 'could not keep his fear of women and disgust with sex from breaking through' so that 'his queasiness before the sexuality of women' arises 'unbidden to the surface of [his] work'.[13] Just a glance at Shakespeare's numerous delightful and vigorous heroines belies such generalizations.

Shakespeare, of course, also depicted wickedness such as seen in his adulterous and cruel Tamora, Queen Margaret, Goneril and Regan, and in Lady Macbeth who sponsors murder and fantasizes infanticide. Noting this range of portrayals only reinforces how Shakespearian treatments of gender and sexuality are so wide-ranging as to render speculations that these treatments are psycho-autobiographical unsupportable.

Nevertheless there is *one* gap in the range of Shakespeare's representations of erotic love. This is that he never presents it in a sentimental light, and on the contrary reveals that anxieties and challenges arise in all sorts of erotic attachments. These challenges may derive from ('star-crossed') bad luck, or from blocking fathers, or from shipwrecks or accidents of war, but more often they are portrayed as emotionally deep-rooted. For instance, in *A Midsummer Night's Dream* a vortex of troubles beset four marionette-like young lovers, illustrating that 'The course of true love never did run smooth' (1.1.134), but beside their mechanical-seeming difficulties with attraction and their wooing problems Shakespeare represents the profounder woes of the estranged married pair Oberon and Titania and hints at ominous incompatibilities between the affianced Theseus and Hippolita.[14]

However, despite difficulties that may result in hurt, anger or temporary estrangement, numerous pairs of Shakespearian lovers achieve mutual erotic connections. These include Rosalind and Orlando, Antony and Cleopatra, Pericles and Thaisa, Perdita and Florizel, Ferdinand and Miranda.

Therefore Shakespeare's frequent representations of 'scorns and mislike' focused on mutual erotic love stand in opposition to an alternative of love fulfilled. In order to explore the nature of that alternative I will next examine a terminology and mythology widely available in Shakespeare's time, but not in ours, that delineates a particular kind of erotic success.

# Who or what was *Anteros*?

The target of the prejudices explored in this chapter was personified in the Renaissance by *Anteros*, who was the classical deity or patron of fulfilled mutual erotic desire. In some contexts '*Anteros*' was not a proper noun, but rather a common noun indicating 'returned love' or 'counter-love', which is what the Greek term Ἀντέρως means. The earliest preserved use of this term appears in Plato's *Phaedrus* 255d where Socrates describes the inevitable reciprocation of a strong attraction to a beautiful youth (a homosexual attraction which is not necessarily physically consummated).

Plato notwithstanding, strong erotic attractions are not always mutual. The ancients knew that, and so sometimes represented Anteros as a deity who avenges the non-reciprocation of love.[15] At other times they represented him in competition with his elder brother *Eros*. In a common motif in classical and Renaissance visual art these two brothers, both born of Aphrodite, are depicted striving for the possession of a palm leaf (see Figure 5.1).[16]

FIGURE 5.1 *Engraving by Vinceno Cartari of Eros and Anteros made after a painting by Guiseppe Salviati (c. 1502–c. 1575) in Vinceno Cartari, Le imagini de i dei de gli antichi (Venetia, 1571).*

In a not infrequent 'conscientious' Renaissance misreading of this tradition described by Erwin Panofsky 'the rivalry between Eros and Anteros ... was often misinterpreted as a struggle between Sensual Love and Virtue'. This variation is not of interest here, for as Panofsky writes, 'The function of the classical Anteros ... had been to assure reciprocity in amorous relations; but while this was clearly understood by scholarly antiquarians, moralists and humanists with Platonizing leanings were apt to interpret the preposition ἀντί as "against" instead of "in return," thus turning the God of Mutual Love into a personification of virtuous purity'.[17] Such an error, figuring Anteros as *anti*-Eros, was more prevalent among continental Renaissance authors,[18] but also appeared in a few seventeenth-century English literary contexts (including one spectacularly disastrous one).[19]

Shakespeare's England also received, contrary to this erroneous revision, a 'graceful' counter-myth transmitted (and possibly originated) by the mid-fourth-century rhetorician Themistius. Themistius' version emphasizes mutual dependence and support, rather than conflict, between Eros and Anteros, thus:

> When Aphrodite bore Eros, the lad was fair and like his mother in every way, save that he did not grow to a stature befitting his beauty, nor did he put on flesh; but he long remained at the size which he had had at birth. This matter perplexed his mother and the Muses who nursed him, and presenting themselves before Themis (for Apollo did not yet possess Delphi) they begged for a cure to this strange and wondrous mischance. So Themis spoke: 'Why', said she, 'I will solve your difficulty, for you have not yet learned the nature of the child. Your true Eros, Aphrodite, might indeed be born by himself, but could not possibly grow by himself; if you wish Eros to grow you need Anteros. These two brothers will be of the same nature, and each will be cause of the other's growth; for as they see each other they will alike grow, but if either is left alone they will both

waste away.' So Aphrodite gave birth to Anteros, and Eros shot up at once; his wings sprouted and he grew tall. The circumstances of his establishment being so remarkable, he often passes through incredible vicissitudes, now waxing, now waning, and again increasing. But he needs his brother always beside him; seeing him large, he strives to prove himself greater, or finding him small and slight he often wastes unwillingly away.[20]

Scholars have indicated how Themistius' Anteros, 'the partner and not merely the avenger of Eros', influenced the 'amoristic literature of the Italian and French Renaissance',[21] but here our concern will be the impact of Themistius' myth of Anteros and Eros' mutuality on English Renaissance literature.

That impact is seen in the writings of Abraham Fraunce, Ben Jonson, John Milton and possibly William Davenant.[22] Thus Fraunce's *The third part of the Countesse of Pembrokes Yuychurch* (1592) first fluently echoes Themistius version above, and then adds a further allegorization of the motif of a struggle over a palm branch:

Eros was figured with a branche of palme in his hand: Anteros contended to wrest it from him, but could not. Hee that will be loved, must love ... We must contend to overcome and get the palme and victory, by loving more, then we be loved so shall we still be loved more.[23]

Overall, the thrust of Fraunce's re-telling emphasizes the interdependence and mutuality of the two brothers.

In two of the works of Shakespeare's colleague Ben Jonson Anteros is introduced as 'Love's Enemy' or 'anti-Cupid',[24] but, in addition, in two of the elaborate entertainments that Jonson devised for aristocratic patrons Eros and Anteros are dramatized as attaining concord, each growing stronger in the presence of the other. The first of these, Jonson's *A Challenge at Tilt*, was played for the ill-fated 26 December 1613 marriage of Frances Howard and Robert Carr.[25] In this two 'Cupids' who are in the service respectively of a newly married bride and groom at first accuse one another of being impostors. They therefore will meet at tilt with champions for contention. However, their conflict is resolved when *Hymen* reveals to these Cupids 'something of your own story, and what yet you know not of yourselves':

> You are both true Cupids, and both the sons of Venus by Mars, but this the first-born, and was called Eros; who upon his birth proved a child of excellent beauty, and right worthy his mother, but after, his growth not answering his form, not only Venus, but the Graces who nursed him, became extremely solicitous for him, and were impelled out of their grief and care to consult the oracle about him. Themis (for Apollo was not yet of years) gave answer there wanted nothing to his perfection but that they had not enough considered or looked into the nature of the infant, which indeed was desirous of a companion only; for though love, and the true, might be born of Venus single and alone, yet he could not thrive and increase alone. Therefore if she affected his growth, Venus must bring forth a brother to him and name him Anteros; that with reciprocal affection might pay the exchange of love. This made that thou wert born her second birth. Since when your natures are that either of you, looking upon the other, thrive, and by your mutual respects and interchange of ardour flourish and prosper; whereas if the one be deficient or wanting to the other it fares worse with both. This is the love that Hymen requires, without which no marriage is happy: when the contention is not who is the true love, but (being both true) who loves most; cleaving the bough between you, and dividing the palm. This is a strife wherein you both win, and begets a concord worthy all married minds' emulation, when the lover transforms himself into the person of his beloved, as you two do now.[26]

This explicitly states that Eros and Anteros divide the victor's palm so that, like a loving couple, they both win.

Jonson revisited the same myth in his 1634 masque *Love's Welcome at Bolsover* in which, amusingly, 'TWO CUPIDS present themselves' and 'stand silent awhile, wondering at one another'. Then 'the lesser begins to speak':

EROS    Another Cupid?
ANTEROS                Yes, your second self,
A son of Venus, and as mere an elf
And wag as you.
EROS            Eros?
ANTEROS                No, Anteros,
Your brother Cupid, yet not sent to cross,
Or spy into your favours here at court.
EROS    What then?
ANTEROS            To serve you, brother, and report
Your graces from the Queen's side to the King's,
In whose name I salute you.
EROS                Break my wings
I fear you will.
ANTEROS        Oh, be not jealous, brother!
What bough is this?
EROS                A palm.
ANTEROS                    Give me't.
ANTEROS *snatches at the palm but* EROS *divides it.*

EROS                    Another
You may have.
ANTEROS        I will this.
EROS            Divide it.
ANTEROS        So.
This was right brother-like! The world will know
By this one act both natures. You are Love,
I, Love-Again. In these two spheres we move,
Eros, and Anteros.

EROS                 We have cleft the bough,
And struck a tally of our loves, too, now.
ANTEROS   I call to mind the wisdom of our mother
Venus, who would have Cupid have a brother —
EROS   To look upon and thrive. Me seems I grew
Three inches higher sin' I met with you.
ANTEROS   It was the counsel that the oracle gave
Your nurses, the glad Graces, sent to crave
Themis' advice. 'You do not know', quoth she,
'The nature of this infant. Love may be
Brought forth thus little, live awhile alone,
But ne'er will prosper if he have not one
Sent after him to play with.'
EROS                      Such another
As you are, Anteros, our loving brother.
ANTEROS   Who would be always planted in your eye:
For Love, by Love increaseth mutually.
EROS   We either, looking on each other, thrive!
ANTEROS   Shoot up, grow galliard –
EROS                      Yes, and more alive!
ANTEROS   When one's away it seems we both are less.
EROS   I was a dwarf, an urchin, I confess,
Till you were present.
ANTEROS               But a bird of wing
Now, fit to fly before a queen or king.
EROS   I ha' not one sick feather sin' you came,
But turned a jollier Cupid –
ANTEROS               Than I am.
EROS   I love my mother's brain could thus provide
For both in court, and give us each our side,
Where we might meet.
ANTEROS               Embrace.
EROS                      Circle each other.
ANTEROS   Confer and whisper.
EROS                      Brother with a brother.
ANTEROS   And by this sweet contention for the palm,
Unite our appetites, and make them calm.

EROS  To will and nill one thing.
ANTEROS                                    And so to move
Affection in our wills as in our love.²⁷

Here, again, the ancient palm branch motif is modified so that, as D. J. Gordon puts it, 'the struggle for the palm ... ends with a division of the palm: the harmony of mutual love'.²⁸ Also, little Eros' modest (or immodest) claim to have 'grown three inches higher' probably would have drawn smiles from the masque's original spectators,²⁹ especially as they were placed to view the elaborate iconographic decorations of that entertainment's venue at Bolsover which included a representation of Eros and Anteros.³⁰

Elaborating on the ensemble of emblematic artworks at William Cavendish's Bolsover, Timothy Raylor argues that this symbolized how 'sensuality and refinement, levity and idealism' may be 'curiously reconciled', thus bridging 'Neoplatonism and Ovidianism, the sacred and the profane, the ideal and the actual'.³¹ Among many complex artistic details described by Raylor, a depiction of the 'smiling embrace' of Eros and Anteros, he says, 'expresses the triumph of mutual affection and the reconciliation of spiritual and earthly love' (427).

The same emphasis on a 'triumph of mutual affection' pertains when John Milton mentions Eros and Anteros in his (at first scandalous³²) treatise *The Doctrine and Discipline of Divorce* (1633–4). Milton focuses on the mutuality in good marriages and vehemently decries the absence of such mutuality in bad marriages, which, he argues, should be dissolved. Thus Milton writes 'that Love, if he be not twin-born, yet hath a brother wondrous like him, called Anteros' and stated that 'no doubt' 'matrimonial love' was 'parabled' in this myth of the 'ancient sages'. Milton then adds that Love, because half-blind, can be misdirected and thereby become

> despoiled of all his force; 'till finding Anteros at last, he kindles and repairs the almost faded ammunition of his deity by the reflection of a coequal and homogenial fire.³³

Despite some radically different readings of Milton's mythography here,[34] I think Lena Cable right in finding that Milton uses the Eros and Anteros myth 'to illustrate the nature of ideal love'.[35]

It might be objected that while Abraham Fraunce, Ben Jonson and Milton were notably erudite writers, Shakespeare (although grammar school educated and certainly very curious) was not. Indeed, even the deeply learnèd of our own era are not quite certain where Jonson found all of his materials on Eros and Anteros.[36] It is nevertheless certain that Shakespeare and his culture praised reciprocated erotic love capable of growth and increasing strength.[37] So, at least for convenience, I will employ the term 'Anterotic' to indicate such mutual love in the following examinations of Shakespeare's portrayals of prejudices against Anterotic love.

# Mistaken conceptions of manliness

Shakespeare repeatedly represents characters who pursue an anxious quest for what they take to be manliness. Such characters, some female as well as male, become subject to rigidities that exclude Anterotic love, and thus express anti-Anterotic prejudices.

Several among these figures are young male characters who resist both Eros and Anteros on account of youthful callowness. One such is Shakespeare's 'Rose-cheeked' Adonis who is identified as a 'boy' nine times in *Venus and Adonis*. The poem starts by noting, 'Hunting he loved, but love he laughed to scorn' (3–4), thus indicating the derision in a typical negative prejudice. Immediately after we are told that the powerful and sex-hungry goddess Venus ''gins to woo him' (6). When thwarted she 'pluck[ed] him from his horse. / Over one arm, the lusty courser's rein; / Under her other was the tender boy'. Thus assaulted, Adonis, 'blushed and pouted in a dull disdain / With leaden appetite, unapt to toy' (30–4). The subsequent tragedy evolves from that disdain.

In common with Adonis, the exiled young princes Arvigraus and Guiderius in *Cymbeline* display squeamish attitudes to sexuality similar to those that have been identified with what is now called the 'latency period' of psycho-sexual development.[38] As mentioned before, these two country-bred brothers display preferences for physical prowess (in hunting and, when insulted, in fighting), over the use of 'wench-like words' (4.2.231). Their taboo-like anti-female orientation prevents them from discerning the true gender of the disguised 'Fidele', whom they take to be a male youth even though Guiderius describes him/her with 'O sweetest, fairest, lilly!' (4.2.202). So these two lads – whose voices have only recently 'got the mannish crack' (4.2.237)[39] – exhibit an exaggerated version of what they believe to be the hardness required of adult males.

Shakespeare also exhibits some women who aspire to what they take to be a proper masculine 'hardness'. However, these manifestations are portrayed as less benign (and less transient) than when adolescent lads strive to become 'manly'. Thus, shockingly, Lady Macbeth pleads 'unsex me here ... Come to my woman's breasts, / And take my milk for gall, you murd'ring ministers' (1.5.40–7). Underscoring her bizarre views of gender, she proclaims to her husband, who is hesitating to murder:

When you durst do it, then you were a man;
And to be more than what you were, you would
Be so much more the man. (1.7.49–51)

and adds

    I have given suck, and know
How tender 'tis to love the babe that milks me.
I would, while it was smiling in my face,
Have plucked my nipple from his boneless gums
And dashed the brains out, had I so sworn
As you have done to this. (1.7.54–9).

After the regicide, she again challenges Macbeth with 'Are you a man?' (3.4.57). This sentiment is paralleled when in the quarto text of *King Lear* Goneril taunts her husband with 'Marry your manhood, mew' (S.16.67).

Like Goneril, the Empress Tamora in *Titus Andronicus*, Queen Margaret of Anjou in *2 Henry VI* and Regan in *King Lear* all intend to become as vicious as they think men are or ought to be. All four of those women are adulterous wives who choose bellicose lower-born paramours, so choosing Eros but giving no place to Anteros.

The would-be militarist Count Bertram in *All's Well that Ends Well* also pursues Eros but rejects Anteros. Bertram is the King's ward, which, under English law makes him less than twenty-one years old.[40] His lament over his status as a ward may indicate that he is much younger than that, for his majority seems to him a long way off when he complains, 'I must attend his majesty's command, to whom I am now in ward, evermore in subjection' (1.1.4–5). When a marriage is imposed on him in accord with wardship, the fatherless Bertram flees his native country to the join Italian wars, leaving behind his mother, new wife and the King. He has been convinced to do this by the fraudulent Paroles, actually a coward, who intones:

> To th' wars, my boy, to th' wars
> He wears his honour in a box unseen
> That hugs his kicky-wicky here at home,
> Spending his manly marrow in her arms,
> Which should sustain the bound and high curvet
> Of Mars's fiery steed. To other regions!
> France is a stable, we that dwell in 't jades.
> Therefore to th' war.
>
> (2.3.275–82)

Following this Bertram speaks of his 'hate' for his 'detested wife' (284–9), but more likely he shuns not so much her as the married state and its possibility of Anteros. Not wishing to be Paroles' weak 'jade' but rather a manly 'steed', Bertram becomes an undomesticated warrior, but does not repudiate Eros, only Anteros. So, in Italy, he attempts to seduce Diana, having refused to bed his wife Helena in France. Perhaps partially excusing him, Shakespeare's play identifies Bertram as 'young' more than a dozen times, and in its ending his adultery is not achieved and he is led back to marriage.

Thus several Shakespearian characters possessing false concepts of manliness reject or defy the dictates of Anterotic love. Some others, conceiving prejudices against Anteros in the light of pseudo-intellectualism, will be considered next.

## 'Scholarly' despisers of Anterotic love

Both *The Taming of the Shrew* and *Love's Labour's Lost* feature fashionably pseudo-intellectual young men who intend to become ascetic scholars. All these quickly fall into the snares of Eros, and all fail to achieve a happy mutually loving ending in accord with Anteros.

The youthful Lucentio is first met in *The Taming of the Shrew* idealizing study, having just arrived in 'fair Padua, nursery of arts' (1.1.2). Comically soon after, upon setting eyes on Bianca Minola, he falls headlong into idealizing and confides to his witty servant that 'I burn, I pine, I perish, Tranio, / If I achieve not this young modest girl' (1.1.153–4). Thus he puts himself on track for marriage with an envious and vain manipulator; thanks to his infatuation, Eros wins the palm from Anteros when he marries a controlling and calculating minx. Uniquely among Shakespeare's marriageable young women, Bianca Minola is portrayed as wholly unfit for real mutuality, and she, rather than her notorious sister, proves in the end to be the play's most balky, 'froward and unable' (5.2.174).[41] Yet she charms almost all the men in the play, and only eccentric Petruchio resists her manipulative charms.

In *Love's Labour's Lost* witty Lord Biron is at first a denigrator of Anteros, although he is also an outspoken sceptic concerning the benefits of the agreement forced on him to remain cloistered from all contact with women during three ascetic years of study (1.1.33–159). Biron praises rather the delights of studying 'where I well may dine / ... / Or study[ing] where to meet some mistress fine' (1.1.61–3). This 'mistress fine' is imaged as a tasty dish in parallel with 'where I well may dine', and is therefore an object of Eros, as opposed to Anteros.

Biron, who at first professes himself the enemy of Anteros, suddenly finds himself strongly attracted to the visiting 'stranger' Lady Rosaline of France. On their first encounter Rosaline reveals herself to be charming and highly intelligent (2.1.116–27). Well aware of the insincerity and shallowness of stereotypic Petrarchan tropes, she wittily derides Biron's complaint that he 'would' that she 'hear' his 'heart ... groan' (2.1.179–93). Following this, Biron laments in a long soliloquy (3.1.169–200) that 'I that have been love's whip' has now fallen 'in love'. He recalls ruefully that he had formerly mocked and scorned those falling prey to 'Signor Junior, giant dwarf, Dan Cupid', and condemns himself as 'perjured'. In this last remark he describes himself not so much a traitor to the ascetic pact to which he had reluctantly subscribed as he is a traitor to his own self-declared identity as the 'critic' and 'domineering pendant o'er' Cupid.

Biron's soliloquy then becomes distinctly anti-Anterotic when he intones ruefully 'What? I love, I sue, I seek a wife?' (3.1.184). Clearly, his emphasis here is on the egotistical 'I'. In order to defend his self-image Biron next directs scorns and mislike against not just Rosaline, but also against all marriageable women:

What? I love, I sue, I seek a wife? –
A woman, that is like a German clock,
Still a-repairing, ever out of frame,
And never going aright, being a watch,
But being watched that it may still go right.
Nay, to be perjured, which is worst of all,
And among three to love the worst of all –

A whitely wanton with a velvet brow,
With two pitch-balls stuck in her face for eyes –
Ay, and, by heaven, one that will do the deed
Though Argus were her eunuch and her guard.
And I to sigh for her, to watch for her,
To pray for her – go to, it is a plague
That Cupid will impose for my neglect
Of his almighty dreadful little might.

(3.1.184–98)

Here, as often in prejudice, 'someone other' represents 'something else'; these denunciations arise not only because charming dark-eyed Lady Rosaline's undeniable attractions have disrupted Biron's smugly prejudiced self-image, but also because Rosaline frightens him sexually. Thus Biron's anticipations of inevitable cuckoldry accompany a dismayed reference to female sexual function (taking the form of an allusion to a clock-like menstrual cycle). As will be seen, Biron heads a parade of woman-fearing and sex-denouncing, males who appear in later-written Shakespeare plays.

Before turning to those and their anti-Anterotic prejudices I want to point out yet another area of overlapping prejudices emerging during Biron's panicked soliloquy about having fallen 'in love'. This is signalled when he caps the soliloquy with a couplet expressing resigned submission: 'Well, I will love, write, sigh, pray, sue, groan: / Some men must love my lady, and some Joan' (199–200). Because Shakespeare repeatedly applied the name 'Joan' to a countrywomen or servants,[42] this couplet links to a motif running through *Love's Labour's Lost* concerning differences in social standing. Biron's allusion to this is redoubled when later, lying to his king, he avers that *he* will never be seen to 'write a thing in rhyme / Or groan for Joan' (4.3.179–80). Here again his choice of a name betrays offhand snobbism, an attitude never approved of by Shakespeare.[43]

In the psychically healthier world of the Princess of France and her ladies there is a better recognition that Eros is not subject to caste barriers. Hence in a hunting scene (where the hunt is an outdoor erotic venue, as often in Shakespeare) the Princess first admires the King of Navarre's gallant horsemanship, finding him distinctly physically attractive (4.1.1–5). Next in this natural setting, the Princess interacts almost flirtatiously with an attendant 'Forester' by eliciting a compliment on her appearance. The Forester seems embarrassed by that, but the Princess reassures and thanks him (4.1.10–23). This interchange might have reminded Elizabethans of Fulke Greville's lyric (to be discussed presently) containing: 'And Love as well the foster can, / As can the noble Noble-man'.

However, a satirical motif also runs throughout *Love's Labour's Lost* when the erratic love life of the country wench Jaquenetta concludes in her match with the grandiloquent Don Adriano de Armado of Spain. Armado's besotted wooing of Jaquenetta (who is pregnant by another) may allude to a legal concept known in Shakespeare's England as 'disparagement' – this was a basis for objecting to a marriage with a person of lower social rank.[44] In any case, Armado's misalliance in *Love's Labour's Lost* is framed as a ludicrous reduction of this fantastical 'stranger's' self-proclaimed elevated social and intellectual status.

Self-ridicule arises when Count Biron of Navarre berates himself as a 'fool' when admitting to his subjection to erotic desire (4.3.205). Biron then explains the necessity of resignation to forces that are indifferent to lofty cultural ideals as well as to caste: 'We cannot cross the cause why we were born, / Therefore of all hands must we be forsworn' (4.3.216–17). Despite the high status of his own and his fellow courtier's love objects Biron's remark suggests that procreative nature (*natura naturans*) forces all men to succumb to degrading abnegation, whether they love 'my lady', or 'Joan'. Continuing in the same unhealthy vein, the King and courtiers of Navarre attempt to take shelter from their newly acknowledged emotional dependency by competitively blazoning the supreme excellence of their own mistresses and dispraising their peers' mistresses, so converting their unnerving desires into masculine vying for pre-eminence (4.3.219–70). Alongside that they all also deploy the Ovidian trope of love as war (4.3.339–62), again attempting to replace feared abjection with 'manly' assertion or aggression. In this way Biron and his friends attempt to sidestep erotic neediness by assuming the guise of heroic knights-errant of love.

Pursuing further reassurance (that is, diversion from neediness), Biron also attempts to merge the former 'intellectual' pretentiousness of the Navarre cabal with their newfound cult, thus finding in 'women's eyes' 'the books, the arts, the academes / That show, contain, and nourish all the world' (4.3.326–9). Hence even when they acknowledge themselves in love these men are still the self-glorifiers who had lauded their magnificent intentions for ascetic study, and the formulistic gestures they make of erotic humility are hypocritical.

For instance, in a passage discussed in Chapter 2 in relation to prejudices against 'art', Biron promises Rosaline that he will eschew henceforth 'maggot ostentation', and then feigns to speak using countrified diction. Attempting to sham low or 'broad' diction (as some now do using 'Mockney'), he concludes:

Henceforth my wooing mind shall be expressed
In russet yeas, and honest kersey noes.
And to begin, wench, so God help me, law!
My love to thee is sound, sans crack or flaw.

(5.2.412–15)

The last line here reveals, however, that Biron has not rid himself of 'ostentation' for in it he slips (for the sake of meter) into using the high-sounding French 'sans'. Witty Rosaline promptly corrects him with 'Sans "sans", I pray you' (5.2.416), providing a brilliant meta-theatrical joke.[45]

Rosaline goes on to correct Biron more seriously in the long passage spanning 5.2.827–55. Here she demands that Biron delay his wooing for a 'twelvemonth' during which time he must learn to eschew his tendencies to indulge in the 'mocks ... / and wounding flouts, / Which you on all estates will execute'. This demand for Biron learning to be considerate toward 'all estates' recalls the play's motif of social snobbery, and a reference to his 'mocks' and 'flouts' points toward his former supposedly witty prejudicial demeaning of the demands of Anteros.

Thus the social and cultural preciousness of young noblemen in *Love's Labour's Lost* is linked with their resistances to Anterotic love. In their continuing egotism those men replaced their original self-regarding anchoritic intentions with equally self-congratulatory pursuits of what Robert Stoller called 'romance' (which is antithetic to genuine Anterotic love). In consequence, their matrimonial hopes are defeated, or at least deflected, at the play's end. Biron must then admit that their 'wooing doth not end like an old play. / Jack hath not Jill'. He thus remarks, meta-theatrically and correctly, that this outcome cannot conclude a full-blown 'comedy' (5.2.860–2).

# Sex-suspicion and prejudice against Anteros

Biron's just noted soliloquy in 3.1.184–98 laments falling in love in terms of fears of cuckoldry, and expresses a parallel aversion to Rosaline's corporality. A similar combination appears in darker and deeper forms in several later Shakespeare plays in which deluded men rage against Anteros, female sexuality and imagined infidelity. Like Biron, these male accusers all descend to misogynistic rants against women in general.

When greatly amplifying Biron's hints about potential cuckoldry and his uncomfortable corporal imagery these dangerously indignant men are not, like him, semi-serious but rather obsessively committed to deep prejudices. Their furious and toxic denunciations of women, and prejudicial attacks on Anteros, include:

CLAUDIO
    I'll lock up all the gates of love,
  And on my eyelids shall conjecture hang

To turn all beauty into thoughts of harm,
And never shall it more be gracious.
                    (*Much Ado About Nothing* 4.1.105–8)


OTHELLO
                    I am abused, and my relief
Must be to loathe her. O curse of marriage,
That we can call these delicate creatures ours
And not their appetites! I had rather be a toad
And live upon the vapour of a dungeon
Than keep a corner in the thing I love
For others' uses.
                              (*Othello* 3.3.271–7)


POSTHUMUS
                              Could I find out
The woman's part in me – for there's no motion
That tends to vice in man but I affirm
It is the woman's part; be it lying, note it,
The woman's; flattering, hers; deceiving, hers;
Lust and rank thoughts, hers, hers; revenges, hers;
Ambitions, covetings, change of prides, disdain,
Nice longing, slanders, mutability,
All faults that man can name, nay, that hell knows,
Why, hers in part or all, but rather all –
For even to vice
They are not constant, but are changing still
One vice but of a minute old for one
Not half so old as that. I'll write against them,
Detest them, curse them, yet 'tis greater skill
In a true hate to pray they have their will.
The very devils cannot plague them better.
                              (*Cymbeline* 2.5.19–35)


LEONTES
                    Should all despair
That have revolted wives, the tenth of mankind

Would hang themselves. Physic for 't there's none.
It is a bawdy planet, that will strike
Where 'tis predominant; and 'tis powerful. Think it:
From east, west, north, and south, be it concluded,
No barricado for a belly. Know 't,
It will let in and out the enemy
With bag and baggage.

(*The Winter's Tale* 1.2.199–207)

In two of these four outbursts anti-Anterotic dismay is laced with voyeuristic anatomical disgust,[46] and *Othello* also strongly evokes voyeurism at 1.1.88–9, 3.3.365 and 399–401. Similar corporal disgust features in other misogynistic and anti-erotic outbursts in *Hamlet* and *King Lear*:

HAMLET

Nay, but to live
In the rank sweat of an enseamed bed,
Stewed in corruption, honeying and making love
Over the nasty sty –

(3.4.81–4)

LEAR

Behold yon simp'ring dame,
Whose face between her forks presages snow,
That minces virtue, and does shake the head
To hear of pleasure's name.
The fitchew nor the soiled horse goes to 't
With a more riotous appetite. Down from the waist
They're centaurs, though women all above.
But to the girdle do the gods inherit;
Beneath is all the fiend's. There's hell, there's darkness, there is the sulphurous pit, burning, scalding, stench, consumption. Fie, fie, fie; pah, pah! Give me an ounce of civet, good apothecary, sweeten my imagination.

(4.5.116–27)

Only some of the above outbursts that are saturated with prejudices against Anteros allude to suspicions of cuckoldry, but all appear in contexts suggesting another common element. Hamlet's disgust openly derives from his dismay at his mother's sexuality. King Lear, who has demolished his hoped-for 'kind nursery' (1.1.124) at the hands of Cordelia, becomes terrified lest his mental aberration will become the swelling 'mother' (2.2.231) and he then curses procreation (3.2.8–9). Othello becomes convinced that Desdemona has cuckolded him when he misconstrues the trajectory of his mother's handkerchief. Leontes suffers a paranoid nervous breakdown when his wife is just about to become a mother. Posthumus prefaces his misogynistic rant with a supposition that his mother conceived him whorishly (2.5.6). The duped Claudio in *Much Ado* might seem an outlier in this pattern, but not if parallels are noted between Claudio's and Hero's inarticulate erotic connection and the hyper-articulate anti-Anterotic wrangling between Beatrice and Benedick that includes her jibe that she rejects him 'lest / I should prove the mother of fools' (2.1.266–7). Moreover, Count Bertram in *All's Well* defies and abandons his mother when fleeing from Anterotic love. More will be said about such patterns presently.

## Shakespeare on sex-terror

Several theories have been brought to bear on the miserable Shakespearian men who proclaim beliefs in the failure of, the falsity of or the worthlessness of Anterotic love. With the usual motive of highlighting alternatives I will first mention some views that I think deficient before summarizing other theories that I think more explanatory of phenomena represented by Shakespeare.

Regarding Elizabethan dramatizations of men's mistaken sexual suspicions, Leslie Fiedler suggests that Shakespeare's own personal 'bad conscience' fed into his depiction of

Othello's unfounded jealousy. Fiedler claims that this bad conscience echoes the bad conscience of Shakespeare's 'whole culture', and that it arises from:

> [Elizabethan] men's awareness that women are the victim of a marriage system in whose making they had no voice, and of a double standard concerning chastity on which they were not consulted. And it is aggravated by the suspicion that women, being conscious of these indignities, are eager for the kind of revenge which is always in their power, the revenge of adultery, and that in any case they cannot keep those marriage vows which male idealism and selfishness in strange concert invented, but which have always striven in vain against the hairy beast between their legs, the *anima avidam generandi*.[47]

Contrary to such a notion, however, is the fact that when Shakespeare portrays restrictions and disabilities placed specifically on women he consistently implies imaginative sympathy with them.[48] Since this sensitivity to unfairness is at variance with Fiedler's notions of a culture-wide fearful male 'bad conscience', there must be another explanation of why some (but not all) of Shakespeare's male characters develop prejudicial beliefs in the universal inconstancy of womankind.

Another even more universalizing account of such fears is offered in Robert Stoller's above-mentioned 1991 essay on love and lovers. In this Stoller concludes there is a universal male opposition to Anterotic love by generalizing from an account of male rearing and socialization in a particular New Guinean society. Extrapolating from this, Stoller concludes that:

> Sambia men respond to their sense that mothers and sons have been too much merged. They recognize it is late in the game and stage a massive separation ritual – first stage initiation – with equally massive indoctrination. (Except in degree, in doing so they do as do other cultures/religions.) They thereby provide the next generation with the symbiosis

barrier – beware the mortal danger of intimacy with women – needed for the culture to survive its brutal physical (non-human and human) circumstances. It is easy – we need no scholarly demonstration here – to see how, throughout history and in all cultures, masculinity has been shaped by the same dynamics with the same resultant deformations.[49]

So, according to Stoller, men 'throughout history and in all cultures' are naturally wary of 'the mortal danger of intimacy with women'.

Stoller's views of love and sexuality thus derive from a premise that erotic difficulties in later life begin with the difficulties inevitably experienced by very young children in their relationships with primary caregivers, most often mothers. In other words, insuperable later resistances to love derive from a traumatic first love.[50]

In the course of her study of mothers in Shakespeare, Janet Adelman narrows down on Stoller's trans-historical universalizing pronouncement that masculine anti-Anterotic tendencies appear 'throughout history and in all cultures',[51] but in other ways follows him closely. Thus Adelman cites Stoller, and like him finds infantile resentments crucially reflected in Shakespeare's plays. However, unlike him, she locates the sources of these resentments specifically in Elizabethan culture and society, and so maintains that Shakespeare's male characters are averse to, fearful of, horrified by and hateful toward femininity on account of specific Elizabethan child-rearing practices. This thesis derives it main support from allegations about uncaring Elizabethan family life in Lawrence Stone's 1977 *The Family, Sex and Marriage in England 1500–1800*. There Stone holds that in response to frequent childhood mortality early modern parents' attachments to their children were typically low-keyed, unaffectionate, undemanding and unstable. Adelman goes even further by alleging that, typically, Elizabethan parents were actually cruel to infants.[52]

Standing against such claims of callousness is the ample evidence provided by Shakespeare and many other writers that Elizabethan parents cared very much for their offspring (for instance, by mourning them intensely if they died).[53] Moreover, Stone connects his theory of early modern parental indifference to Philippe Ariès's 1960 argument that childhood was a late-developed concept, but Ariès's book specifically denies that children were 'neglected, forsaken or despised', and states categorically that 'The idea of childhood is not to be confused with affection for children'.[54] Following the 1977 publication of Stone's book many scholars have rejected Stone's thesis on varied historical grounds. These include Alan Macfarlane (1979), Keith Wrightson (1982: 104–18), Peter Laslett (1983: 119–20), Eileen Spring (1984) and Ann Jennalie Cook (1991: 12–13). For instance, viewing the matter from a legal-historical perspective, Spring concludes that Stone's 'impressionistic' theory of unaffectionate early modern parenting 'is largely misperceived'.[55] Apparently undeterred by his critics, Stone repeated his former position in his 1993 *Broken Lives: Separation and Divorce in England 1660–1857*, and indeed his theories about uncaring early modern parents continued to impress many – including Adelman – for some time. Perhaps the appeal lay in the 'materialistic' nature of Stone's economic theory of unprofitable emotional investments combined with his allegations that in a better-run economy (one with numerically fewer child deaths) there is a great improvement in emotional life. However, such a quantitative view of the history of emotions is not endorsed in Amanda Vickery's detailed study of women's intimate lives, in which she comments that 'Lawrence Stone's assertion that high infant and child mortality cauterized parental affection is doubtful, and his belief that "the value of children rises as their durability improves" highly questionable'.[56]

A further, more important, lacuna also appears in Stoller and Adelman's accounts of masculine resistances to Anterotic love. This is that both accounts derive from truncated and distorted versions of 'object relations' theories of mother–child relations, and in particular they bypass an understanding of the above-summarized Kleinian 'depressive position'. Thus both Stoller and Adelman overlook or invert Kleinian insights regarding infants' emergence from an initial sense of fusion with their first caregiver whereby they learn that they have selves that may interrelate as independent whole persons, rather than only in terms of the gratification of needs or else terrifying frustrations due to the delaying of gratification. The process involved in learning this, although difficult and painful, helps to develop capabilities of giving, receiving and sharing love and concern, and helps to produce a sense of having a good self that inhabits a tolerable world.[57]

On the contrary, Janet Adelman agrees with Robert Stoller that entrapment of, in particular, male infants by overwhelming mothers permanently hinders mutual adult loving based on affection, generosity and concern. Against that, evidence-based psychoanalytic studies have shown that although infantile terrors and anger may be elicited by dependency and thwarted phantasies of merger and omnipotence, these are normally mitigated and transformed by a caregiver who can 'contain' and assuage the infant's projected-out fears and hostilities. In consequence, the 'paranoid-schizoid position' which is noted in the Introduction above as characterized by the 'splitting' of internal objects gives way to the also noted 'depressive position' in which broken 'part objects' are reinstated as 'whole objects' that can be successfully loved.

Despite the pessimism of Stoller and Adelman, such a process, known as 'reparation', may allow 'the course of true love' to 'run' on, even though inevitable minor oscillations between converse 'positions' mean that it cannot always 'run smooth'.

The converse psychic 'positions' described by Klein and her followers are not developmental 'phases' that may be left behind, or fixated, or regressed to, but are rather emotional constellations that repeatedly recur in varied forms long after infancy and childhood. Therefore re-entry into the reparative 'depressive position' remains possible throughout life. Although some have denied that entering the remorseful depressive position may allow adults to repair damaged love and gratitude, and thus to realize that wholeness and separateness are consistent with loving, Shakespeare himself did not overlook such possibilities. Therefore the next two sections of this book will contrast a portrayal in *Hamlet* of unredeemed paranoid-schizoid splitting of love objects with a stunning representation in *The Winter's Tale* of the reparative overcoming of splitting and of dire anti-Anterotic prejudices.

# Anti-Anterotic prejudices in *Hamlet*

The resistance to Anterotic love seen when Ophelia's offered love is rejected in Shakespeare's *Hamlet* presents a mystery of inaction even more elusive than Hamlet's famously delayed revenge. In an unpublished letter directed to Fleiss in 1897, Freud discussed 'Hamlet the hysteric' who, in response to the 'sexual alienation in his conversation with Ophelia', becomes 'typically hysterical',[58] and this suggests one useful way to understand his behaviour, as will be seen.

In the same letter Freud makes his earliest known mention of the Oedipus complex.[59] I think, however, that when examining the hysterical behaviour that signals Hamlet's anti-Anterotic prejudices it is best not to follow the well-worn path of interpreting him as an Oedipal son incapable of killing a father figure.[60] I will to seek rather to uncover the roots of Hamlet's catastrophic rejection of Ophelia's love by applying more appropriate Freudian and post-Freudian understandings.

In Elisabeth Young-Bruehl's threefold division of prejudices outlined in the last chapter prejudices against Anterotic love belong to category of id-dominated prejudices in which hysterical traits predominate. Characteristic of hysterical traits are the splitting of objects and the denigration of 'bad' objects. To illustrate this from Shakespeare it may be observed that splitting and denigration are evident when King Lear first divides his daughters into the all-good Goneril and Regan and the all-bad Cordelia, and then, not finding his desired 'kind nursery' (1.1.124) with those two daughters, Lear reverses the splitting and takes the absent Cordelia to be all-good and her two sisters all-bad. This leads to Lear's hysterical dash into a storm and his fear of madness.

Hamlet also repeatedly splits his love objects into two, one part presumed to be all-good and the other all-bad. Thus, when he has berated and bullied his mother into her exclamation 'O Hamlet, thou hast cleft my heart in twain!', he replies, 'O, throw away the worser part of it' (3.4.147–8). In the same gruelling scene he shows Queen Gertrude miniature portraits of both his late father and of his uncle Claudius, contrasting these two as images of 'Hyperion' and a 'mildewed ear' or a 'moor' (3.4.62–6). Earlier Claudius had said that Hamlet should 'think of us / As of a father' (1.2.107–8), so here Hamlet contrasts two father images, splitting them apart and denigrating one. While doing so Hamlet expresses outright racism (which is rarely portrayed by Shakespeare) – and according to Young-Bruehl (34 and 269–72) racism is characteristic of hysterical character types.

Ophelia is also split into two by Hamlet. At first she is for him 'the celestial and my soul's idol, the most beautified / Ophelia' (2.2.110–11), yet later he associates her with a face-painting, ambling, lisping, wanton fit for a 'nunnery' or brothel (3.1.137–49). Hamlet equally splits and denigrates his mother when he eventually proclaims her 'whored' (5.2.65). Even the corporal remains of the long-dead jester Yorick, in connection with whom Hamlet recalls fond memories of childhood tenderness, are associated by him with the revolting sexual vanity of 'my lady' in her 'chamber' (5.1.180–90). So throughout the play Hamlet is seen splitting nearly all his objects, the sole exception being his strictly rational friend Horatio.

Ophelia must notice this, and where does that leave her? I suggest that that it is crucial to consider the possibilities of Ophelia's perspicacity, intelligence and independent agency (which Elaine Showalter complains far too many critics have failed to do).[61] Thus, with Showalter, I think that the very common reading of Ophelia as an excessively innocent and pliable young woman is mistaken. I would point out, on the contrary, that Shakespeare's Ophelia is a young woman possessing the spirited resourcefulness to show an interested (but not physical)[62] response to Hamlet's erotic advances, and that she does so without parental guidance (see 1.3.91–100). Therefore it is plausible that when Ophelia later withdraws from Hamlet she acts wisely, not just on advice but also for her own sensible and good reasons.

Her reasons for doing this may be clarified if the failure of Hamlet's wooing is compared with somewhat similar failures or mishaps seen in *Love's Labour's Lost*. That play begins with the King of Navarre and his three attendant nobles intending to establish an austere homosocial academy, their self-idealizing fantasies leading them to imagine that their callow pursuits of 'philosophy' will elevate them above 'the gross world's baser slaves' (1.1.30–2). As has been noted, this puerile project to 'buy' immortal fame and attain such 'honour' as to make Navarre 'the wonder of the world' (1.1.5–12) is disrupted before it takes off it by the intervention of Biron's depreciatingly named 'Dan Cupid' (3.1.175).

Hamlet, by contrast, had long inhabited Wittenberg's established academy (where all his schoolfellows were male). His desire to return there is at first thwarted by his tyrannous uncle, but (unlike the Navarre coterie) he seemingly remains a studious reader (2.2.198) who moreover has the humility to admit to his fellow student that 'There are more things in heaven and earth, Horatio, / Than are dreamt of in your philosophy' (1.5.169–70). This scepticism, bordering on cynicism when Hamlet avers he is reading just 'Words, words, words' (2.2.195), contrasts with the inflated vision of all-conquering philosophy mooted in Navarre.

Nevertheless, important parallels still pertain. One involves a theme of 'disparagement' in marriage pervading *Love's Labour's Lost* that impacts in *Hamlet* as well. Prince Hamlet indeed seems a snob when he berates himself with 'O, what a rogue and peasant slave am I!' in 2.2.552, yet he still fastens his erotic interest on a woman coming from a station lower than befits a Prince's wife. His Ophelia is no 'country maid' like Armado's Jaquenetta (3.1.127), nor any 'Joan', yet her relatively lower birth does become visible when she describes Hamlet in terms of

> The courtier's, soldier's, scholar's eye, tongue, sword,
> Th' expectancy and rose of the fair state,
> The glass of fashion and the mould of form,
> Th' observed of all observers.
>
> (3.1.154–7)

Her admiration here is certainly not as abject as that of middling-class Helena in *All's Well* who finds Count Bertram an out-of-reach 'bright particular star' (1.1.85), yet misalliance becomes an issue when Ophelia's father Polonius (operating in his characteristic politic-opportunist mode) reports to King Claudius that he has admonished her with 'Lord Hamlet is a prince out of thy star. / This must not be' (2.2.142–3).

Hypocritical Polonius would allow his son Laertes some mild 'drabbing' in Paris (2.1.27), yet still insists on keeping '*my*' marriageable daughter strictly chaste (1.3.95–7). He thus tells Claudius that he 'precepts gave her' to keep clear of Hamlet and to repel his 'tokens' and 'messengers', adding the self-satisfied remark that Ophelia 'took the fruits of my advice' (2.2.143–6).

Ophelia's compliance with this 'advice' has often been read as evidence of her pliability, but as I say I think otherwise. Quite aside from social issues, in *Love's Labour's Lost* the Princess of France and her three attending ladies are certainly wise when they exercise caution in response to the overblown love advances of the King and courtiers of Navarre. There is no sense that they act out of weakness or immaturity. I believe that Ophelia repulses Hamlet on a similar or even stronger basis than theirs, having to do with a suitor's behaviour, and *his* immaturity or unreadiness.

Thus the four young women in *Love's Labour's Lost* are rightly concerned about the sincerity of the men who profess love by showering them with letters, gifts and poems, enacting a stereotypic courtly style of wooing. One of those women, Catherine, actually labels her receipt of 'Some thousand verses of a faithful lover' as 'A huge translation of hypocrisy' (5.2.50–1). Catherine also more darkly suggests that the King of Navarre once fatally betrayed her sister: 'He made her melancholy, sad, and heavy, / And so she died' (5.2.14–15).[63] Recognizing the shallowness and potential danger in conventional and self-regarding tropes of courtship, the four Frenchwomen are justifiably dubious of the capabilities of their admirers to enter into genuinely reciprocal relationships. In consequence they wisely refuse, or at least defer, their acceptance of the four wooers' frantic love pleas.

Comparisons are suggested between *Love's Labour's Lost* and *Hamlet* arise not only because the death of Ophelia resembles that of Catherine's unfortunate sister. For one, Hamlet's initial approaches to his beloved are even more overblown and conventional than those of the four men of Navarre. So, when his verses and their superscription sent to Ophelia are read out in 2.2.116–19 they appear even more conventional and less accomplished than the missives and poems of the Navarre courtiers.[64]

There are stronger reasons, as well, for Ophelia conceiving even more deep-seated reservations than those of the young women visiting Navarre, and therefore accepting advice to deter Hamlet's further advances. This is not only for the social reason that Ophelia lacks the spirited self-confidence of the aristocratic Frenchwomen in *Love's Labour's Lost*, for beyond that a far deeper problem lies in the intractable nature of Hamlet's particular anti-Anterotic prejudices. In consequence Ophelia is unable to educate her immature suitor in love as do many other Shakespearian young women (Rosaline, Portia, Viola, Rosalind and Helena).

Comparing evidence of the mental conditions of the four men of Navarre with that of Hamlet finds the former responding to their beloveds' resistance by producing the jackanapes of costume switching at a masked dance, or in Biron's case imitating a strange speaking voice. These men are even willing to accept demands placed on them to withhold their suit for a year in order to prove the seriousness of an 'offer made in heat of blood' (5.2.792).[65] By contrast, Hamlet becomes overwhelmed when he fails to gain all that he demands and as soon as he is thwarted immediately enters into a manic mode. Thus when in contention with his mother he lashes out murderously (3.4.23), and when discouraged by Ophelia he adopts a terrifyingly wordless 'antic disposition' (1.5.173) and bursts into her private 'chamber' half dressed (recounted in 2.1.78–101). His behaviour with Ophelia subsequently becomes insultingly verbal during their seemingly private 'nunnery' encounter in the lobby (3.1.105–52), and finally becomes obscenely public during the performance of *The Mousetrap* (3.2.107–15, 146–7, 234–8).

All this rightly dismays poor Ophelia. Hence, although her father does not take Ophelia's best interests primarily into account when he asks her to withhold her affections, she is not at all naive or overly compliant when agreeing to do this.

Hamlet's mode of wooing involves idealization only fragilely divided from denigrations of women and marriage that reveal misogynistic and anti-Anterotic prejudices. Thus, provoked by Ophelia's rejection of his gifts and letters, Hamlet fulminates against all women:

> You jig, you amble, and you lisp, and nickname God's creatures, and make your wantonness your ignorance. Go to, I'll no more on't. It hath made me mad. I say we will have no more marriages.
>
> (3.1.147–50)

Upon hearing this Ophelia laments, 'O what a noble mind is here o'erthrown!' (3.1.153), but that 'overthrow' is not due to her behaviour. Rather, what is revealed is more characteristic than consequential.

Throughout the play Hamlet's loving intentions regarding women are easily converted to despising. So, early on he develops the misogynistic theme that 'frailty, thy name is woman' (1.2.146). He continues this theme in his semi-jovial claims that 'woman ... delights me not' (2.2.310–11). Later he cruelly quips to Ophelia that 'woman's love' is exceedingly brief (3.2.147), and still later he dismisses his qualms before the fencing match as those that 'would perhaps trouble a woman' (5.2.162).[66]

At the same time Hamlet does love Ophelia. Given his radical ambivalence it is no surprise that his love verses addressed to her emphasize the concept of doubt, beginning: 'Doubt thou the stars are fire, / Doubt that the sun doth move, / Doubt truth to be a liar' (2.2.116–19). Hamlet's self-depreciation as a poet included in the same missive as these verses runs: 'I am ill at these numbers. I have not art to reckon my groans' (2.2.120–1). This is not just a Renaissance author's conventional gesture of self-'naughting' or humility; Hamlet really does have problems with self-expression. For, despite his clearly superior verbal talents, Hamlet's words, written or spoken, always seem inadequate for the true expression of his amours. One might ask why.

In common with Meg Harris Williams, I believe that Hamlet's failures as a lover to communicate and persuade dovetail with out-of-control emotions arising in him whenever he encounters a frustrating woman.[67] So Williams suggests that Hamlet's rage against Ophelia in the nunnery scene partly derives from 'his own failure to communicate with her – the conventional absurdity of his love letters, which belong as much to the realms of courtly artifice as do Polonius' manoeuvres, rather than to the true expression of feeling' (105).

Whenever he feels disappointed, unheard or rejected, Hamlet's behaviour and speech become as overblown and unconvincing as the thrasonical excesses that he himself counsels the visiting players to avoid.[68] But oddly, despite the fact that he repeatedly fails to rein in his own immoderate ranting, when he is not stung by imagined or actual rejections Hamlet can be a trenchant critic of inflated speech. Thus he mocks Osric's affected courtly circumlocutions (in the second quarto text at A.N. 7–17), and during Ophelia's funeral sarcastically threatens to surpass Laertes in 'rant' (5.1.271–81).

Moreover, when Hamlet is not berating Ophelia, Gertrude, Claudius or Polonius in a brittle and insulting manner, he appears to be a fluently spoken if melancholy searcher after inner and outer truth. This inwardness might suggest that if Hamlet had been allowed to live he might have achieved a reparative state of mind and so developed capabilities for a truer recognition of others, and for forgiveness, gratitude and apology.

That is made impossible because – however time in this play is measured[69] – the events in *Hamlet* swiftly culminate in nearly universal deaths. Near the end of his theatrical career Shakespeare allowed himself far greater dramaturgic leeway, and so in his late Romances portrayed vastly longer story arcs extending up to sixteen years. That allowed a much happier outcome for the initially violently anti-Anterotic protagonist of *The Winter's Tale* than is seen in *Hamlet*. I will next, nearly finally, consider Shakespeare's portrayal of that outcome.

# How anti-Anterotic prejudices are overcome in *The Winter's Tale*

Anti-Anterotic prejudices have dire consequences in *The Winter's Tale* when King Leontes tries his innocent wife for treason and expels his infant daughter Perdita, apparently causing the death of both. With no external Don John or Iago present to deceive him, Leontes starts the play by becoming falsely self-convinced of his wife's infidelity. He then expresses the anti-Anterotic fantasy that most married women cuckold their husbands:

And many a man there is, even at this present,
Now, while I speak this, holds his wife by th' arm,
That little thinks she has been sluiced in 's absence,
And his pond fished by his next neighbour, by
Sir Smile, his neighbour.
(*The Winter's Tale* 1.2.193–7)

In pronouncing this Leontes is very similar to Hamlet, King Lear and also Othello, who proclaim respectively: 'if thou wilt needs marry, marry a fool; for wise men know well enough what monsters you make of them' (*Hamlet*, 3.1.139–42); 'Down from the waist / They're centaurs, though women all above. / But to the girdle do the gods inherit; / Beneath is all the fiend's' (*King Lear*, 4.5.116–24); and, 'O curse of marriage, / That we can call these delicate creatures ours / And not their appetites!' (*Othello*, 3.2.472–9). My former comments on these similar outbursts may be expanded by noting that all of these men have in common the intrusion of a new third party into a relationship with a significant woman who, in their phantasy, had been exclusively devoted to themselves. Those new third parties, creating new triangles, are, respectively: King Claudio who, in Hamlet's belief, has 'whored' his mother (5.2.65); cashiered Cassio who intrudes into Othello's marriage when Desdemona vigorously advocates for his reinstatement (in 3.3.19–27, 41–86, 3.4.32–3, 48–9, 88–90, 124–9, 163–4); the King of France, to whom Cordelia says she will hereafter owe a wife's allegiance (1.1.100–3). Likewise, Leontes will have to share his wife's affections with his soon-to-be-born daughter Perdita.

Also in common, all of these four men split their affectional objects into two fragments, one of which is wholly good and the other wholly bad. Hamlet, famously, idealizes his deceased father and despises his uncle (so, according to some, revealing an unresolved Oedipus complex). Othello's wholly good object is his mourned-for former 'unhoused free condition' (1.2.26), a military 'occupation' that is 'gone' (3.3.352–62). Lear's good objects each in turn become bad ones, starting with Cordelia who says she will love her future husband. Next Goneril, and then Regan, flatter Lear by declaring him the sole object of their love, then each proves otherwise. In a remarkable contradiction, the madly jealous Leontes places all his positive affections on the small shoulders of his uncomprehending little boy Mamillius (whose very name refers to motherhood).

Thus, exactly when first expressing his delusions about cuckoldry, Leontes remains sure of the legitimacy of his first child, and so acknowledges Mamillius's remark, 'I am like you, they say', with 'Why, that's some comfort' (1.2.209). He next addresses his little boy with great tenderness: 'Come, sir page, / Look on me with your welkin eye. Sweet villain, / Most dear'st, my collop!' (1.2.132, 137–9). Following that, Leontes intersperses a wild rant against women and marriage with 'Go play boy, play' and 'Go play, Mamillius, thou'rt an honest man' (1.2.188–211).

Others in the play claim that Leontes is almost indistinguishable from his first child, that he and the boy Mamillius are 'Almost as like as eggs' (1.2.131–2). In fact, this father and son alike suffer from very similar distress when Hermione is on the brink of giving birth to new rival child.[70] Mamillius so fretfully acts out his anxieties about being displaced that the heavily pregnant Queen Hermione is driven at one point to ask her gentlewomen to 'Take the boy to you. He so troubles me / 'Tis past enduring' (2.1.1–2). One of these attendants then unwisely teases troublesome Mamillius with 'Hark ye, / The Queen your mother rounds apace. We shall / Present our services to a fine new prince / One of these days, and then you'd wanton with us, / If we would have you'. Another lady adds, more graciously, 'She is spread of late / Into a goodly bulk, good time encounter her' (16–21). After that, no doubt observing her son's dismay at the first lady's suggestion, Hermione rallies. Exemplifying Donald Winnicott's 'good enough mother',[71] she then says 'What wisdom stirs amongst you? Come sir, now / I am for you again. Pray you sit by us, / And tell's a tale' (22–4).

Hermione then encourages her son to invent and tell her intimately 'in mine ear' a frightening story involving 'sprites and goblins', thus illustrating perfectly a pattern described by W. R. Bion in which a good mother can accept and contain the inchoate projected terrors of her child in order to transform them and allow them to be re-introjected in a bearable, knowable, form.[72]

Unhappily, however, when her husband reacts frighteningly to her pregnancy Hermione cannot hold and contain, and thus assuage, his excessive anxieties. An attempt on her part to do so fails miserably in the opening court scene where Leontes flares up in anger because she, not he, is able to persuade visiting King Polixenes to remain in Sicily 'One sennight longer' (1.2.17). A theme of procreation launches this scene when Polixenes announces that his visit has extended over the exact period of human gestation, comprising 'Nine changes of the wat'ry star' (1.2.1). This, and Hermione's advanced pregnancy, thus set the stage for a theme of cuckoldry.

In this first full scene of the play tensions between the old friends are immediately implied by Polixenes' stilted locutions and Leontes' curt replies (1.2.1–10). Sensing this, Hermione attempts to cajole her husband and his friend into a better mood by eliciting reminiscences of their shared closeness in boyhood. Polixenes then says they were like 'twinned lambs', but adds ominously that they were innocent of sexual awareness (61–72). Hermione's reply defends women against accusations that they are temptresses, 'lest you say / Your queen and I are devils' (82–8). In this context Leontes asks ambiguously 'Is he won yet' and, learning that he has agreed to stay on, adds with implicit sarcasm, 'Hermione, my dearest, thou never spok'st / To better purpose' (88–91).

Here Hermione's reply and Leontes' rejoinder become critical. Using her own keyword 'grace', Hermione says that she is hungry for 'praise' and indeed does deserve praise for having spoken better once before. Leontes correctly gathers that she refers to her first acceptance of his love suit, but instead of expressing gratitude for that he complains bitterly about having had to suffer a delay before she pronounced her choice, saying:

> Why, that was when
> Three crabbed months had soured themselves to death
> Ere I could make thee open thy white hand
> And clap thyself my love. Then didst thou utter,
> 'I am yours for ever'.
>
> (1.2.103–7)

In an attempt to counter this expression of a sharply remembered anger, Hermione completes Leontes' final half-line above with her characteristic ''Tis grace indeed'.

Backtracking to enlarge on Polixenes' just-mentioned reply when asked to recall his shared boyhood with Leontes, it is notable that when he denies that boys have sexual imaginations he identifies the rise of such imaginations with original sin:

> We were as twinned lambs that did frisk i' th' sun,
> And bleat the one at th' other. What we changed
> Was innocence for innocence. We knew not
> The doctrine of ill-doing, nor dreamed
> That any did. Had we pursued that life,
> And our weak spirits ne'er been higher reared
> With stronger blood, we should have answered heaven
> Boldly, 'Not guilty', the imposition cleared
> Hereditary ours.
>
> (1.2.69–77)

The imagery here anticipates the play's pastoral scenes in Act Four, but those show that country life saturated with erotic love (just as does *As You Like It*). This contradicts Polixenes' claims about primal 'innocence', as indeed does little Mamillius' display of sexual awareness in his interchanges with two gentlewomen in 2.1.6–16. Polixenes' views of childhood are both theologically and psychologically heretical – and this anticipates Paulina's accusation in 2.3.115 that the madly jealous Leontes is a 'heretic'.

Leontes' 'Three crabbed months' complaint, scathingly denying a former benefit, finds a 'twin' later in the play when Polixenes becomes furious with old Camillo (who had earlier rescued him from assassination) because this councillor will not now assist him in a further covert operation. Polixenes expresses his resentment and ingratitude pointedly: 'Better, not to have had thee than thus to want thee' (4.2.12–13), and this of course mirrors Leontes' denial of the gratitude owed to Hermione.

At the end of *The Winter's Tale* a pattern of frustration-driven bitterness and envious resentment is reversed, and so Leontes' former violently anti-Anterotic prejudices are overcome. The play moves toward that outcome though a series of turning points, multiple moments of anagnorisis. The first of these occurs when Hermione is brought to trial for treason and adultery. Courtiers have been sent to 'Delphos' to consult Apollo's oracle (2.1.185), and return during the trial with the message that 'Hermione is chaste, Polixenes blameless, Camillo a true subject, Leontes a jealous tyrant, his innocent babe truly begotten, and the King shall live without an heir if that which is lost be not found' (3.2.132–5). Leontes rejects the oracle and orders the trial to continue, but only a moment after that is told that his son Mamillius 'with mere conceit and fear / Of the Queen's speed' has died (143–4). Leontes then exclaims, 'Apollo's angry, and the heavens themselves / Do strike at my injustice', and at that moment Hermione also apparently falls dead (145–7). Leontes thus suddenly loses his split-off good 'part object' Mamillius and he apparently loses his (no longer bad-object) wife. He has also discarded his legitimate infant daughter, the loyal Camillo and his erstwhile friend Polixenes.

Following this first radical turnaround in the play, Leontes enters into a long depression, sixteen years of 'saint-like sorrow' and 'penitence'. His courtiers beg him to overcome this sorrow and marry again for the sake of royal succession, but the Lady Paulina forbids it. Leontes then swears that he will never remarry unless Paulina permits it (5.1.1–84). Thus a pact apparently forswearing Anterotic love is agreed in the court of Sicilia.

The second great turnaround in the play occurs when the infant Perdita, abandoned on a Bohemian seashore, is rescued and adopted by an old Shepherd who presumes that she is the bastard child of some courtly 'waiting gentlewoman'. The Shepherd remarks that 'They were warmer that got this than the poor thing is here. I'll take it up for pity' (3.3.73–4), showing compassion mixed with worldliness. Tellingly, this charitable Shepherd resolves to adopt the 'very pretty bairn', a 'thing ... new-born' (68–9, 111), *before* he discovers the wealthy trappings and substantial 'fairy gold' left with her (119).

The third turnaround in the play occupies the pastoral festival scenes 4.3 and 4.4. The first scene introduces the frank eroticism of the rogue Autolycus who sings of tumbling with his 'aunts' (e.g. doxies) 'in the hay' (4.3.1–12). The festival itself reveals the sexual rivalries, jealousies and passionate longings of young country folk, and centrally displays the passionate Anterotic love between Florizel and a Perdita 'now grown in grace / Equal with wond'ring' (4.1.24–5). These lovers frankly acknowledge their mutual erotic desires (4.4.24–35 and 4.4.130–5) and then join hands to plight troth (4.4.382–98). Florizel's father Polixenes, observing his son's apparent misalliance, misinterprets this love affair as lewd, and becomes furiously destructive. Thus the play's pattern of Anterotic love under attack is recapitulated.

Florizel and Perdita then escape by ship from (land-locked) Bohemia to Sicily on the advice of Camillo, just as Polixenes had escaped in the opposite direction sixteen years earlier on

Camillo's advice. The couple arrive in Sicily with Perdita lovely as always (5.1.94–5, 110–11), and Leontes then briefly casts desirous eyes on her. But he is restrained by Paulina, and so resolves to help the young couple (5.1.222–31).

The play's next major turning point, disclosing that Perdita is Leontes' and Hermione's lost daughter, occurs offstage and is only reported. This revelation fulfils Apollo's oracle's condition that 'the King shall live without an heir if that which is lost be not found'.

However, in addition to Perdita, 'that which has been lost' is also a belief in Anterotic love. The recovery of that, symbolically begun at the sheep-shearing festival, is completed in a remarkable way at the play's culminating turning point, which occurs *just before* the reanimation of Hermione's supposed statue.

Immediately before Hermione's 'statue' becomes alive, Leontes' contemplation of it as an artwork reveals total reversal of the position he had had taken in his bitter 'three crabbed months' speech. Exactly contradicting that speech, Leontes now recalls Hermione having 'stood' during their courtship just as her 'statue' does now:

> O, thus she stood,
> Even with such life of majesty – warm life,
> As now it coldly stands – when first I wooed her.
> I am ashamed. Does not the stone rebuke me
> For being more stone than it?
>
> (5.3.34–8)

Here Leontes exposes not only his remorse and repentance, but also a newborn awareness of the autonomous interior life of the young woman he had wooed. In other words, he shows that he has repaired his love object so that she becomes a whole good object rather than a part object split into good and bad fragments. This realization sets the scene for Paulina's final command, as follows:

PAULINA                    It is required
You do awake your faith. Then, all stand still.
Or those that think it is unlawful business
I am about, let them depart.
LEONTES                         Proceed.
No foot shall stir.
PAULINA           Music; awake her; strike!

(5.3.94–8)

Paulina then commands the 'statue' to 'Descend. Be stone no more' (99), and demands of Leontes, 'Nay, present your hand. / When she was young, you wooed her. Now, in age, / Is she become the suitor?'. Here we encounter the second miracle in the scene, for when Leontes does as he is bidden he proclaims, 'O, she's warm!' (107–9).

To repeat, Leontes' physical, tactile, hand-holding recognition of an Anterotic connection restored, leading to the embrace described in 5.3.112–13, derives from his newfound recognition of wrongs he had done and the identities he had misconstrued. When Leontes at last comes to admire the splendid autonomy of his beloved, he is able to take her by the hand; previously Leontes suffered perverse anger when recalling her hesitation in offering her hand, igniting scorns and mislike targeting Anterotic love. Thus in the first scene Leontes' bitter phrase, 'open thy white hand / And clap thyself my love' (1.2.105–6), led on to an egregious misinterpretation of Polixenes' and Hermione's normal courtly taking by the hand, which Leontes saw as revoltingly sexual 'paddling palms and pinching fingers' (1.2.117).[73] What he attacked then was married Anterotic love, because in Shakespeare's age hand-fasting was a legal means to consent to the formation of a valid marriage.[74]

Here in *The Winter's Tale* Anterotic love is revived and becomes 'warm' again after vile prejudices have assaulted it. Shakespeare has shown as well that other sorts of prejudices, for instance Theseus' prejudices against art and imagination, can be reversed. Prejudice is always possible because the human race is not perfectible, but the human species is not despicable either. Einstein's alleged quip about cracking a prejudice being harder than cracking an atom should be placed against the fact that humans *have* cracked atoms. I am very happy to (nearly) conclude this book about negative prejudices by noting that these need not win out in the end.

## Much of the above about Anterotic love is condensed in the lyrics of three Elizabethan songs

The ditties of three songs of Shakespeare's period, one written by Shakespeare himself, encapsulate a number of the above concepts, and thus prove that those notions were appreciated in his time.

The first of these songs is John Dowland's setting of a poem by Fulke Greville that begins: 'Away with these selfe-loving Lads, / Whom *Cupids* arrow never glads'. This first saw print in Dowland's hugely popular 1597 *First Booke of Songes*. It appears again as 'sonnet' LII in Greville's 1633 posthumously printed sonnet sequence *Caelica* that may have circulated in manuscript as early as 1586.[75]

This tetrameter lyric is typical of Greville's densely constructed poetry, for it develops in varied directions after decrying the 'selfe-loving Lads' who resemble the callow Eros-deniers discussed above. Thus this lyric's third stanza concludes, 'Where Honor *Cupids* rivall is / There miracles are seen of his'. This is to say that Cupid's unholy 'miracles' are his triumphs over sex-defying 'Honor'. That cynicism accords with the anti-idealizing stance expressed at large in Greville's *Caelica*.[76] Likewise this lyric's second stanza concludes with: 'What fooles art they that have not knowne / That love likes no lawes but his owne?' – referring to the anarchic and dangerous powers of Eros.

Greville's poem's last stanza offers another turn, placing a democratic sentiment alongside an anti-abstinence barb against a 'Saint':

> The worth that worthinesse should move
> Is Love, that is the bow of love,
> And Love as well the foster can,
> As can the noble Noble-man.
> Sweet Saint 'tis true you worthy be,
> Yet without Love nought worth to me.

Greville's complex lyric expresses overall that resistance to all-conquering Cupid is both unworthy and futile.

A warning, resembling that heard from Robert Stoller, that Eros might ignite an unstable, short-lived 'romance' is heard in the song performed while Bassanio chooses a casket in *The Merchant of Venice*:

> Tell me where is fancy bred,
> Or in the heart, or in the head?
> How begot, how nourished?
> [Reply, reply.]
> It is engendered in the eyes,
> With gazing fed; and fancy dies
> In the cradle where it lies.
>
> (3.2.63–9)

This lyric, famous for rhyming in its first three lines with 'lead', may call to mind the initial cynical resistances of the rueful lover Biron in *Love's Labour's Lost*.

On the contrary, another wonderful song lyric asserts the possibility of wanton, wandering Cupid giving way to lifelong lasting affection. This song was published by Thomas Ford in 1607, and it begins, 'There is a Ladie sweet & kind, / Was never face so pleasde my mind; / I did but see her passing by, / And yet I love her till I die'. The last stanza of the ditty reasserts true constancy: 'Cupid is winged and doth range, / Her country so my love doth change: / But change she earth, or change she sky, / Yet will I love her till I die'.[77]

These three lyrics vary between acknowledging Cupid's irresistible if fickle power and asserting constant Anterotic love's power to defy the instabilities of 'ranging' Cupid. However, Cupid has a role to play, for the 'face' of the 'Ladie' in Ford's lyric distinctly 'pleasde my mind'. So in this vision Eros and Anteros are reconciled, and potential prejudices against both are overcome.

# Afterword: interpreting chapter overlaps

As noted, Richard Mulcaster commented that the targets of a genuine 'prejudice' are not ignorantly unknown but are rather 'things' well known. This aligns with a strange characteristic exhibited in several of Shakespeare's representations of prejudices. I will cite one instance of that from each of the chapters that consider prejudices against learning, art, strangers, peace and love – and will then attempt to account for this patterned repetition. The first chapter suggests that Shakespeare's Jack Cade's violent animus against education sits strangely alongside indications that Cade himself has been exposed to a typical humanistic education. The second chapter notes that Hotspur's scornfully dismissive remarks on poets and poetry are suspiciously or ironically expressed in truly excellent blank verse. The third chapter remarks that Iago's denigrating remarks about Othello and Cassio accompany Iago at other times admitting that both men have excellent qualities. The fourth chapter notes that during his family's 'old-accustomed feast' (1.2.18) the head of the combative Capulet clan in *Romeo and Juliet* suppressed his nephew's truculence in order to maintain civility and peace (1.5.64–87). Lastly, while scoffing about and protesting against 'Dan Cupid's' demands for dependency in *Love's Labour's Lost*, Biron still remembers 'the cause why we were born' (4.3.216), paralleling furious Troilus' 'Think, we had mothers' in *Troilus and Cressida*

(5.2.132). All of these apparent contradictions can be appreciated as related to the envious splitting off and denial of good things that has been described by object-relations psychoanalysts as central to an infantile or later reawakened 'paranoid schizoid' process.[1]

Other overlaps between the varied sorts of prejudices discussed in the chapters above arise when one and the same Shakespearian figure exhibits more than one of the prejudices detailed in those five chapters. For instance, Mercutio in *Romeo and Juliet* is typical of several Shakespearian young men whose prejudices against peace seem to work in tandem with their prejudices against Anterotic or mutual love. Combining denigration of Anterotic love with despising foreign cultures is also possible, as for instance when King Polixenes in *The Winter's Tale* describes another nation as 'that fatal country Sicilia' (4.3.30–1) and soon after demeans the Anterotic love between his son Florizel and Perdita by designating her a 'knack' or doxy (4.4.425–8). Such linkages are not inevitable, however, for Leontes in the same play visciously rejects his wife's Anterotic affections, yet he does not attribute her imagined misdeeds to the fact that she is the daughter of 'The Emperor of Russia' (3.2.118). On the contrary, Othello murderously rejects Desdemona's love, and *does* associate her supposed infidelity with nationality when referring to 'that cunning whore of Venice / That married with Othello' (4.2.93–4). To mention one last example, Chapter 3 outlines a theory of subtle connections in *A Comedy of Errors* between rejections of Anterotic married states and anti-stranger delusions or fantasies.

These possibilities of the overlapping of my five sorts of negative prejudices do not arise because those categories are blurred, but rather because the pathologies involved in negative prejudices often involve projection or splitting or other difference-confounding psychic mechanisms. Thus, when a Shakespeare character becomes 'so bewitched with his own fantsie' (as Richard Mulcaster puts it) as to exhibit prejudicial 'scorns and mislike' (as Shakespeare puts it) more than one of the following deficiencies or perverse orientations may be combined:

1. An unwillingness to increase understanding and an adherence to unfounded beliefs. Resistance to and scorning of formal education resembles the more widespread embracing of ignorance labelled - K in W. R. Bion's study *Learning from Experience*, for both derive from attacks on a basic epistimophilic instinct.[2]

2. Stubborn unresponsiveness to representations of complexity. Although especially evident in those who deny or scorn the value of artistic expression, this is again a widespread deficiency.

3. A lack of empathy with those perceived to be 'other'. This often extends beyond avoidance to denigration and even demonizing of those deemed to be 'strangers'. Such reviled 'strangers' in Shakespeare's plays are often stand-ins for quite different denied or repressed elements of mental life.

4. A relishing of violence and the substitution of naked aggression for thoughtful responses to difference or contention. Shakespearian figures who celebrate and enjoy fighting typically split off and scorn as weak and despicable any appreciation of peaceable modes of interaction.

5. A denial of the possibility of close relatedness and physical warmth in interpersonal relations. This expresses the splitting of internal objects in the so-called 'paranoid-schizoid position'; the same disturbance of libidinal life often motivates other sorts of prejudices.

Hence those who Shakespeare shows 'wedded unto' their prejudices (in Mulcaster's phrase) may seem caught by multiple mental snares.

Shakespeare, however, also shows that escape from such ensnarement is possible.

# Appendix: Renaissance and modern takes on false and true knowledge

The particular prejudices studied here in relation to Shakespearian representations all involve misjudgements in which good things are seen as bad things. Of course, those must be distinguished from proper judgements of good and bad things, and therefore the question of knowledge arises. It follows that in the scheme investigated here a prejudice is a failure of perspicacity.

This Appendix will consider several views of the opposition between false judgements and true knowledge.

## Richard Mulcaster on prejudice, ignorance and knowledge

As noted in the Introduction, Richard Mulcaster's 1582 *First Part of the Elementarie* distinguishes between *misliking* that 'commeth upon desert, when the thing is such, as for verie naughtinesse it is to be misliked' and *misliking* 'upon opinion, when error in the partie mislikethe that thing, which is of it self well worthie the liking'.[1] Mulcaster then subdivides erroneous opinions that arise from 'mere ignorance' from those that arise from 'prejudice'. Following this Mulcaster pursues a theme that 'Ignorance & prejudice [are] the greatest enemies and mislikers of sound learning', writing:

> what greater enemies hath learning euen in natur, then prejudice & ignorance? whence is there more open shew of implacable hostilitie to knowledge, then from prejudice and ignorance? Ignorance knoweth nothing, and therefore is no friend to ane unknown good: prejudice knoweth and will not, and therefor is a great fo to a not favored good. Ignorance yet in part deserueth som excuse for all hir disfrindship, bycause infirmitie is hir falt, not bolstered with ill will, and the worst is hir own, ane ordinarie case, where euen enimitie pityeth. But prejudice is a poison to anie common weall, so far as it stretcheth, which being at the first infected with the incurable disease of a cankred and a corrupt opinion gathered by confluence of sundrie ill humors will neither it self yeild to a right iudgement, nor will suffer anie other, where hir persuasion can take place. For by yeilding hir self she feareth the emparing of hir misconceiued estimation, and by suffring other to yeild, she feareth the encrease of knowledges frinds; whereby hir self shall com in danger to be oppressed, both with truth of matter, and number of patrons. Wherefor she opposeth hir self, she bendeth all hir eloquence, she mureth up all passages, so much as she maie, both by persuasion and entreatie, that none shall iudge right, which will hear hir speak, & regard hir autoritie, but shall take that musik to sound the swetest, which commeth from hir, tho she be but a mearmaid, which by offring of delite endevoreth to destroie.
>
> (46)

Here Mulcaster distinguishes that ignorance is an 'infirmitie ... not bolstered with ill will', while 'prejudice' inexcusably 'knoweth and will not, and therefor is a great fo to a not favored good'.

Mulcaster then further explains why prejudice attacks 'not favoured good', and describes its deceptiveness in employing seductive eloquence with an aim of walling up 'all passages' to truth, laying out the 'diverse grounds' on which poisonous prejudices are founded:

> But that same perverse prejudice is a sutle fo to knowledge like a manieheaded hydra, and as the venim of his autoritie is gathered of diverse grounds, so the sting of his poison infecteth diverse waies. The person himself which is thus caried awaie by a pevish opinion is commonlie no heavie head, but either superficiallie learned, and yet loth to seme so: or enviouslie affected and still carping at his better: or ambitiouslie given and presumeth upon countenance: or he measureth knowledge by gain, and setteth naught by ante more, that himself shall nede, to compas that he coveteth, where a litle cunning will compas much more then reason thinks enough in corruption of mindes. All which four causes mean learning glad to make great shew, enuious affection glancing at good things: vane presumption plaing the peicok: covetous desire carelesse of great cunning, as theie corrupt the iudgement, so theie maintain prejudice, while the partie so corrupted will seeke by all means to continew his credit.
>
> (47–8)

Thus, Mulcaster distinguishes between prejudices based on pretensions to knowledge, those based on envy, those based on vain presumption and those based on greed. He claims that any of these four 'causes' may produce prejudices masquerading as knowledge and attacking true knowledge. Instances of all of these 'causes' have been seen at work in the preceding discussions of Shakespearian depictions of prejudices.

## Adding groups to Mulcaster's picture of the 'sutle fo to knowledge'

As seen in Jack Cade's rebellion discussed above, group concurrence may offer strong support to anti-knowledge prejudices. As Ronald Britton put it in 1998:

> I suspect that there is a basic desire for the corroboration of belief and an innate wish to share beliefs with others that bind us all into groupings of one sort or another. The snag is that we can substitute concurrence for reality testing, and so shared phantasy can gain the same or even greater status than knowledge.[2]

The anti-knowledge certainties of some believers in wild conspiracies may fit this pattern; more striking is the violent militancy of those, like Cade's followers, who would kill under the banner of wholly fantastical slogans.

## Other modern ideas resonating with Mulcaster's views

As noted, Mulcaster's division of prejudice from false but ignorant misapprehensions resonates with distinctions between kinds of 'discrimination' made by Thomas Sowell. In addition, Mulcaster's claims that learning and knowledge are the enemies of 'prejudice', and vice versa, resonate with sophisticated psychoanalytic views of false thinking.

Psychoanalytic concepts are derived from observations and empathic interpretations of actual mental states and human development, but also sometimes look to literature for insights and illustrations. In fact, the *Psychoanalytic Electronic Database* locates almost 3,500 references to Shakespeare, dating back to 1873. Conversely, the invaluable *World*

*Shakespeare Bibliography* that includes citations back to 1960 locates over 600 references to psychoanalysis. In accord with that, this study has been inspired by the work of several psychoanalytic thinkers briefly noted here.

These include Donald Meltzer who discusses a 'delusion of clarity of insight' and Ronald Britton who describes 'overvalued ideas'.[3] A seminal earlier thinker in the same British school of psychoanalysis, W. R. Bion, claimed that the establishment of an emotional link supporting a human predisposition toward learning and knowing truth is equally essential, as is feeding for human growth.[4] Bion labelled this mental-growth-supporting link 'K',[5] and also posited an opposite to K, which he labelled minus K, involving attacks on thinking or inabilities to think or learn. According to Bion, minus K may entail 'an envious assertion of moral superiority without any morals'.[6] Such envious superiority supports misrepresentations, false suspicions and prejudices – here envy attacks the true knowledge of other persons and things. Such attacks surely resemble the subversive work of Mulcaster's 'sutle fo to knowledge'. This 'foe' also personifies what the psychoanalyst Ronald Fairbairn described in 1944 as an anti-libidinal 'internal saboteur'.[7]

# NOTES

## Introduction

1  See Meltzer, 1990, 130–1.
2  See Brearley, 2018; Kahneman, 2011, 22.
3  See DeMolen, 1972 and Bradbrook, 2005, 11.
4  Mulcaster, 1582, 44.
5  Ibid., 46.
6  The mysterious, beautiful and immutable Idea of the Good discussed in Plato's *Republic* VI–VII, *Gorgias* (especially 499c), *Timeaus* and *Philebus* was a live topic in the Renaissance. Varied critiques of such a notion continue down to our time, but for a wholly approving account see Demos, 1937. This comments that 'We are dealing with the theory of value, not with ethics' (245), and argues that for Plato 'the Good is the source of being' (267).
7  Sowell, 2018, 21–3.
8  Doleac, 2021, 575.
9  See Yates, 1936, 137–40.
10 In 1H6, 3.7.91, AIT 1.1.182 and 2.4.151, and TNK at 5.5.88 'prejudice' is either 'Injury, damage, hurt loss' or 'to affect injuriously or unfavourably by doing some act' (OED2 n. I.1.b or v. I.1).
11 See the 1578 *Gorgeous Gallery of Gallant Inventions*, A.ii. recto and verso, reprinted in Proctor, 1926, 3–4.
12 The earliest citation for this in OED2 is dated 1643.
13 Davids, 2011, 196.
14 I have discussed many other approaches to Shakespeare and 'race' in Sokol, 2008, 113–68.

15  For an example of such an approach one might look to Robert Brustein's *The Tainted Muse: Prejudice and Presumption in Shakespeare and His Time* (Brustein, 2009). Here belief in the great achievements of modern Western civilization leads to the invention of a William Shakespeare who (until his conversion late in his life to better, more modern-like attitudes) personally endorsed all the repugnant prejudices expressed by his dramatic characters and who also shared all the prejudices expressed by numerous other bigoted writers of his time – even the views of the poetry-despising Stephen Gosson (248n18). Thus Brustein castigates an Elizabethan dark age, and contrasts it with far more enlightened times. He sometimes illustrates this by referring to permissive 'blue-state' and repressive 'red-state' United States local politics (160), and Barack Obama's electoral strategies (149–50 explicated in 259n5). Adopting a precisely opposite view of America and the West, Little, 2016, applies an impassioned response to current events in the USA (the killing of Michael Brown) to Shakespearian reflections. Sokol, 2008, 201–2n8, notes how the similar stance seen in Little, 2000, is critiqued in Bassi, 2003.

16  Egan, 2013, 39.

17  For instance England's burgeoning involvement in the Atlantic slave trade in the years following about 1650 undoubtedly has considerable bearing on current day prejudicial attitudes and concerns, but as others and myself have argued this historical background cannot have been foreseen by Shakespeare who died in 1616 – see Sokol, 2008, 142–67, and the dozens of sources cited there. See also ibid., 113–41, on discussions of differences between race awareness in Elizabethan and later times. I did not remark there on Kaplan, 2007, which acknowledges views that 'identif[y] the nineteenth century as giving rise to the modern formulation of race, constructed in terms of physical difference and inferiority that are "biologically" inheritable' (3), yet applies this very formulation to MV.

18  In a new Introduction to OTH, Thompson, 2016, 108, applies this viewpoint especially to a theatrical production, stating, 'it is not merely Shakespeare's politics that needs to be addressed in contemporary performances of *Othello*, but also the ensuing

history of racial portrayals'. Cultural memory is certainly a topic deserving of scholarly attention as well as possibly theatrical attention.

19 Thus Demeter and Thompson, 2017, 575, hold that the 'vacillating' term race 'from Shakespeare's time … could evoke and invoke lineage, nationality, religion, sexuality, class, language, and/or skin colour', and go on to say of the critical movement they represent that 'we continue to track its radical instability into the twenty-first century'. The overlapping or interactions over time between these diverse areas of human difference leading to potential dislikes are of particular interest to Thompson. In my Chapter 3, Shakespearian treatments of just such a range of dislikes are considered with the aim of detecting structures of prejudice held in common.

20 See, for instance, Thompson, 2011, Thompson, 2016, Demeter and Thompson, 2017, and portions of Thompson, 2021. These focus much of their attention on matters concerning race relations in the United States. For a personal and personal-political account of the adoption in the UK of the associated *RaceB4Race* movement see Karim-Cooper and Price, 2021.

21 See Sokol, 2008, xi–xiv, and Kennedy, 2019, 142–4.

22 See Britton, 2015, 45–54, 50–2.

23 Cited from Bion, 1967c, 111.

24 See Money-Kirle, 1978; Traub-Werner, 1984; Ryan and Buirski, 2001; and Steiner, 2016, 387.

25 Klein, 1986 (1946/1952).

26 Spillius, et al., 2011, 63.

27 Steiner, 2016, 287.

28 Klein, 1986 (1935). Idealization, which evades pain, guilt and a sense of limitations, is not depressive in Klein's sense, and may create Ronald Britton's 'false whole objects' (private communication). Steiner, 2016, 287, quotes Isaiah Berlin: 'Few things have done more harm than the belief on the part of individuals or groups … that he or she or they are in sole possession of the truth'.

29 See Shakespeare, 1989, which usefully includes variant texts and passages, and see Hinman, 1968.

# Chapter 1

1. Bion, 1962, 64.
2. The Appendix discusses further Elizabethan and modern thinking about this delusion.
3. These are lacking only in STM and 1H6 (as usual SON is taken to be a single text).
4. Negative associations appear in SHR 3.1.18–20 and in CYL 4.4.35.
5. MV 1.2.110, MM 3.1.406–7 and HAM 3.1.154.
6. SON 77, SON 106, ROM 3.3.159, MV 2.2.59 and 4.1.156, LLL 4.2.31, MND 5.1.53, SHR 1.1.9, 1.2.157, 1.2.167, 1H4 5.2.64, 2H4 4.1.44, WIV 3.1.53, TRO 1.2.250, TIM 2.2.80, CYM 1.1.43 and 4.2.269, AIT 2.4.57, 3.1.72, 4.2.58.
7. MND 3.2.203, MM 1.4.46–7 and JC 5.5.26–8.
8. From Aubrey, relaying the report of William Beeston, discussed in Schoenbaum, 1986, 110–11.
9. Proposed in Honigmann, 1985, refuted in Bearman, 2002 and Winstanley, 2017, re-argued in Honigmann, 2003.
10. See Baldwin, 1944, Rutter, 2013, 141–4, Enterline, 2016a, Enterline, 2016b.
11. Baxandall, 2010, 49.
12. Bion, 2014, 119. Bion, 1986, 33ff., recounts the author's misery at school due to separation from family, bullying and repression. Also see Klein, 1945.
13. Bion, 1967c, 118.
14. Ascham, 1570, B1r–v.
15. See Orme, 2006, 146.
16. See Hackett, 2017, especially appendices a–d.
17. Ibid., section 28.
18. Burrow, 2004, 11.
19. Ibid.
20. Schoenbaum, 1986, 64, adds that schoolboys in ADO 2.1.208–9 'are overjoyed … with finding birds' nests rather than with their lessons'.

21 See Sokol, 2018, 97–107, on weak love poetry in LLL, ROM, AYL and VEN.
22 TIT 2.3.28–9, ADO 3.3.62–3, ANT 303–5 and SON 22.
23 Harbage, 1973, 17.
24 Carlson, 2013, 44, connects Pinch's failed exorcism with the exorcists in Ephesus described in Acts 19:13–20.
25 See Sokol, 1991.
26 Plutarch, 1919, 595 (at 65.1 in 'The Life of Julius Caesar'). In North's translation, Plutarch, 1579, 793–4, Artemidorus is 'a Doctor of Rethoricke in the Greeke tongue' whose written warning to Caesar is accidentally unread, not rejected.
27 In ANT 3.12.4 Dolabella calls this schoolmaster 'so poor a pinion of [Antony's] wing'.
28 See Newton, 1933, and DeMolen, 1972.
29 These are noted in PER 9.34–6, 19.206–10, 20.1–11 and TMP 1.2.172–5 and 1.2.355–60. See Lindsay, 2016, 408–10.
30 Shin, 2008, 375. Shin suggests that rather than resenting his education Caliban resents its breaking off (381).
31 See Shin, 2008, 389.
32 See McCutcheon, 2015, 260–2; Jardine, 1987.
33 Mulcaster, 1581, 168.
34 See McCutcheon, 2015.
35 See Bowker, 2017.
36 See Ascham, 1570; Parks, 1938, 323–4.
37 See Kingsley-Smith, 2016; Sokol, 2018, 123–4.
38 Shakespeare's private tutors are: 'Cambio' and 'Licio' in SHR; an unnamed tutor in ANT 3.11.71 and 3.12.2ff who corresponds with Plutarch's Euphronius; Pericles (9.33–6) and Marina (20.5–11) in PER; Prospero (1.2.172–3) and Miranda (1.2.353–64) in TMP. None of these are clerics.
39 See Sokol, 2019b.
40 Simon, 1966, 284–5; Moran, 1985, 142–4; Jewell, 1998, 32, 80; Cressy, 1973, 66.
41 Cressy, 1973, 66. See also Cressy, 1987, 129–53, 148–9 and Simon, 1966, 382.

42  The dates of the realm of Henry IV mean Fenton 'kept company with the wild Prince and Poins' (3.2.66–7) before 1413, yet the Host exclaims 'Am I a Machiavel?' (3.1.93) referencing the author of The Prince written c. 1513, and published in 1532.

43  See Melchiori, 2000, 4. Sokol, 2009 finds *Merry Wives* mirroring Warwickshire events of 1600.

44  According to Baldwin, 1944, 1:466, William Smart left the Stratford school to become a vicar in 1565, and a former teacher John Bretchgirdle baptized Shakespeare (1:490) – both, as usual, left teaching when becoming ministers, unlike Hugh Evans.

45  Cressy, 1987, 148.

46  See Anglin, 1985, 142–55, especially 154.

47  Ibid, 1985 155, 156; see also 155–67.

48  On cross gartering and a 'Pedant ... i' th' church see: notes in Lothian and Craik, 1984, 70–1 and 88; notes in Elam, 2008, 247; Linthicum, 1927, 92.

49  See Sokol and Sokol, 2003, 35–43, on how such behaviour was seen as scandalous.

50  See Sternfeld and Chan, 1970.

51  See Sokol, 2019a.

52  See Hardy, 1979.

53  'Envy' appears in 27 of the 44 texts in the Oxford Electronic Shakespeare, 26 texts contain the lexeme based on 'to learn', and these two subsets are *nearly identical*.

54  See Sokol, 2020 on Middleton's *A Chaste Maid* and Sokol, 2019a on H5.

55  Private communication.

56  See Oliver, 1979, 120–1n67, which contrasts this with tln 2563.

57  See Sokol, 2008, 2–10.

58  It is, however, paradoxical in relation to the historical records. According to Caldwell, 1995, 58, Shakespeare's 'Cade scenes attacking clerks, lawyers, those who erect grammar schools and speak of nouns and verbs – in short, anyone who can write – and lines referring to burning the records of the realm and having law (however sore, stinking, or biting) issue from

Cade's mouth, derive mainly from accounts of the Peasants' Revolt of 1381' (see also ibid., 57). Caldwell also claims (and documents) that historically 'Cade's rebellion [was] the first "popular" up-rising in England in which the rebels articulated a set of demands and disseminated them widely in writing' (19). In other words, Cade and his followers seem to have been the opposite of illiterate. This may accord with a strange claim made concerning 'John Cade' in one of Shakespeare's two main sources for his play. Hall, 1548: 'This capitayn not onely suborned by techers, but also enforced by pryuye scholemasters, assembled together a great company of talle personages' (fol. clix). Could Shakespeare have inverted the historical record deliberately?

59  Chigas and Mosyakov, 2018.
60  Hampton-Reeves, 2014, 65.
61  See Harvey, 2006.
62  In 4.2.129–44 Cade falsely claims to descend from Edmund Mortimer, Earl of March.
63  See Ascham, 1570, B1v and B2r.
64  Chandler, 2018, 21.
65  Cade may have been a 'shearman' (4.2.132) or a 'clothier' (4.2.5).
66  See Sokol and Sokol, 2004, 41–4.
67  Britton, 1998, 2. See Appendix for more on the topic of prejudices and beliefs.

# Chapter 2

1  Altschuler and Jansen, 2005, describes an exception when it notes that in the first dedication to his *Madrigals of 5 and 6 Parts* (1600) 'Thomas Weelkes claims that his work is "untouched by any other arts [than music]"' (83). It is particularly fascinating that this denial (false, in fact, as Weelkes was a proficient lyricist) was illustrated by what these authors call 'one of the earliest instances of Shakepeariana –

a reference to the unique character of Jack Cade from *Henry VI, part 2*' (ibid.). This dedication contains '*I confesse my conscience is untoucht with any other arts ... and, if* Jack Cade *were alive yet some of us would live*' (fac. ibid., 86), thus alluding specifically to Shakespeare's Cade.

2  See Sokol, 2018, 4–8 on this nomenclature and category – this notes another possible exception in PER 7.13–14.

3  See Sokol, 2008, 4–8, 59–64, on several other such indications.

4  For detail on Shakespeare and *paragone*, see Blunt, 1939; Salerno, 1951; Hunt, 1988; Tassi, 2005; Sokol, 2008, 13–21 and passim.

5  See T. S. Eliot, 'Little Gidding', section III, lines 1–7.

6  Shakespeare alluded to sectarian controversies over the Prayer Book in AWW, debates about settlement in Virginia in TMP, divided views concerning witchcraft in MAC.

7  See AYL 4.3.126–57 and 5.4.149–64, OTH, LRF, PER, CYM, WT and TMP.

8  On the date of MND see Brooks, 1989, xxxiv–xxxv, and Taylor and Egan, 2017, 520.

9  Schoenbaum, 1986, 184.

10  However, see Taylor and Egan, 2017, 446, on novelty expected in the court performances of 1603–4.

11  Reproduced in Melchiori, 2000, 295, and commented on in Dutton, 2016, 253.

12  See Gombrich, 1977, 154–244, and on Renaissance anticipations, see Sokol, 1994, 12–13, 15–16, 22–3, 28, 90, 92, 142, 188n23. On Shakespeare's treatments, see Sokol, 2018, 3, 22–4, 28, 33–7, 39, 64, 75 and 91.

13  Carlson, 2018, 194.

14  Klause, 2008, 60. Carlson, 2018, 198, credits Klause and also notes Michael Wood's less nuanced comment on this echo. Klause, 2008, 64–70, claims that further connections between Shakespeare, Southwell and Southampton are reflected in LUC, ERR, TIT, HAM, AWW and MM, and MND.

15  Carlson's 'wonderworld' (202) is borrowed from 'wonderworld' in Duffy, 2005, 540.

16  See Barber, 1963, 3–4 and passim. Carlson, 2018, 202, admits that 'vestiges' remained in 1575.

17  Chesterton, 1904.

18  On the other hand, Nuttall, 2000, 52, claims 'The suppression of dark forces is not only incomplete at the beginning of the play; there is a sense in which it remains incomplete throughout', and so refers to MND as 'this play of nervous delight' (55), whereas Wilson, 2007, 150–60, attributes a trivialization of grim myths in MND to Shakespeare being a class-traitor and lackey of the Elizabethan establishment.

19  Quoted in Alpers, 1978, 114 from William Empson's 1935 *Some Versions of the Pastoral*.

20  See Sokol, 2018, 149–51, 154, 155–8 and 189.

21  A contrast may be noted between this line, which has nothing at all to do with Rosaline's actual complexion in terms of black versus white, and a former line of Biron that exhibits a far inferior verbal quality. In that line, also monosyllabic but much clumsier, Biron plays the courtly paradox-making game when competitively asserting a preference for her in 'No face is fair that is not full so black' (4.3.251). A press reader points out that here 'Shakespeare connects blackness with beauty'. I have exhibited similar instances in Sokol, 2008, 113–21, and indicated that the complex Shakespeare canon implies that 'something like racial tolerance must have been an alternative to intolerance, and an alternative perceivable to Shakespeare's audiences' (117).

22  See Sokol, 2018, 99–101, on this glorious monosyllabic line.

23  See Skinner, 2014, 111–17 on Mark Antony's political rhetoric.

24  Shakespeare's 'Poet' derives from North's Plutarch's account of the Homer-quoting but derided Marcus Phaonius (reprinted in Daniel, 2006, 349–50).

25  But see Latham, 1975, xxxiii–xxxiv.

26  Hilliard, 1911–12, 18.

27  This term was coined in Burrow, 1971.

28  The notion of Elizabethan audiences' uncritical acceptance of a triumphalist 'Tudor myth' idealizing Richard II is still echoed in Brustein, 2009, 135–6, although Rosenstein, 2004, for instance, reads Shakespeare's Richard II in relation to non-partisan accounts of a complex historical figure.

29  Steel, 1941, 7.
30  These scholars' works include Scattergood, 1983, 33–42; Doyle, 1983; Eberle, 1999; Schiefele, 1999; and Bowers, 2001, especially 77–132.
31  Aston, 1971, 317. Evans and Taylor are quoted (disapprovingly) in Sherborne, 1983, 6.
32  Mathew, 1968, 5 and 38–9.
33  Bennett, 1992, 3.
34  Sherborne, 1983, 6. This accuses all former studies of imprecision in argument and definition.
35  Scattergood, 1983, 29, noting a tendency for literary-historical evidence to degrade over time. Doyle, 1983, 181, agrees.
36  Bennett, 1992, 3.
37  See Matthews, 2007, which charts a subsequent decline in Chaucer's reputation.
38  See Ormrod, 2004, especially 292–3.
39  Bennett, 1992, 1997; Barr, 2000 and Bowers, 2001.
40  Edwards, 1997, 198, dates this MS, BL Cotton Nero A.x., to before 1614, and Levy, 2004, proposes Savile may have inherited it from his father Henry Savile (d. 1607). Robbins, 1943 and 1950 report on lines from Gawain in an early Tudor commonplace book.
41  According to Levy, 2004, Henry Savile of Banke 'matriculated from Merton College, Oxford, in 1588, during the wardenship of his distant cousin and namesake, Sir Henry Savile' and Goulding, 2004, traces *this* Sir Henry's friendship with Essex 'to at least 1591'. Shakespeare was connected with the Essex circle through Southampton.
42  See Fraunce, 1588, Puttenham, 1936 (1589), 26, 60, 62 and 145, and Anderson, 1976, 5.
43  See Moore, 2004.
44  Palmer, 1982, 28–30 doubts that Lydgate impacts on TRO but Pittock, 1986, proposes Lydgate as a possible a source of one phrase in TMP. Tambling, 2004, 94–118, notes thematic overlaps between Shakespeare and Thomas Hoccleve.
45  Puttenham, 1936 (1589), 60–2.

46 Sidney, 1961 (1595), 3, 51.

47 Spenser, 1966, 3.

48 Burrow, 2003, 278–9, regrets a newer tendency to ignore 'criteria of literary and aesthetic excellence'.

49 Saintsbury, 2005 (1902), 1.

50 Lewis, 1954, 120–47, 127. This finds exceptions in Skelton and Thomas More (133).

51 Pinto, 1966, 10.

52 Green, 1980, 126.

53 Wells, 1994, 63–80.

54 See Siemens, 2009.

55 See Jenkins, 1982, 548–51, on HAM 5.1.61–4, 71–4, 91–4.

56 See Forker, 2002, 152–4 and the somewhat more dubious Ure, 1961, xxxiv–xxxv.

57 Froissart, 1525, 251v.

58 On Richard's predilection for sumptuary objects, see Steel, 1941, 7, Eberle, 1985, Schiefele, 1999, 255–60, and PRO E 101 144/9.

59 Dubiousness about this is expressed in Saul, 1999, 43, Bowers, 2001, 81, and Green, 1980, 64–5, 70.

60 See Goodman, 2004 on Richard's courtier John Montagu confirmed to be a 'fine poet' whose work is lost, and see Green, 1980, 65 and 216n24; Robbins, 1978, 113n.

61 See Bennett, 1992, 14 and 15; Bowers, 2001, 190.

62 Thomas Berthelette's 1554 edition of John Gower's *Confessio Amantis* was a major source for *Pericles* (Hoeniger, 1977, xiv n5). This edition, Gower, 1554, remarks that the prologue to *Confessio* in Gower's MS (reproduced in Gower, 1554, fol. 2r) was 'cleane altered' in Caxton's edition Gower, 1483, fol. 2v, so that the credit Gower originally gave to Richard II for inspiring his poem is suppressed and replaced by credit given to Henry IV. See Eberle, 1999, 236, on this.

63 Camden, 1600, c.2r. I am grateful to Westminster Abbey and Tony Trowles and David Burden for allowing me to study this monument, which is too fragile for public access.

64 Green, 1980, 109.
65 Forker, 2002, 152–8, and Ure, 1961, xliv–xlviii discuss Creton as a possible main source, and Lisak, 2002, strongly supports this.
66 Robbins, 1978, 113–17n87. See Thompson, 1904, 267 and Bowers, 2001, 165. The possibility of a transcription verbatim is supported by Creton explaining elsewhere that his chronicle changes from using verse to prose 'so that I can set down better the words that these two [Richard and Bolingbroke] spoke when they met together. For I believe I can remember them well'. See Given-Wilson, 2004, 146, on this.
67 Yeats, 1903, 156.
68 Contradicting such views, Brooke, 1968, 110, claims 'The conception of Richard as a wilting poet is completely out of place in Act I, which opens in terms of high rhetorical splendor'. Certainly, Richard deflects all attention from the lists to himself there.
69 Pater, 1889, 193. But 'exquisite' is used over three dozen times in Pater's *Appreciations*.
70 John, 1912, xxxvi. Van Doren, 1939, and Ure, 1961, lxix–lxxi, make similar suggestions.
71 Draffan, 1971, 39. This is not indicated by Cottrell's director's notes at www.mckellen.com/stage/r2/quotes.htm (accessed 11 September 2021).
72 Draffan not only reads Pater's judgements one-sidedly, but also those in Raleigh, 1953, 185 and Van Doren, 1939, 68–79.
73 Saintsbury, 1907, xx.
74 Wilson, 2008, 104–5.
75 Forker, 2002, 55–64, discusses poetic diction in *Richard II* without mentioning that Richard might be a poet. Kehler, 1985, 7, finds 'unfit' King Richard 'albeit a gifted actor-poet', and Budra, 2000, 90, similarly claims that Richard 'writes himself into several roles … to author himself in different ways'. Blanpeid, 1983, 128, also claims that Richard is a self-scripting actor-poet, but seeing Richard as a self-author does not address if he is imaged as a poet.
76 Cooke, 1972 and Marshall and Thompson, 2011, 63 decry placing constraints on 'character criticism'.

77  Saul, 1992, 50–1.
78  Saul, 1999, 43, 44. 'No bibliophile' seems contradicted by Froissart, 1525, fols 255v–256r, discussed above.
79  Saul, 1999, 44; this is contradicted by Eberle, 1999.
80  Saul, 1997, 449.
81  Saul, 1998, 16.
82  Saul, 1998, 22, repeats 'it is possible to see Tudor chivalry as a posthumous vindication for Richard'.
83  Similarities of other sorts are alleged in Gurr, 2003, 50–6; Hammer, 2008, 9. Lane, 1995, finds the 1590s succession crisis reflected also in JN.
84  Chambers, 1930, 2:326–7.
85  Chambers, 1930, 2:325. Because of calendar difference this was dated 1600.
86  Also, Hammer, 2008, 23–4, argues that even if her conversation with Lambarde occurred (which is not certain) the Queen might not refer to Shakespeare's play, or any 'particular play'.
87  Campbell, 1947, 170–91.
88  Chambers, 1930, 1:353. Coke's prosecutor's speech at Essex's trial, in Chambers, 1930, 2:325, also deploys this analogy.
89  Vasari, 1855, 1:32–3.
90  Fischlin, 1997, 21.
91  Robbins, 1978, 113n.
92  See Middleton, 1978, 96–7, and also Green, 1980, 112, 203–6.
93  Bowers, 2001, 166. Bowers adds that the authorship of the parting poem in Creton's Chronicles is moot because 'both Richard and [Creton] knew the rhetorical formulas that were properly delivered by noblemen on occasions of public separation'.
94  Examples include *Astrophil and Stella* 71 (Sidney, 1962, 201), Drayton's Sonnet 61 (Esdaile, 1908, 128) and Shakespeare's Sonnet 29.
95  Strier, 2019.
96  Ewbank, 1971, 104.

97 Ginsberg, 2011, describes a rare exception where Chaucer embeds a translated Petrarch sonnet in his *Troilus*.

98 Leonard Foster writes that Elizabethan Petrarchanism was in vogue because the Queen 'herself wished it so', and adds that while King James in Scotland preferred 'the Platonic line in the Pléiade', Elizabeth's 'attitudes encouraged the development of the passionate and temporal Petrarchan vein' (quoted in Jack, 1976, 802, 805).

99 Richard seeking to impress even when relinquishing his crown accords with the view in Tuck, 2004, that the historical Richard continually struggled to assert his prerogative.

100 It seems reductive to me when Middleton, 1978, 112, and Cox, 2007, 151–3, find that this expresses only convention.

101 Hockey, 1964, 190, although this finds Richard's poetic imagination far more intense.

102 Brockbank, 1983, 64–7.

103 Staley, 2000, 94. This article attributes the many cultural interests of Henry and his father to their political ambitions.

104 Data on rhyming was very kindly supplied to me by David Crystal, who warned me to 'bear in mind that the decision about what counts as a rhyme is not always clear-cut'. Here only orders of magnitude are significant.

105 Some, including Phialas, 1961, Hapgood, 1963 and Eberle, 1985, 178, hold that Shakespeare stresses only faults and injustice in Richard's realm, but I find Shakespeare's portrayal of his flawed protagonist more complex.

106 The persons in these two-handed dramas are a father and son while relations between a father and son are deeply embedded in 1&2 H4.

107 This was historically possible because in 1381, when the very young Richard proved himself a determined leader during the Peasant's Revolt, Glendower at twenty-two years old might have been a student in London. According to Holinshead (reprinted in Humphries, 1968, 167) he became 'an vtter barrester'.

108 Doran, 1942, 122. See Sokol, 2018, 91–7, on verses embedded as opposed to verses inserted in verse drama.

109 The phrase 'as lustrously as possible' is borrowed from Ure, 1961, lxix and lxxi, although Ure claims 'the poetry in Richard' is 'there' only 'because he is a character in a poetic drama'.

110 Hotspur admits in 1.3.28–68, 1.3.123–6, 1.3.251–2, 3.1.144–60 and 3.1.186 that his rash and disdainful outbursts have undermined his faction, and his friends warn him about such behaviour in 3.1,50, 3.1.143, 3.1.161–85, and 3.1.229–31.

111 'Swaddling-clothes', indeed! The historical Henry Percy (Hotspur) was only three years younger than Henry IV and was twenty-two years older than Prince Hal. Shakespeare makes Hal and Hotspur contemporaries to allow contrasting them, especially in in 3.2.93–128.

# Chapter 3

1 Novy, 2013, 2.

2 See ibid., 155; Sokol, 2008, 62–5; Tudeau-Clayton, 2012.

3 In AWW 1.3, on which see Sokol, 2008, 58–68 and 103–8.

4 H5 1.2.258, 2.4.24–5, 3.2.21–2, 3.7.130 and 4.2.29; MV 1.2.63–73; AWW 2.3.95–6; HAM 5.1.145–51; MAC 5.3.8; OTH 2.3.70–8; TMP 2.2.28–30; AIT 3.1.144.

5 Sokol, 2008, 57–89, finds these gestures mainly humorous but Hoenselaars, 1998, 98, claims that satiric inversions of national stereotyping common in much Elizabethan and early Stuart drama convey 'A pervasive national identity crisis'. A third possibility is that these 'jokes' are embedded in texts in order to represent the double consciousness involved in typical shameless 'taunting' behaviours that involve a boastful vaunting of negative judgements alongside half-admission that those judgements are not only unwarranted in terms of logic or evidence, but also wilfully transgressive of civilized predilections. The main purpose of taunting, in such cases, is vaunting.

6 Davids, 2011, 82. In particular, ibid., 175–80 confronts notions that racism correlates to anal fixations and finds that in varied cases sibling rivalry or Oedipal or pre-Oedipal elements are operative instead.

7  Allport, 1954, 7.
8  Money-Kyrle, 1978, 354 and ff.
9  Freud, 1977 (1917), 272.
10 Freud, 1973 (1930), 51–2.
11 Available at https://archive.org/details/LoveAffair (accessed 11 September 2021). This original version of the film has had several remakes, one directed by McCarey himself.
12 'It is he, not I' exemplifies the 'attributive projective identification' described in Britton, 1998, 5–6.
13 In R2 Queen Margaret calls Richard 'this poisonous bunch-backed toad' (1.3.244), partly on account of his self-confessed (1.1.27) 'deformity'. Terry is not so vehement.
14 Freud, 1958 (1919)-c, 122–31.
15 Freud, 1958 (1910)-a, finds that certain important 'primal words' convey antithetical meanings. Freud's examples include Latin *altus* which can mean 'high' or 'low' and Latin *sacer* which can mean 'holy' or 'accursed'. Likewise, in English 'cleave' can mean either stick together or sunder apart (60). Edward W. Tayler detected that use of 'cleave' in *Areopagitica* (Milton, 1941 (1644), 13).
16 Haughton, 2003, xliv–xlv.
17 Maguire, 1997, 384n7, notes that in one of the two Plautine sources of ERR, *The Brothers Menaechmus*, the identical naming of one set of twins is rationalized but in ERR it is redoubled and unexplained. Less farce, more projection, I would say.
18 This deadline ensures accord with 'the unity of time', met only in Shakespeare's ERR and TMP.
19 Meltzer, 1990, 130, offers 'a list of the adverbs of unobservant un-thought: clearly, obviously, self-evident, of course, naturally, we think, how else, what could you expect, as I always say, where there's smoke …'.
20 OED3 '*cozenage, n.*' lacks this remark, but the headnote to '*cozen, v.*' in OED3 gestures towards it, citing Cotgrave's 1611 dictionary.
21 See Sokol, 2008, 71, on this speech defending 'Strangers and Aliens' made probably by Henry Jackman.

22  Plautus, 1595, sig. F1v.
23  Hennings, 1986, 92–3. This argues that, in common with Montaigne and the Elizabethan *Homilie on Marriage*, ERR promotes companionate marriage above the 'pleasant *licentia*' championed in Plautus' 'Saturnalian' farce (96–8).
24  Freedman, 1980, 374.
25  Freedman connects Egeon's non-payment of a 'marital debt' with the play's chaotic circulation of monetary debt.
26  This *Elegy* was composed in the earlier 1590s (Donne, 1990, 422), the same time as the likely composition of ERR.
27  *Paradise Lost*, 3.307–18, based on *Hebrews* 1.9, and 5.665.
28  Allport, 1954, 14–15. Allport offers a similar colloquy (195), and remarks 'Whatever Jews are like, are not like, do, or don't do, the prejudice finds, its rationalization in some presumed aspect of "Jewish essence"'.
29  Novy, 2013, 53.
30  See Sokol, 2010.
31  Accusations of insanity (even that *all* the English are 'mad' made in HAM, 5.1.150–1) seem generally unanswerable in Shakespeare. Sokol, 1996, traces how witchcraft phenomena were increasingly understood in terms of mental illness when MAC was written.
32  See ERR 2.1.34–41, or OTH 4.3.85–102.
33  Young-Bruehl, 1998, 201ff.
34  Freud, 1961 (1931), 217.
35  See Sokol, 2010, on Shylock's claimed 'suffrance'.
36  See, for instance, Freeman, 2002, 155–7, 162–4, or Fisch, 1987, 243–5.
37  Sokol, 2015, connects the Marsyas myth with prejudice in MER, and Sokol, 2018, 179–218, adds connections with OTH.
38  In Natalie Conti's Renaissance retelling Apollo suddenly demands that the competing musicians sing to their own accompaniment – which is easy with the lyre and impossible with a wind instrument. See Sokol, 2015, 349 and 356.
39  Apollo cheats in his contest by appointing his cronies the Muses as judges while the 'civil doctor' Balthazar in MV

pretends to be an impartial legal expert (4.1.171, 5.1.210) but is actually the disguised wife of Bassanio, Antonio's kinsman and 'dear friend' (3.2.259). See Sokol, 2018, 184 and 210.

40 Comparisons are often made with Barabas in Marlowe's *Jew of Malta* but Barabas is actually a less successful Machiavellian devil than his Muslim or Christian rivals. Nevertheless TIT and MV sometimes echo Marlowe's cynical play.

41 See Yaffe, 1997, which places heavy emphasis on Shylock's violation of Jewish dietary laws (4–5, 61, 100, 101, 158, 164, 180n23, 181n39). MV shows awareness of those laws at 1.3.31–5 and 4.1.302–8, 321–2. Some in Shakespeare's audiences might have reacted negatively to Shylock's fastidiousness, or responded in accord with a Christian 'vision of purity and exclusivity [that] was destined to compete with that of the Jews' (Stow, 2006, 10, 133–57).

42 See, in *The Bible*, 1587, Lamentations 3:30, Isaiah 50:6, Matthew 5:39 and Luke 6:29 that all counsel turning the cheek. Leviticus 19:18 enjoins, 'Thou shalt not auenge, nor be mindful of wrong against ye childre of thy people, but shalt loue thy neighbour as thy selfe'. The translation 'neighbour' in this passage has been much debated, with Alter, 2019 rendering it rather as 'other people'. Deuteronomy 32:35, 'To me belongeth vengeance, and recompence' is echoed in many places including Psalms 58, 94, and 149. Sokol, 2010, considers inversions of these doctrines in MV, and adds that Shylock also inverts admonitions in Ecclesiasticus 8:2–5 and some injunctions in the Talmud. Nevertheless, Heschel, 2006, holds that the theological problem of the continuing existence of Jews infused the reception of MV both in Shakespeare's age and in later times.

43 See Sokol, 2010.

44 See Hirsch, 2011, 150–61.

45 See Collinson, 1994, 228. Queen Elizabeth also showed reluctance to grant her assent to the 1571 Subscription Act (13 Elizabeth, Cap. 12) that demanded clerical assent to the Thirty Nine Articles intended 'for the avoiding of the diversities of opinions, and for the establishing of consent touching true religion put forth by the queen's authority'. Elizabeth's reluctance may have accorded with her famous 'I would not open windows into men's souls', but Hardwick, 1876, 146–9,

claims that she was motivated by protection of her royal prerogative, not tolerance.

46  See Greenblatt, 2001, 239–40; Marotti, 2003; Hopkins, 2003; Hunt, 2004.

47  See Sokol, 2008, 103–11, on AWW, 1H4, 2H4 and SHR.

48  Yaffe, 1997, 61.

49  Shakespeare invested in a share of his theatre company, real estate and tithes. Schoenbaum, 1986, 272–5, details how a mortgage was involved in his 1613 purchase of the Blackfriars' gatehouse.

50  Thomas and Evans, 1984, 316.

51  Taking interest was allowed by statutes of 1545, 1571, 1597 and 1623 (the period of the loan not being specified). See Thomas and Evans, 1984, 316, on complications arising between 1552 and the mid-1570s.

52  See Sokol and Sokol, 2004, 238–43, describing actions 'on the case' that after Slade's Case (1597–1602) allowed the common law court of King's Bench to enforce all sorts of obligations, including debts. This explains the deliberate error in ERR 4.2.41–51 where arrest 'on the case' is confused with arrest 'on a bond'.

53  MV 3.2.282–8. Yet Nevo, 1980, 130–1, holds that Shylock's murderous intent arises only after Jessica and Lorenzo's elopement.

54  Yaffe, 1997, 61. Supersessionism is discussed in relation to MV in Heschel, 2006.

55  See Sokol and Sokol, 1999, and 2004, 112–17.

56  See Sokol and Sokol, 2004, 252–6.

57  Foakes, 2001, 110, cites A Stationers' Register entry of 26 November 1607 noting a court performance of 'Kinge Lear' on 'St Stevens night at christmas Last'. Egan and Taylor, 2017, 559, dates the LRQ text to 1604–6 and offers a 'best guess' of 'late 1605'.

58  For details and references, see Sokol and Sokol, 1999, 436–9.

59  Competition arose between the two main common law courts of Common Pleas and King's Bench, between these courts and the equity courts of Chancery and Requests and the prerogative

courts of Admiralty, High Commission and Star Chamber, between the Queen's courts and the Church courts, etc.
60 Thus Sokol and Sokol, 1999, argues that the suppression of the mock trial in LRQ evidences a dating of the LRF text to after 1610.
61 Sokol and Sokol, 2003, 189n2, notes that every adult person in Shakespeare's England was involved on average in about one litigation annually.
62 See Baker, 1990, 370.
63 See note 42 above.
64 1 Dyer 51a, Baker and Milsom, 1986, 257–8.
65 Shylock's awareness of his outsider status also emerges when he swears by '*our* holy Sabbath' (4.1.35, my italics). His insistence that Venice's prosperity requires international confidence in its legal institutions corresponds with the high value put on the city's 'policy of right' in Edmund Spenser's preparatory poem for Lewkenor's *The Commonwealth and Government of Venice* (in Spenser, 1966, 482).
66 See Sokol, 1992 for more details, including that in Southampton 'owing to the use of the town-hall for theatrical purposes by stage-players, the mayor and bailiffs coming to the hall to administer justice in the piepowder courts ... cannot sit down in decent order' (62).
67 Jonson, 1979, 42–3.
68 See Sokol, 2008, 62 and 187 n35 and n36. Smith, 2013, 212–19, even argues that Antonio's anti-Shylock sentiments allude only to intolerance of Elizabethan Protestant refugee aliens, and not Jews. I doubt this claim because Shylock recalls being called a 'misbeliever' (1.3.110). Contrarily, Shapiro, 1992, and Heschel, 2008, find perceptions of Jewish identity central to the play.
69 Yaffe, 1997, 62, adding that Shylock is 'less an example of a law-abiding Jew than of what Plato's Socrates would call an oligarchic or moneymaking man'.
70 Ibid., 83. Oddly (since he several times comments on *kashrut*) Yaffe overlooks the materialistic sacrilege in Launcelot Gobbo's quip that 'This making of Christians will raise the

price of hogs. If we grow all to be pork-eaters we shall not shortly have a rasher on the coals for money' (3.5.21–4), and also Gobbo's deception of his blind father for 'fun' in 2.2, a blasphemous parody of Jacob's deception of Isaac in Genesis 27:8–30.

71 Gross, 2006.

72 Yaffe, 1997, 62, finds this only a 'loose and self-serving reading of a biblical text', but Sokol, 1998, 162–4, finds Shylock's biblical reading particularly pointed. See below.

73 *The Bible*, 1587.

74 For instance Shylock remarks, 'These be the Christian husbands' when Bassanio and Graziano's express willingness to 'sacrifice' their wives to save Antonio (4.1.279–92). Less obvious sarcasm appears at 3.1.89–96 when Shylock parodies by inversion Jewish rules concerning the good treatment of bondsmen or slaves, as is discussed in Sokol, 2010, 371–2.

75 Gobbo's 'It is much that the Moor should be more than reason, but if she be less than an honest woman, she is indeed more than I took her for', means that even if 'less than an honest woman' she is 'more than I took her for', so Gobbo claims that he took her for less than a woman, less than a human being at all. In a play replete with repugnant images of animals breeding (as is discussed in Sokol, 1998, 165–8 and 173), this quip displays the nadir in Shakespeare's representations of anti-stranger prejudices.

76 This is discussed in Sokol, 2008, 152–5.

77 The next chapter will discuss a distinction between 'libidinal' and 'destructive' narcissism that is summarized in Spillius et al., 2011, 412–13.

78 Silvayn, 1977 (1596), 170.

79 See Freud, 1967 (1900), 387.

80 Stephens, 1993, 93. See also 97 and 99–101 and Sokol, 1995, 381–2.

81 Stephens, 1993, 100.

82 See Spillius et al, 2011, 126–46 and 453–6 on this central Kleinian concept.

83 MV shows a tendency to conflate 'thrift' in the sense of 'the fact or condition of thriving or prospering' (OED3 1.a) with 'thrift' in the sense of 'frugality' (OED3 3.a), which were both current senses in Shakespeare's time. However, these words may overlap categories, as other complex words do in *The Merchant of Venice*. On other complex words in MV, see Sokol, 2010, on 'suffer/suffrance', and Sokol, 1998, 169–73, on 'good'.

84 See Greene, 1985.

85 Although this nomenclature might seem paradoxical, Queen Elizabeth opened Gresham's commercial 'Royal Exchange' in London in 1571.

86 See Pettet, 1945.

87 Yaffe, 1997, 55–7, proposes that Antonio 'prefers to treat his friends as charity cases', and hopes to increase rather than decrease 'Bassanio's reliance on his charity' by encouraging his reckless spending.

88 Although Shylock is in many ways the opposite of Barabas in Marlowe's *The Jew of Malta*, they share abandonment by a daughter and a servant.

89 3.1.110–14. Like Antonio at the play's start, Jessica finds herself 'never merry' toward its end (5.1.69). Does she suffer from guilt or remorse?

90 Sokol, 1995, 384–5, concludes that 'Antonio's compulsive generosity' is 'an envious parody of femininity: he gives his all, without any real charity', and remarks on reflections in MV of 'Freud's original concept of the fetish: the fearful matter of potency for women'.

91 Adelman, 2003, accepts that this is 'axiomatically true' (25n9) yet argues that Jews are viewed in 'protoracialized' (11) in MV, and repeatedly omits the prefix 'proto' in her further discussions there. Also regarding OTH, Adelman, 1997, 125, premises a 'racist ideology everywhere visible in Venice'. Sokol, 2008, 113–41 maintains that the racialist theories known to us were not represented by Shakespeare, citing numerous studies in support. However, see below on the 'comic' interchange that begins when the newly converted Jessica is accused by the egregious Lancelot Gobbo of raising 'the price of hogs'

(MV 3.5.36–41) and Jessica's husband Lorenzo retaliates by accusing Gobbo of 'the getting up of the Negro's belly'.

92  Cervantes, 1964, dramatises how the elite of a Spanish town pretend to enjoy a non-existent 'Wonder Show' put on by a fraudulent stage manager in order to affirm that they are 'pureblood Christian[s]' (113) of untainted 'old Christian stock' (115).

93  Earlier Jessica confesses herself 'ashamed to be my father's child!', denying that 'blood' is crucial in her, 'But though I am a daughter to his blood, / I am not to his manners' (2.3.15–21). Kaplan, 2007, attributes Jessica's full conversion to Christianity despite her 'race' to theories alleging the biological inferiority of women. This overlooks, while still citing, a view that 'identifies the nineteenth century as giving rise to the modern formulation of race, constructed in terms of physical difference and inferiority that are "biologically" inheritable' (3).

94  Adelman, 2003, 6–7, notes that Gobbo and Graziano explicitly question Jessica's conversion, and that Bassanio and Portia 'do not register' Jessica's presence in Belmont, perhaps snubbing her. Heschel, 2008, 76, claims that 'the converted Jew, at least in the popular imagination, was not a Christian' and argues that the image of Jessica as a *converso* in combination with her 'transgendering' 'call our attention to a broader question of transracial, transreligious identity … destabilizing Christian as well as Jewish identities and throwing into question the boundary between them'. See also Hirsch, 2009.

95  Floyd-Wilson, 2003, 35 and passim. Also see Hoenselaars, 1992, 18–19, 180–1, 202, 226, 232, 2250n21, 279–80n93.

96  See Sokol, 2008, 79, 123–4, 156–63 and 123 on Morocco's denial.

97  See Sokol, 2008, 123–4 and Floyd-Wilson, 2003, 36–8. In TMP African-derived Caliban is more astute and focused than, as well as more sexually inclined than, the European drunkards Stepheno and Trinculo.

98  For instance, Morse, 1998, 75, calls the racialization insisted on in some interpretations of OTH 'disgusting'.

99  Cassio is thus identified by Iago in 1.1.19 and 3.1.39, but at 2.1.27 he may be alternately identified by a gentleman as

'Veronessa'. However, the Folio punctuation shows it more likely that this gentleman identifies the type of ship he is arriving in.

100 I agree with this overall claim of Hyman, 1971, and would extend it generally to Shakespeare.

101 In 1.1.113–14 Iago equates Othello with a 'Barbary horse' and in 1.1.88–9 with 'an old black ram ... tupping your white ewe', attributing animalistic sexuality to black Othello (and white Desdemona). But Brabantio angrily objects, 'This is Venice / My house is not a grange' (107–8, meaning 'not a farm'), rejecting Iago's imagery.

102 Rosenfeld, 1987, 22.

103 However, some critics claim that Iago is stung into rancour by being snubbed. They include Babcock, 1965, 299, holding that Iago's dry response to the brevity of Lodovico's salutation at 4.1.218–21 indicates that he has an acute sense of being snubbed; Zender, 1994, 328–31, claiming that Iago is humiliated by his failure to respond in an appropriately courteous manner to Desdemona's challenge 'what praise couldst thou bestow on a deserving woman' at 2.1.147–8; and Empson, 1995, 222, alleging that 'Iago feels he has been snubbed' when learning at 3.3.102 that Cassio has been chosen, and not himself, as Othello and Desdemona's go-between.

104 Rosenfeld, 1987, 274–5.

105 See Britton, 1998, 46–54. This comments further that some may oscillate between 'thick-skinned' and 'thin-skinned' narcissistic modes (46).

106 Jorgensen, 1950, 566, notes the irony of Iago playing the role of personified Honesty when he is actually a Vice figure.

107 See Morse, 1998, 65–9. In Shakespeare's work *moor* is used negatively only in TIM and once each in MV 3.5.38–40 and HAM 3.4.66 and is used positively many times in OTH.

108 In Shakespeare's era inhabitants of widely varied places remote from Europe could be identified as 'moors', on which see Sokol, 2004, 115–17, 133, 202n10 and n11.

109 'Shakespeare and the Stoicism of Seneca' in Eliot, 1934, 33–54 characterizes Othello's last speech is an attempt to '*cheer*

*himself up*' (39–40), but this claim that Othello aims to 'think well of himself' ignores the despair arising from recognizing an 'enemy within'.

110 Vickers, 1979, 70, claims that once seduced Othello 'takes over [Iago's] language ... with its bestial images', but Streir, 2019, 116–18, maintains that the fallen Othello only occasionally becomes Iago-like in language use. Strier maintains generally that 'The transformation that Iago effects in Othello occurs not at the level of style or mode but at the level of attitude' (114).

111 An 1867 emendation replacing 'fair wife' with 'fair life' at the crux at 1.1.20 where Iago asserts Cassio is 'almost damned in a fair wife' (noted in Babcock, 1965, 301n6) would locate Iago's recognition of Cassio's charisma or 'beauty' at both ends of the play.

112 Pace Zender, 1994, 323, nowhere in OTH does Iago pay serious erotic attention to Desdemona, or any woman.

113 Empson, 1995, 247, agrees that harming Desdemona is only Iago's means to an end, but see the next note.

114 Other readings include Zender, 1994, 328–31, that finds Iago seeking revenge against Desdemona because he thinks he has been humiliated by her (but Zender alternately claims that 'Iago can only ensure Othello's continuation in torment by destroying ... Desdemona' (333), with which I agree). Adelman, 1997, 139, asserts 'the destruction of Desdemona's generativity has been Iago's ultimate goal from the beginning' and that Iago's 'ultimate game is to make father destroy mother on that bed in a parody of the life-giving might have taken place there'. Although this essay attempts to distinguish triangular jealousy from bilateral envy (138n34), it confuses Oedipal with pre-Oedipal configurations. Adelman, 1992, 269n45, is more convincing in alleging Iago's envy resembles 'infantile rage at a mother who has failed him'.

115 Inciting Cassio's drunken brawling is only the beginning of Iago's campaign to bring him down. Thus Sokol, 2018, 211–18, identifies Cassio's further abject disgrace when he follows Iago's malign advice and inappropriately hires raucous wind-instrument players to disturb the newlywed Othello and Desdemona.

116 Adelman, 1997, 153, alleges 'we never see Iago taking the miser's or even the spendthrift's ordinary delight in this treasure; detached from any ordinary human motivation, the money accrues almost purely psychic meaning, becoming the sign not of any palpable economic advantage but of Iago's pleasure in being able to empty Roderigo out, to fill himself at will'.

117 See Girard, 1991, and for a pungent illustration of 'mimetic desire' see Castiglione, 1975, 125–6.

118 See Mallett and Hale, 1984, 315–17. Lewkenor, 1599, 15 and 130–3, defends those arrangements.

119 In a modern analogue some sub-segments of disadvantaged groups have espoused anti-Semitism, on which see Young-Bruehl, 1998, 481–5.

120 See Babcock, 1965, 297–8, which adds that it is derogatory when Iago is addressed using the familiar pronoun 'thee', rather than 'you' (298–9). Empson, 1995, 219, explains that a 'patronizing use' of honest 'carried an obscure social insult as well as a hint of stupidity' while exploring how 'honest' and 'honesty' become complexly overloaded terms when used 52 times in OTH (218–49).

121 Orwell, 1936, concerns itself with a different motive but describes the same condition.

122 See Fairbairn, 1944, 78–9.

# Chapter 4

1   For instance Marx, 1992; White, 1999; Wells, 2000b; Zimmermann, 2006; Kullmann, 2008; Morse, 2008; Meron, 2017; Randall, 2019.

2   Foakes, 2003, 17.

3   For example, see Dewey, 1922.

4   Quoted in Holmer, 1994, 170.

5   Quoted in Tiffany, 2011, 301.

6   See Kilgour, 1937, 10–11.

7   See Chambers, 1930, 2: 153.
8   See Sokol and Sokol, 2004, 10–12, 212–18.
9   Ibid., 214–15.
10  See R2 1.1 and 1.3; CYL 1.3.27–39, 1.3.180-226 and 2.3.59–109; LRF 5.3.83-145. See also 1H6 2.4.96–8; PER S.9.51–3; TMP 1.2.467–76; SHR 4.3.143–50. Sokol and Sokol, 2004, 9–12 and 212–18 discusses these unfulfilled challenges.
11  See ibid., 212 and 216.
12  Snyder, 1980, 201.
13  However Tiffany, 2011, 295, holds that when Hal vanquishes Hotspur unmounted 'Shakespeare subtly implies that the single combat does not reliably demonstrate the moral superiority of the champion'. Tiffany suggests that at one point Hal may even have planned to shoot Hotspur (314–15).
14  Snyder, 1980, 203 and Tiffany, 2011, 296–315. Critically, in 1H6 1.6.50–67 two experienced English heroes are shot to pieces by a mere Gunner's boy only recently schooled to do so (1.4.1–20).
15  Tiffany, 2011, 300–1, notes proclamations of 1566, 1600 and 1613. Peltonen, 2003, details proclamations of 1613 and 1614 and associated treatises published in 1614, 1614 and 1618.
16  See Peltonen, 2003, 82–4.
17  See ibid., 61–3, and Tiffany, 2011, 300–1.
18  In addition 'sword' appears over 300 times in Shakespeare, featuring in every play and poem except TGV, MV, VEN and LC. Also 'foils' are weapons in H5 4.0.50, ADO 5.2.12–13, and HAM 4.7.109, and 5.2.136, 200, 206 and 212. Ovens, 2015, 85n3, claims that 'At the time Shakespeare was writing . . . 'sword' and "rapier" were often used interchangeably or inconsistently' and Edelman, 1992, 27–8, 182, 184, 185, 190, details where 'rapier' referred specifically to a duelling weapon.
19  See Holmer, 1994, 178.
20  Tiffany, 2011, 301.
21  Holmer, 1994, 178, quoting Craig Turner and Tony Soper, *Methods and Practice of Swordplay* (Carbondale and Edwardsville, IL, 1990), 6.

22  Ovens, 2015, 81.
23  Peltonen, 2001, contrasts Bacon's wish for full suppression with the more moderate anti-duelling position of the Earl of Northumberland.
24  Bacon, 1614, 6–7.
25  Edelman, 1990, 118.
26  Anglin, 1984. 393. See also Potter, 2012, 66 and Tribble, 2017, 16 and 82.
27  Soens, 1969, 126.
28  See Holmer, 1994, 166, and Anglin, 1984, 407–9.
29  Soens, 1969, 126, which cites as well the evidence of technique derived from the nature of Mercutio's wound.
30  Tribble, 2017, 86.
31  See Holmer, 1994, 174–5.
32  Augustine, 2008b, 107–9. In the less vivid translation Augustine, 2008a, 100–1, this 'forceful horseplay of friends' (107) becomes 'friendly violence' (100).
33  In Augustine, 2008a, 147–8, Augustine says sinful weakness arises because 'the will that commands is incomplete, and therefore what it commands does not happen'. Alipius eventually overcomes this, as does Augustine himself.
34  Snyder, 1996, 88.
35  Sokol, 2018, 102–67, argues that the counterpoised vapid and anguished oxymora in ROM 1.1.173–8 and ROM 3.2.73–85 are contrived to be heard as contrasting in quality. It holds generally that poetic forms that are embedded in Shakespeare texts (such as the sonnet and the aubade spoken by the lovers ROM) are intended to illustrate how identical verse formats or conventions may produce poems of widely different quality. Led by theory, Snyder, 1996, 95, asserts the opposite.
36  Snyder, 1996, 93–4, allows that the lovers in ROM are 'less fixed by constant conditioning than are their elders'. Earlier Snyder, 1972, 133, admits that 'Othello violates his own peculiar essence and yields to Iago's law of the many', so seemingly Othello could have been free. However, Snyder then insists on

37. the 'tragic inadequacies and contradictions of all human love' (141). Such prejudicial beliefs are treated in Chapter 5.

37. For instance, when discussing COR, Hatlen, 1997, 397, asserts 'The political ... makes possible personal identity: for human beings there is no "self" outside of or prior to the political order'.

38. Walter Raleigh's poem 'The Lie', in Raleigh, 1951, 45–7, captures the reductive qualities of cynical pessimism – interestingly, by formally parodying a challenge to a duel.

39. Snyder, 1996, 95. This is not so absolutely reductive as a Lacanian position paraphrased in Lear, 2017, 154, as: 'ego-formation as such is a form of imprisonment in alienating signifiers'.

40. In Greville, 1939, 1:151. Greville's *A Treatise on War* includes bitter accounts of warfare, but also condemns of the 'weeds of *Peace*', including 'Opinions freedome, full of prejudice' (stanza 37, 1:223).

41. Meron, 2017, 939. White, 1999 and Merriam, 2007 also hold that Shakespeare did not first become opposed to chivalric fighting and warfare in mid-career, as is proposed in Marx, 1992 and Wells, 2000b. However Meron allows that 'Shakespeare seems to approve of the war of Malcolm on Macbeth and that of Henry of Richmond against Richard III, both bloody tyrants.'

42. White, 1999, 137–42 and Marx, 1992, 52–7.

43. Wells, 2000a, 399–407, 409, 420–1.

44. Kullmann, 2008, 52, and see 44–5 and 48.

45. See respectively Martin, 2019, and Morse, 2008.

46. Meron, 2017, 941.

47. Snyder, 1980, 201. Potter, 1990, 91, likewise comments, 'The single combat is synecdoche for war, with each fighter representing his army'.

48. In fact their exploits are to subdue a villain in self-defence, and then to rescue their father thereby enabling the conclusion of a war with a treaty granting peace and amity.

49. Thus Freud, 1958 (1915)-b, 92–9, suggests that a theme of childlessness permeates MAC.

50 Sidney, 1961, 42.

51 North's translation is reprinted in Philip Brockbank's edition of *Coriolanus*, listed here as Plutarch, 1978 (1579). Brockbank also supplies detailed notes on textual connections to Shakespeare's play.

52 George, 2013, and Barton, 1985, remark on divergences between North's translation and COR. For a parallel see Sokol, 1996, 264–5, on Shakespeare's 'radical pruning of his source materials' in MAC.

53 See, for instance, treatments of the play's historical, political, constitutional or sociological dimensions in Pettet, 1950; Norbrook, 2017; and George, 2013.

54 Milward, 1979, iii.

55 Although stage directions at tln 1475 and 1530 indicate three citizens are present at this time, they do not seem to hear this speech.

56 Stockholder, 1970, 231.

57 The word 'honour' appears in 43 speeches in COR, which is near the top end of the frequency scale (48 in MM, 43 in AWW, 40 in TIT). See https://www.opensourceshakespeare.org/concordance (accessed 11 September 2021).

58 Peltonen, 2001, 7.

59 As Plutarch, 1978 (1579), 314, asserts.

60 Britton, 2004, 163.

61 Rosenfeld, 1971, 174.

62 See Rosenfeld, 1971, and Britton, 2004, 156–7.

63 Thus Shakespeare's Achilles boasts about vanquishing Hector, but his Coriolanus is indifferent to fame (despite an opposite view of him taken in North's Plutarch).

64 Barton, 1985, 119.

65 S. H. Butcher's translation of *Poetics* 1416b at http://classics.mit.edu/Aristotle/poetics.mb.txt (accessed September 11, 2021) is clearer than Aristotle, 1941, 1485–6 or Aristotle, 1995, 135.

66 Huffman, 1982, 174, cites suggestions that this forgetfulness humanizes Coriolanus.

67  See COR 1.1.228–36 and 3.1.12–21.

68  Adelman, 1980, 138.

69  Barton, 1985, 124–5, explains this anomaly by referring to Volscian's non-urban culture. See also Huffman, 1982, 173n3.

70  Likewise in TIM Shakespeare's Alcibiades relishes resentful motives for action, averring 'Tis honour with most lands to be at odds. / Soldiers should brook as little wrongs as gods' (3.6.114–15).

71  Barton, 1985, 123. Historically, the Volscians were a semi-nomadic, cattle-raiding people, hill-dwellers to the south who envied the rich lands of the Latin campagna.

72  Although OED3 online at https://www-oed-com.libproxy.ucl.ac.uk/ (accessed 22 March 2019), appends 'Draft additions 1997' to 'lonely' citing a 1634 passage containing 'lonely bed', which it says figuratively indicates 'feelings of loneliness', OED3 traces 'loneliness 3' meaning 'dejection arising from want of companionship or society', and the similar 'lonely 4.a' furthest back to Byron in 1811 and Wordsworth in 1814 respectively.

73  George 2013, 43, connects COR, PER, CYM and WT and TMP thematically with 'the recognition of humaneness, driven home to the wayward male who must renounce power for family and love'.

74  See Lear, 2000, 106–65.

75  Plutarch, 367, reports that Aufidius thinks this outcome is likely, and so conspires to cut it off.

76  Spillius et al., 2011, 360, on 'Pitfalls of idealization'.

77  Klein, 1986 (1945), 132–3.

78  Britton, 2004, 157.

79  Folio stage directions tln 3804–5, 5.6.133–4.

80  For example, see Plotz, 1996, and for more nuanced disapproval of Rome, see Brockbank, 1978, 45 or Vickers, 1976, 38, 56–8.

81  Such critics also often comment on Volumnia's oral-sadistic remark following her son's exile: 'Anger is my meat. I sup upon myself / And so shall starve with feeding' (4.2.53–4). See

Harding, 1969, 252–3; Cavell, 1983, 3; Adelman, 1980, 131, 135; and Stoller, 1966, 271.

# Chapter 5

1. See Aristotle, 1941, 804. 'The Definition of Love', in Marvell, 1971, 1:39–40, wittily contrasts these modes of definition, on which see Sokol, 1988.
2. English Petrarchanism produced poems about unfulfilled desire and led to other poems mocking these complaints. See Fischlin, 1997, 103–7, 124–5 and 336–7n53, and Sokol, 2018, 97–107.
3. 'The Definition of Love' in Marvell, 1971, 1:39–40, echoing *Symposium* 200 (which Socrates revises at 203b–c).
4. Sokol, 2018, 97–107 and 118–20 discusses love complaints in bad verse seen in VEN, LLL, ROM, AYL and TN. But an Elizabethan tradition of excellent love complaints as seen in Sidney's *Asrophil and Stella* and in the ditties 'If my complaints could passions move', 'Can she excuse my wrongs' and 'Now, O now, I needs must part' in Dowland, 1597, also persisted.
5. Stoller, 1991, 414–15.
6. Klein, 1977, 72.
7. Lear, 2015, 72.
8. Sidney, 1961 (1595), 11, adding that excellent poets 'imitate borrowing nothing of what is, hath been, or shall be, but range, only rayned with learned discretion, into the divine consideration of what may be and should be'.
9. The claim in Frye, 1962, 53, that Shakespeare's Sonnets 'are a poetic realization of the whole range of love in the Western world' may be overstated, but in any case Wells and Edmondson, 2012, 213–16, makes a case against them being autobiographical, while Sokol, 2018, 124–38, finds them structured and disposed in quite other ways than autobiographically. Even an artist who self-dramatizes (unlike Shakespeare) may fictionalize their artistic self-depiction, as did the Elizabethan composer John Dowland according to Wells, 1994, 20 and 189–207, and Wells, 1985.

10   Cheney, 2004, 279.

11   For instance, Fiedler, 1974, 17, finds Shakespeare's Sonnets 'The very scriptures, the holy text, of his personal mythology' a mythology derived from Shakespeare's 'anti-feminist bias'.

12   Brustein, 2009, 13, remarks on the attitudes of 'Shakespeare's misogynistic contemporaries', claims Hamlet is 'Eager to endorse his culture's identification of women and demonic spirits' (16) and holds that when depicting misogynistic attitudes Shakespeare was 'echoing a prejudice of his age' (21).

13   Fiedler, 1974, 44. Here Fiedler reiterates the theses of his *Love and Death in the American Novel* (1960) and *The Return of the Vanishing American* (1968).

14   See Nuttall, 2000, 52–3, on this incompatibility.

15   Merrill, 1944, traces Anteros' transmutation from a personification to a minor god.

16   See De Tevarent, 1965.

17   Panofsky, 1972 (1939), 126.

18   Von Koppenfels, 1999, 7–8 and passim, relates this to an anti-Petrarchan tradition having precedents in Ovid, Horace, Martial and Catullus.

19   Catastrophe accompanied the 1631 premiere in Cambridge of Peter Hausted's *The Rivall Friends*, played before the King and Queen. Hausted himself performed the part of an insultingly antifeminist 'Anteros', and as Adams, 1912, relates the outcome was a near riot that led to the suicide of the Vice-Chancellor Henry Butts (434). The undergraduate John Milton probably attended this theatrical disaster (433).

20   Translated in Merrill, 1944, 271–2. See also Stephenson, 2012, 10–11.

21   Merrill, 1944, 272–3. See Stephenson, 2012, 21–38 and 39–48 on impacts in Italy and France.

22   Kingsley-Smith, 2010, 180–1, claims the appearance of 'Amianteros' in Daveant's 1635 *The Temple of Love* 'recalls Cupid's old sparring partner and brother, Anteros'.

23   Fraunce, 1592, unpaginated.

24  'Anteros' introduces himself as 'Love's Enemy' in the 1601 quarto version of Jonson's *Cynthia's Revels*, and a 'brother' of Cupid is called 'anti-Cupid' in Jonson's 1612 masque *Love Resored*.

25  Kingsley-Smith, 2010, 178, describes Hymen's intent in the masque to secure 'the happiness of the married couple'.

26  'A Challenge at Tilt', 1.1.152–72, ed. David Lindley, in Jonson, 2015.

27  'The King and Queen's Entertainment at Bolsover', 1.1.68–120, ed. James Knowles, in Jonson, 2015.

28  Gordon, 1980, 99.

29  Orvis, 2018, 37–8, over-literalizes this, adding that Jonson was 'intrigued by Eros and Anteros' penises' (44n26).

30  See James Knowles's commentary to 'The King and Queen's Entertainment at Bolsover'.

31  Raylor, 1999, 404, 435.

32  See Cable, 1981, 173–4 and passim.

33  From the enlarged 1644 edition of *Doctrine*, reprinted in Milton, 1957, 711.

34  Patterson, 1990, finds only male chauvinism in *The Doctrine and Discipline of Divorce* and remarks on Milton's 'peculiar interpretation of the Eros / Anteros model, a tale of passionately incestuous love between brothers, as an image of human *marriage*' (96). Orvis, 2018, 41, alleges that Milton's allusion to Eros and Anteros refers to a 'disconnection between mutual love and marriage', so that 'the primacy Milton affords mutual love irrespective of cultural expectations appears strikingly similar to queer critiques of marriage and the neoliberal state' (27).

35  Cable, 1981, 148, continuing: 'Love and Anteros are mutually regenerative, hence each is spiritually incomplete without the other'.

36  See Gordon, 1980, 272–4.

37  For instance, see Hennings, 1986, 95–107, on ERR and Anglican approval of affectionate marriages (96) and Maguire, 1997, 366, on ERR and St Paul's *Ephesians*.

38  See Etchegoyen, 1993, on the 'the latency period'.
39  According to CYM 1.1.58–63, 3.3.68–73 and 3.3.100–1 the brothers' ages are twenty-two and twenty-three, but 4.2.199–200 makes the younger brother sixteen. Puberty and adolescence may have arrived much later in Shakespeare's England than now; on average marriage occurred very late then (see Sokol and Sokol, 2003, 194n5), and the average age for menarche was about fifteen then (see Sokol, 1990, 311n5).
40  See Sokol and Sokol, 2004, 404–6 and 2003, 43–55 on wardship.
41  As is noted in Sokol, 1985, the antithetical adjectives 'froward' and 'forward' appear eight and nine times respectively in SHR, alluding to concepts explored in Spenser's *Faerie Queene* books II and III where 'forward' refers to vigorous life-affirming impulses and 'froward' to destructive ego-affirming ones.
42  See 1H6 1.3.51, LLL 3.1.200, 4.3.180 and 5.2.904 and 912, SHR I.2.107, and JN 1.1.184. However, Pentland, 2014, 27, suggests that in LLL 'The joke is that in England "Joan" was… a "proverbial name for a lower-class woman," whereas in Navarre it was commonly associated with royalty'.
43  See Patterson, 1989, 1 and Patterson, 2017, 260.
44  See Sokol and Sokol, 2003, 52 and 200n50, 200n51 on the possibility that 'disparagement' may partly explain the ward Bertram's reluctance to marry middling class Helena in AWW.
45  See Sokol, 2021, on this joke.
46  See Maus, 1987, 564–6 and 569–72, on the representations in English Renaissance drama of the voyeurism of real or imaginary cuckolds.
47  Fiedler, 1974, 130–1. Eager female revenge is hardly universal as claimed, and when mentioned in OTH 4.3.83–102 it does not provoke Desdemona's sympathetic response. See Parten, 1984, on female revenge for male adultery.
48  I have discussed this in Sokol, 1995 on MER; Sokol, 2008, 27–56 on SHR, WIV, MM, MER, JN, CYM, LLL, and WT; Sokol, 2004, 120–4 on LC; and Sokol and Sokol, 2003, 117–38, 164–84 on Shakespeare's take on petty treason, coverture, domestic violence, domestic murder and Elizabethan widows.
49  Stoller, 1991, 429.

50 In Stoller, 1966, 272, an earlier essay on *Coriolanus*, Stoller alleges that the 'universality of the threat that every infant senses (to which we give the name of separation anxiety) – his mother's life-and-death power over him – reverberates in each person of the [Shakespearian] audience'. He adds that 'Men like Coriolanus are deficient in the richness of their personalities. Stereotyped inhibitions, reaction-formations, and the smell of death give their humanity a two-dimensional quality' (263). Thus Stoller claims that Coriolanus pays little or no heed his wife (272), overlooking, for example, the importance, of the passionate kiss between Coriolanus and Virgilia at 5.3.44–8.

51 This position propounded in Stoller, 1991 is much less insisted upon in Stoller, 1966, where Coriolanus is alleged to be 'a man whose identity was an insubstantial image of his mother's phallic fantasy' (271). This earlier essay claims finally only that 'The poet would have sensed that, having such a mother [as Volumnia], her son could not be devoted to any woman'.

52 Adelman, 1992, 4–7 and notes. This includes 'Wet-nursing [was] sometimes tantamount to murder'.

53 Note, for instance, Kyd's *The Spanish Tragedy*, MAC 4.3.217–29 and 'On my First Sonne' and 'On my First Daughter' in Jonson, 1980, 23 and 14–15.

54 Ariès, 1973 (1960), 123.

55 Spring, 1984, 184–7.

56 Vickery, 1998, 122.

57 This condensed summary may suffice to show the insufficiency of Stoller's and Adelman's beliefs that the impossibility of infinite maternal nurture, joined with infantile terrors of being abandoned or displaced (or the frustrations that reality imposes on omnipotent phantasies), lead all human males into woman-hating or woman-shunning hyper-masculinity. For further details and an excellent bibliography exposing this fallacy, see Spillius et al., 2011, 63–84, 348–9, 424–6, 434–6, 456–8, 470–2, 491–7.

58 In this letter, printed in Freud, 1953–74, 1:266, Freud also asks about Hamlet, 'And does he not in the end, in the

same remarkable way as my hysterical patients, bring down punishment on himself by suffering the same fate as his father of being poisoned by the same rival?'.

59  See the editorial note on this letter in Freud, 1953–74, 1:266.

60  That path, opened by Freud, has been surveyed and offered as an 'Explanation of Hamlet's Mystery' many times, as for example in Jones, 1910. There is no doubt that Hamlet has a father problem. For instance, had he married Ophelia then Hamlet would have called Polonius 'father'; instead he kills him and designates his corpse as mere 'guts' (3.4.186), fit to be eaten by 'worms' (4.3.20–5).

61  Showalter, 1985, 77, complains that 'For most critics of Shakespeare, Ophelia has been an insignificant minor character in the play, touching in her weakness and madness'. Even Williams, 1988, 104, finds Ophelia a 'tabula- rasa', while Leverenz, 1980, 112, finds Ophelia similar to 'schizophrenics … whose voices are only the amalgams of other people's voices… or a still more terrifying vacuum'.

62  Billingham, 2015, 160, lists scholars who conclude from the abortifacient powers of the rosemary, rue and willow that Hamlet and Ophelia have had a physical relationship, but thinks otherwise. However, the sexual contents of Ophelia's mad singing may well reflect only fantasies (as do those of the of the songs of the Jailor's daughter's in TNK).

63  David, 1960, xxxiii, describes a probable historical background to Catherine's allusion to her sister's death, and adds that the same historical incident may have prompted 'the story of Ophelia in *Hamlet*'. Another offstage death (the king's conveyed in 5.2.711–13) provides the concluding motivation of LLL.

64  See Sokol, 2008, 99–102 and 113–14 on these verses.

65  In a parody of that, the patient acceptance of a love-trial period is extended to three years (the same duration as the period of study initially agreed upon in Navarre) when Don Armado ends LLL proclaiming, 'I am a votary, I have vowed to Jaquenetta / To hold the plough for her sweet love three year' (5.2.869–70).

66  Misogyny also appears in HAM in 2.1.27 where Polonius approves of 'drabbing' and at 4.7.162 where Laertes calls his own tears womanish.

67  Williams, 1988, 106, holds that Hamlet's 'intrusion into [Ophelia's] closet is less a communication than as species of attack, a type of play-acting or false art in the same mode as the Mousetrap'.

68  Foakes, 1980, 112–14, describes Hamlet's own repeated violations of his advice to the players, while Williams, 1988, 109, proposes that Hamlet is 'swept away by misplaced reforming zeal' in these redundant 'harangues'.

69  HAM 1.2.138 and 3.2.122 seemingly indicate that the play's action extends over only several months. Bradley, 1964 (1904), 319–24, in appendices A and B, considers the play's contradictory time scheme but does not posit a longer overall duration. Fendt, 1996, attempts to resolve some temporal enigmas by referring to the geography, but also does not greatly extend the duration.

70  Sokol, 1994, 42–9, discusses how a wife's *second* pregnancy is not infrequently associated with a husband's paranoid nervous breakdown, and that such husbands may identify with their first child (especially if a boy).

71  Winnicott, 1953, 99–100 and 103–4. On the contrary, Mazzola, 2019, 187, finds Hermione withholding, selfish and demanding, alleging connections with instances of destructive motherhood caused by economic distress.

72  See 'Attacks on Linking' (1959), reprinted in Bion, 1967a, 103–4. See also Bion, 1967c, 116.

73  See Karim-Cooper, 2016, 76, 107 and 189, on this 'paddling'.

74  Gurr, 1966, finds hand gestures in oratory becoming distinguished from those in Elizabethan stage action. Neill, 1995, discusses hands on the Shakespearian stage, but without reference to WT. Karim-Cooper, 2016, 2–3, 60–1, 76, and 107 surveys hands in WT. Sokol, 1994, 177–9, additionally considers Autolycus' filching hands and the statue's posed hands in WT, and Sokol and Sokol, 2003, 15, 17–18, 19, 95, discusses marriages by hand-fasting and Shakespeare's representations of these.

75  Dowland, 1597, L1v–L2r. *Caelica* is edited in Greville, 1939, LII in 1:104. Discussing the dating of the *Caelica* poems (1:34–42), this edition notes (38) that some must have circulated before being praised in Puttenham's 1586 *Arte of English Poesie*.

76  Fischlin, 1997, 105, disagrees, finding 'honor' the referent of 'his' in 'There miracles are scene of his', but see Sokol, 1980, on an anti-idealizing emphasis in *Caelica*.

77  Ford, 1607, song IX.

# Afterword

1  See especially Klein, 1977, and 1986b (1946/1952).
2  See Bion, 1962 and Spillius et al., 2011, 323.

# Appendix

1  Mulcaster, 1582, 46.
2  Britton, 1998, 2.
3  Meltzer, 1976, discusses 'beauty' in true insight and its lack in delusional insight. Britton, 1998, 97–108, investigates 'overvalued ideas' in relation to clinical materials in psychoanalysis.
4  According to Bion, 1962, 36, that link in infancy would be with a mother who is able to process her child's projected-out anxious thoughts in 'reverie' in such a way that her baby can learn to tolerate these thoughts and develop thinking. This suggests that a receptive infant is 'able to profit from reverie as it is able … to profit from the breast and the milk it supplies'. Bion continues that 'reverie' allows for an 'alpha function' which supplies a 'a sense of reality [which] matters to the individual in the way that food, drink, air and excretion of waste products matter' (42).

5   Ibid., 96, describes 'the breast in K' which is able to assuage projected-out infantile terrors so that a child can 're-introject a now tolerable and consequently growth-stimulating part of its personality'. Ibid., 101–2, holds that 'mental development like physical development depends on the efficient working of a mental alimentary system'.

6   Bion's 'K' link recalls Melanie Klein's positing of an 'epistemophilic instinct', on which see Spillius et al., 2011, 323. On the essential function of the infant's K link with a maternal object see Bion, 1962, 94–9, especially 97. Bion remarks here: 'The relationship of K to -K can be epitomized by saying that in K particularization and concretization of the abstract and general is possible, but in -K it is not because the abstract and general, in so far as they exist, are felt to become things-in-themselves' (98).

7   Fairbairn, 1944, 78–9, describes how the author was 'led to set aside the traditional classification of mental structure in terms of ego, id and super-ego in favour of a classification couched in terms of an ego-structure split into three separate egos — (1) a central ego (the "I"), (2) a libidinal ego, and (3) an aggressive, persecutory ego which I designate as the internal saboteur'. Fairbairn continues: 'Subsequent experience has led me to regard this classification as having a universal application'.

# BIBLIOGRAPHY

Adams, Joseph Quincy, Jr. 'Peter Hausted's "The Rivall Friends", with Some Account of His Other Works.' *Journal of English and Germanic Philology* 11.3 (1912): 433–50.

Adelman, Janet. '"Anger's My Meat": Feeding, Dependency, and Aggression in *Coriolanus*.' *Representing Shakespeare: New Psychoanalytic Essays*. Ed. Coppèlia Kahn and Murray M. Schwartz. Baltimore: Johns Hopkins University Press, 1980. 129–49.

Adelman, Janet. *Suffocating Mothers: Fantasies of Maternal Origin in Shakespeare's Plays, Hamlet to The Tempest*. New York: Routledge, 1992.

Adelman, Janet. 'Iago's Alter Ego: Race as Projection in Othello.' *Shakespeare Quarterly* 48 (1997): 125–44.

Adelman, Janet. 'Her Father's Blood: Race, Conversion, and Nation in *The Merchant of Venice*.' *Representations* 81 (2003): 4–30.

Allport, Gordon W. *The Nature of Prejudice*. Reading, MA: Addison-Wesley, 1954.

Alpers, Paul. 'Empson on Pastoral.' *New Literary History* 10 (1978): 101–23.

Alter, Robert. *The Hebrew Bible: A Translation with Commentary*. 3 vols. New York: W. W. Norton & Co., 2019.

Altschuler, Eric Lewin, and William Jansen. 'Shakespeariana in a Thomas Weelkes Dedication from 1600.' *Musical Times* Autumn (2005): 83–91.

Anderson, Judith H. *The Growth of a Personal Voice: Piers Plowman and The Faerie Queene*. New Haven: Yale University Press, 1976.

Anglin, Jay Pascal. 'The Schools of Defense in Elizabethan London.' *Renaissance Quarterly* 37 (1984): 393–410.

Anglin, Jay Pascal. *The Third University: A Survey of Schools and Schoolmasters in the Elizabethan Diocese of London*. Norwood: Norwood Editions, 1985.

Ariès, Philippe. *Centuries of Childhood: A Social History of Family Life.* Trans. Robert Baldick, first published 1962. Harmondsworth: Penguin, 1973.

Aristotle. *The Basic Works.* Ed. Richard McKeon. New York: Random House, 1941.

Aristotle. 'Poetics.' *Aristotle 'Poetics', Longinus 'On the Sublime', Demetrius,On Style'.* Loeb Classical Library. Ed. Stephen Halliwell. Cambridge, MA: Harvard University Press, 1995. 1–141.

Ascham, Roger. *The scholemaster or plaine and perfite way of teachyng children, to vnderstand, write, and speake, the Latin tong.* London: John Daye, 1570.

Aston, Margaret. 'Richard II and the Wars of the Roses.' *The Reign of Richard II: Essays in Honour of May McKisack.* Ed. F. R. H. Du Boulay and Caroline M. Barron. London: The Athlone Press, 1971. 280–317.

Augustine *Confessions.* Trans. and intro. Henry Chadwick. Oxford: Oxford University Press, 2008a.

Augustine *The Confessions, Modern English Version.* Selections. Grand Rapids: Revell, 2008b.

Babcock, Weston. 'Iago – An Extraordinary Honest Man.' *Shakespeare Quarterly* 16 (1965): 297–301.

Bacon, Francis. *The Charge of Sir Francis Bacon ... Touching Duells, Vpon an Information in the Star-Chamber Against Priest and Wright. With the Decree of the Star-Chamber in the Same Cause.* London, 1614.

Bacon, Francis. *Essays.* Ed. Michael J. Hawkins. London: J. M. Dent, 1994 (1625).

Baker, J. H. *An Introduction to English Legal History.* Third edition. London: Butterworths, 1990.

Baker, J. H., and S. F. C. Milsom. *Sources of English Legal History: Private Law to 1750.* London: Butterworths, 1986.

Baldwin, Thomas. *William Shakespere's Small Latine and Lesse Greeke.* 2 vols. Urbana: University of Illinois Press, 1944.

Barber, C. L. *Shakespeare's Festive Comedy: A Study of Dramatic Form in Relation to Social Custom.* Cleveland and New York: The World Publishing Company, 1963.

Barr, Helen. 'Pearl – or "The Jeweller's Tale".' *Medium Aevum* 69 (2000): 59–79.

Barton, Anne. 'Livy, Machiavelli, and Shakespeare's Coriolanus.' *Shakespeare Survey* 38 (1985): 115–29.

Bassi, Shaul. 'Country Dispositions: Ethnic Fallacies in Shakespeare Criticism.' *Shakespearean International Yearbook* 3 (2003): 59–76.

Bate, Jonathan. *Shakespeare and Ovid*. Oxford: Clarendon Press, 1999.

Baxandall, Michael. *Episodes: A Memory Book*. London: Frances Lincoln, 2010.

Bearman, Robert. '"Was William Shakespeare William Shakeshafte?" Revisited.' *Shakespeare Quarterly* 53 (2002): 83–94.

Bennett, Michael J. 'The Court of Richard II and the Promotion of Literature.' *Chaucer's England: Literature in Historical Context*. Ed. Barbara A. Hanawalt. Minneapolis: University of Minnesota Press, 1992. 3–20.

Bennett, Michael J. 'The Historical Background.' *A Companion to the Gawain-Poet*. Ed. Derek Brewer and Jonathan Gibson. Cambridge: D. S. Brewer, 1997. 71–90.

*The Bible*. Known as the Geneva Bible. London: Christopher Barker, 1587.

Billingham, Josephine Elaine. 'Piteous Performances: Representations of Infanticide and Its Contexts in Tudor and Stuart Literature of Stage and Street.' Ph.D. Dissertation. University College London, 2015. Available at https://discovery.ucl.ac.uk/id/eprint/1468973/.

Bion, W. R. *Learning From Experience*. London: William Heinemann, 1962.

Bion, W. R. 'Attacks on Linking.' *Second Thoughts*. Ed. W. R. Bion. New York: Jason Aronson, 1967a. 93–109.

Bion, W. R. 'On Arrogance.' *Second Thoughts*. Ed. W. R. Bion. New York: Jason Aronson, 1967b. 86–92.

Bion, W. R. 'A Theory of Thinking.' *Second Thoughts*. Ed. W. R. Bion. New York: Jason Aronson, 1967c. 110–19.

Bion, W. R. *The Long Weekend 1897–1919: Part of a Life*. London: Free Association Books, 1986.

Bion, W. R. *The Complete Works of W.R. Bion*. Ed. Chris Mawson. 16 vols. London: Karnac Books, 2014.

Bion, W. R. 'Break Up, Break Through, Break Down.' *Three Papers of W. R. Bion*. Ed. Chris Mawson. London: Routledge, 2018. 35–42.

Blanpeid, John W. *Time and the Artist in Shakespeare's English Histories*. London: Associated Universities Presses, 1983.

Blunt, A. 'An Echo of the "Paragone" in Shakespeare.' *Journal of the Warburg and Courtauld Institutes* 2 (1939): 260–2.
Bowers, John M. *The Politics of Pearl: Court Poetry in the Age of Richard II*. Cambridge: D. S. Brewer, 2001.
Bowker, Margaret. 'Roper [née More], Margaret (1505–1544).' *Oxford Dictionary of National Biography*. Ed. H. C. G. Matthew and Brian Harrison. Oxford: Oxford University Press, 2017.
Bradbrook, Muriel C. *The Growth and Structure of Elizabethan Comedy*. Harmondsworth: Peregrine Books, 1963.
Bradbrook, Muriel C. *Shakespeare: The Poet in his World*. Reprint of 1978. London: Routledge, 2005.
Bradley, A. C. *Shakespearean Tragedy*. New York: Meridian Books, 1964 (1904).
Brearley, Mike. *On Form*. London: Constable, 2018.
Britton, Ronald. *Belief and Imagination*. Hove: Routledge, 1998.
Britton, Ronald. *Sex, Death and the Superego: Experiences in Psychoanalysis*. London: Karnac, 2004.
Britton, Ronald. *Between Mind and Brain: Models of the Mind and Models in the Mind*. London: Karnac Books, 2015.
Brockbank, Philip. 'Richard II and the Music of Men's Lives.' *Leeds Studies in English* 14 (1983): 57–73.
Brooke, Nicholas. *Shakespeare's Early Tragedies*. London: Methuen & Co., Ltd, 1968.
Brooks, Harold F., ed. *A Midsummer Night's Dream*. Second Arden edition. London: Routledge, 1989.
Brustein, Robert. *The Tainted Muse: Prejudice and Presumption in Shakespeare and His Time*. New Haven: Yale University Press, 2009.
Budra, Paul. *A Mirror for Magistrates and the de casibus Tradition*. Toronto: University of Toronto Press, 2000.
Burrow, Colin. 'Shakespeare and Humanistic Culture.' *Shakespeare and the Classics*. Ed. Charles Martindale and A. B. Taylor. Cambridge: Cambridge University Press, 2004. 9–27.
Burrow, J. A. *Ricardian Poetry*. London: Routledge & Kegan Paul, 1971.
Burrow, J. A. 'Should We Leave Medieval Literature to the Medievalists?' *Essays in Criticism* 53 (2003): 278–83.
Buxton, John. *A Tradition of Poetry*. London: Macmillan, 1967.
Cable, Lana. 'Coupling Logic and Milton's Doctrine of Divorce.' *Milton Studies* 15 (1981): 143–59.

Caldwell, Ellen C. 'Jack Cade and Shakespeare's Henry VI, Part 2.' *Studies in Philology* 92 (1995): 18–79.
Camden, William. *Reges, reginae, nobiles, & alij in ecclesia collegiata B. Petri Westmonasterij sepulti*. London, 1600.
Campbell, Lily B. *Shakespeare's Histories: Mirrors of Elizabethan Policy*. San Marino: The Huntingdon Library, 1947.
Carlson, Donald. '"For he is our peace which hath made of both one": Echoes of Paul in Shakespeare's Comedy of Errors.' *Ben Jonson Journal* 20 (2013): 38–57.
Carlson, Donald. 'Of Lunatics, Lovers, and Poets: The Conversation about Poetry in Shakespeare's *Midsummer Night's Dream*.' *Ben Jonson Journal* 25 (2018): 194–213.
Castiglione, Baldassare. *The Book of the Courtier*. Trans. Sir Thomas Hoby, 1561. London: J. M. Dent, 1975.
Cavell, Stanley. '"Who Does the Wolf Love?" Reading Coriolanus.' *Representations* 3 Summer (1983): 1–20.
Cervantes, Miguel de. 'The Wonder Show.' *Interludes*. Ed. Edwin Honig. New York: New American Library, 1964. 109–23.
Chambers, E. K. *William Shakespeare: A Study of Facts and Problems*. 2 vols. Oxford: Clarendon Press, 1930.
Chandler, David P. *Brother Number One: A Political Biography of Pol Pot*. Revised edition. Abingdon: Routledge, 2018.
Cheney, Patrick. *Shakespeare, National Poet-Playwright*. Cambridge: Cambridge University Press, 2004.
Chesterton, Gilbert Keith. 'A Midsummer Night's Dream.' *Good Words* 45 (1904): 621–6.
Chigas, George, and Dmitri Mosyakov. 'Literacy and Education under the Khmer Rouge.' At https://gsp.yale.edu/literacy-and-education-under-khmer-rouge, accessed 6 November 2018.
Collinson, Patrick. *Elizabethan Essays*. London: Hambledon Press, 1994.
Cook, Ann Jennalie. *Making a Match: Courtship in Shakespeare and his Society*. Princeton: Princeton University Press, 1991.
Cooke, Katherine. *A. C. Bradley and His Influence in Twentieth Century Shakespeare Criticism*. Oxford: Clarendon Press, 1972.
Cox, John D. *Seeming Knowledge: Shakespeare and Skeptical Faith*. Waco: Baylor University Press, 2007.
Cressy, David. *Education in Tudor and Stuart England*. London: Edward Arnold, 1973.
Cressy, David. 'A Drudgery of Schoolmasters: The Teaching Profession in Elizabethan and Stuart England.' *The Professions in*

*Early Modern England*. Ed. Wilfrid Prest. London: Croom Helm, 1987. 129–53.

Daniel, David. *Shakespeare, Julius Caesar*. Third Arden edition. London: Thomson Learning, 2006.

David, Richard, ed. *Shakespeare Love's Labour's Lost*. Second Arden edition. London: Methuen & Co. Ltd, 1960.

Davids, M. Fakhry. *Internal Racism: A Psychoanalytic Approach to Race and Difference*. London: Macmillan International, 2011.

Demeter, Jason, and Ayanna Thompson. 'Shakespeare and Early Modern Race Studies: An Overview of the Field.' *The Shakespearean World*. Ed. Jill L. Levenson and Robert Ormsby. London: Routledge, 2017. 574–89.

DeMolen, Richard L. 'Richard Mulcaster and the Elizabethan Theatre.' *Theatre Survey* 13 (1972): 28–41.

Demos, Raphael. 'Plato's Idea of the Good.' *The Philosophical Review* 46 (1937): 245–75.

De Tevarent, Guy. 'Eros and Anteros or Reciprocal Love in Ancient and Renaissance Art.' *Journal of the Warburg and Courtauld Institutes* 28 (1965): 205–8.

Dewey, John. 'Classification of Instincts.' *Human Nature and Conduct: An Introduction to Social Psychology*. New York: Modern Library, 1922. 124–30.

Doleac, Jennifer L. 2021. 'A Review of Thomas Sowell's *Discrimination and Disparities*.' *Journal of Economic Literature* 59.2: 574–89.

Donne, John. *Poems*. Ed. John Carey. Oxford: Oxford University Press, 1990.

Doran, Madeleine. 'Imagery in "Richard II" and in "Henry IV".' *The Modern Language Review* 37 (1942): 113–22.

Dowland, John. *The first booke of songes or ayres*. STC, second edition/7091, EEBO. London, 1597.

Doyle, A. I. 'English Books In and Out of Court from Edward III to Henry VII.' *English Court Culture in the Later Middle Ages*. Ed. J. W. Sherborne and V. J. Scattergood. London: Duckworth, 1983. 161–81.

Draffan, Robert A. '"Without taking sides against poetry": *Richard II*.' *English* 20 (1971): 39–44.

Duffy, Eamon. *The Stripping of the Altars: Traditional Religion in England, 1400–1580*. London: Yale University Press, 2005.

Dutton, Richard. 'A Jacobean Merry Wives?' *Ben Jonson Journal* 19 (2011): 1–26.

Dutton, Richard. *Shakespeare, Court Dramatist*. Oxford: Oxford University Press, 2016.
Eberle, Patricia J. 'The Politics of Courtly Style at the Court of Richard II.' *The Spirit of the Court*. Ed. Glyn S. Burgess and Robert A. Taylor. Cambridge: D. S. Brewer, 1985. 168–78.
Eberle, Patricia J. 'Richard II and the Literary Arts.' *Richard II: The Art of Kingship*. Ed. Anthony Goodman and James Gillespie. Oxford: Clarendon Press, 1999. 231–53.
Edelman, Charles. 'Shakespeare's "brawl ridiculous".' *Shakespeare Survey* 42 (1990): 111–18.
Edelman, Charles. *Brawl Ridiculous*. Manchester: Manchester University Press, 1992.
Edwards, A. S. G. 'The Manuscript: British Library MS Cotton Nero A.x.' *A Companion to the Gawain-Poet*. Ed. Derek Brewer and Jonathan Gibson. Cambridge: D. S. Brewer, 1997. 197–219.
Egan, Gabriel. 'The Presentist Threat to Editions of Shakespeare.' *Shakespeare and the Urgency of Now: Criticism and Theory in the 21st Century*. Ed. Cary DiPietro and Hugh Grady. Basingstoke and New York: Palgrave Macmillan, 2013. 38–59.
Egan, Gabriel, and Gary Taylor, eds. *The New Oxford Shakespeare: Authorship Companion*. Oxford: Oxford University Press, 2017.
Elam, Keir, ed. *Shakespeare, Twelfth Night*. Third Arden edition. London: Bloomsbury Arden Shakespeare, 2008.
Eliot, T. S. *Elizabethan Essays*. London: Faber & Faber, 1934.
Empson, William. *The Structure of Complex Words*. London: Penguin Books Ltd, 1995.
Enterline, Lynn. 'Education and Reading in Shakespeare's Work.' *The Cambridge Guide to the Worlds of Shakespeare: Shakespeare's World, 1500–1660*. 2 vols. Ed. Bruce Smith. Cambridge: Cambridge University Press, 2016a. 1:845–50.
Enterline, Lynn. Schooling in the English Renaissance. Oxford Handbooks Online, 2016b. https://www.oxfordhandbooks.com/view/10.1093/oxfordhb/9780199935338.001.0001/oxfordhb-9780199935338-e-76?rskey=dcsRpW&result=3, accessed 14 September 2021.
Esdaile, Arundell, ed. *Daniel's Delia and Drayton's Idea*. London: Chatto and Windus, 1908.
Etchegoyen, Alicia. 'Latency – A Reappraisal.' *International Journal of Psycho-Analysis* 74 (1993): 347–57.

Ewbank, Inga-Stina. 'Shakespeare's Poetry.' *A New Companion to Shakespeare Studies*. Ed. Kenneth Muir and S. Schoenbaum. Cambridge: Cambridge University Press, 1971. 99–115.

Fairbairn, W. Ronald D. 'Object-Relationship Psychology as the Rationale of the Internalization of Objects.' *International Journal of Psycho-Analysis* 25 (1944): 70–92.

Fendt, Gene. 'A Note on the Time Scheme in Hamlet.' *Notes and Queries* 43 (1996): 159–60.

Fiedler, Leslie A. *The Stranger in Shakespeare*. Frogmore, St Albans: Paladin, 1974.

Fisch, Harold. 'Shakespeare and the Language of Gesture.' *Shakespeare Studies* 19 (1987): 239–51.

Fischlin, Daniel. *In Small Proportions: Poetics of the English Ayre, 1596–1622*. Detroit: Wayne State University Press, 1997.

Floyd-Wilson, Mary. *English Ethnicity and Race in Early Modern Drama*. Cambridge: Cambridge University Press, 2003.

Foakes, R. A. '"Forms to his Conceit": Shakespeare and the Uses of Stage Illusion.' *Proceedings of the British Academy* 66 (1980): 103–19.

Foakes, R. A., ed. *Shakespeare, King Lear*. Third Arden edition. London: Thomson Learning, 2001.

Foakes, R. A. *Shakespeare and Violence*. Cambridge: Cambridge University Press, 2003.

Ford, Thomas. *Musicke of Sundrie Kindes: Set Forth in Two Bookes*. London, 1607.

Forker, Charles R., ed. *Shakespeare, King Richard II*. Third Arden edition. London: Cenage Learning, 2002.

Fraunce, Abraham. *The Arcadian Rhetorike*. London, 1588.

Fraunce, Abraham. *The third part of the Countesse of Pembrokes Yuychurch Entituled, Amintas dale. Wherein are the most conceited tales of the pagan gods in English hexameters together with their aunciente descriptions and philosophicall explications*. London: Thomas Woodcocke, 1592.

Freedman, Barbara. 'Egeon's Debt: Self-Division and Self-Redemption in "The Comedy of Errors".' *English Literary Renaissance* 10 (1980): 360–83.

Freeman, Jane. '"Fair terms and a villain's mind": Rhetorical Patterns in *The Merchant of Venice*.' *Rhetorica* 20 (2002): 149–72.

Freud, Sigmund. *The Standard Edition of the Complete Psychological Works of Sigmund Freud*. Ed. James Strachey. 24 vols. London: Hogarth Press, 1953–74.

Freud, Sigmund. 'The Antithetical Sense of Primal Words.' *On Creativity and The Unconscious*. Ed. Benjamin Nelson. New York: Harper & Row, 1958a (1910). 55–62.

Freud, Sigmund. 'Some Character Types Met With in Psycho-analytic Work.' *On Creativity and The Unconscious*. Ed. Benjamin Nelson. New York: Harper & Row, 1958b (1915). 84–110.

Freud, Sigmund. 'The "Uncanny".' *On Creativity and The Unconscious*. Ed. Benjamin Nelson. New York: Harper & Row, 1958c (1919). 122–61.

Freud, Sigmund. 'Libidinal Types.' *The Standard Edition of the Complete Psychological Works*. Vol. 21. Ed. James Strachey. London: Hogarth Press, 1961 (1931). 215–20.

Freud, Sigmund. *The Interpretation of Dreams*. Trans. and ed. James Strachey. London: George Allen & Unwin Ltd, 1967 (1900).

Freud, Sigmund. *Civilization and its Discontents*. Trans. Joan Riviere, ed. James Strachey. London: The Hogarth Press, 1973 (1930).

Freud, Sigmund. "The Taboo of Virginity." *Pelican Freud Library*. Ed. Angela Richards. Vol. 7. London: Penguin, 1977 (1917). 261–83.

Froissart, Jean. *The thirde and fourthe boke of sir Iohn Froissart of the cronycles of Englande, Fraunce, Spaygne, Portyngale, Scotlande, Bretayne, Flaunders, and other places adioynyng. Translated out of Frenche in to englysshe by Iohan Bourchier knyght lorde Berners*. London, 1525.

Frye, Northrop. 'How True a Twain.' *The Riddle of Shakespeare's Sonnets*. New York: Basic Books, 1962. 23–53.

George, David. 'Coriolanus and the Late Romances.' *Late Shakespeare, 1608–1613*. Ed. Andrew J. Power and Rory Loughnane. Cambridge: Cambridge University Press, 2013. 36–55.

Ginsberg, Warren. 'Chaucer and Petrarch: "S'amor non è" and the Canticus Troili.' *Humanist Studies & the Digital Age* 1.1 (2011): 121–7.

Girard, René. *A Theatre of Envy*. Oxford: Oxford University Press, 1991.

Given-Wilson, Chris. *Chronicles: The Writing of History in Medieval England*. London: Hambledon and London, 2004.

Gombrich, E. H. *Art and Illusion*. Oxford: Phaidon, 1977.

Goodman, Anthony. 'Montagu, John, Third Earl of Salisbury (c.1350–1400).' *Oxford Dictionary of National Biography*. Ed. H. C. G. Matthew and Brian Harrison. Oxford: Oxford University Press, 2004.

Gordon, D. J. *The Renaissance Imagination: Essays and Lectures*. Ed. Stephen Orgel. Berkeley: University of Califonia Press, 1980.

Goulding, R. D. 'Savile, Sir Henry (1549–1622).' *Oxford Dictionary of National Biography*. Ed. H. C. G. Matthew and Brian Harrison. Oxford: Oxford University Press, 2004. Online edition. https://0-www-oxforddnb-com.catalogue.libraries.london.ac.uk/, accessed 14 September 2021.

Gower, John. *Confessio Amantis*. London: William Caxton, 1483.

Gower, John. *Confessio Amantis*. Printed and introduced by Thomas Berthelette. London, 1554.

Green, Richard Firth. *Poets and Princepleasers: Literature and the English Court in the Late Middle Ages*. Toronto: University of Toronto Press, 1980.

Greenblatt, Stephen. *Hamlet in Purgatory*. Princeton: Princeton University Press, 2001.

Greene, Thomas M. 'Pitiful Thrivers: Failed Husbandry in the Sonnets.' *Shakespeare and the Question of Theory*. Ed. Patricia Parker and Geoffrey H. Hartman. New York: Methuen & Co. Ltd, 1985. 230–44.

Greville, Fulke. *Poems and Dramas*. Ed. Geoffrey Bullough. 2 vols. Edinburgh: Oliver and Boyd, 1939.

Gross, C. *Select Cases Concerning the Law Merchant, 1270–1638*. London: The Selden Society, 1908.

Gross, Kenneth. *Shakespeare is Shylock*. Chicago: University of Chicago Press, 2006.

Gurr, Andrew. 'Elizabethan Action.' *Studies in Philology* 63 (1966): 144–56.

Gurr, Andrew, ed. *William Shakespeare, King Richard II*. The New Cambridge Shakespeare, second edition. Cambridge: Cambridge University Press, 2003.

Hackett, Helen. '"He is a better scholar than I thought he was": Debating the Achievements of the Elizabethan Grammar Schools.' *Journal of the Northern Renaissance* 9 (2017): n.p.

Hall, Edward. *The vnion of the two noble and illustrate famelies of Lancastre [and] Yorke*. London, 1548.

Hammer, Paul E. J. 'Shakespeare's Richard II, the Play of 7 February 1601, and the Essex Rising.' *Shakespeare Quarterly* 59 (2008): 1–35.

Hampton-Reeves, Stuart. 'Kent's Best Man: Radical Chorographic Consciousness and the Identity Politics of Local History in Shakespeare's 2 Henry VI.' *Journal For Early Modern Cultural Studies* 14.1 (2014): 63–87.

Hapgood, Robert. 'Three Eras in *Richard II.*' *Shakespeare Quarterly* 14 (1963): 281–3.

Harbage, Alfred. 'Shakespeare and the Professions.' *Shakespeare's Art: Seven Essays*. Ed. Milton Crane. Chicago: University of Chicago Press, 1973. 11–28.

Harding, D. W. 'Women's Fantasy of Manhood.' *Shakespeare Quarterly* 20 (1969): 245–53.

Hardwick, Charles. *A History of the Articles of Religion*. Third edition, revised by Francis Proctor. London: George Bell & Sons, 1876.

Hardy, Barbara. *Dramatic Quickleyisms: Malapropic Wordplay Technique in Shakespeare's Henriad*. Salzburg: Universität Salzburg, 1979.

Harvey, I. M. W. 'Cade, John [Jack] [alias John Mortimer; called the Captain of Kent].' *Oxford Dictionary of National Biography*. Ed. H. C. G. Matthew and Brian Harrison. Oxford: Oxford University Press, 2006.

Hassig, Debra. *Medieval Bestiaries: Text, Image, Ideology*. Cambridge: Cambridge University Press, 1995.

Hatlen, Burton. 'The "Noble Thing" and the "Boy of Tears": Coriolanus and the Embarrassments of Identity.' *English Literary Renaissance* 27 (1997): 393–420.

Haughton, Hugh. 'Introduction.' *The Uncanny, by Sigmund Freud*. Trans. David McLintock. London: Penguin, 2003. vii–lviii.

Hennings, Thomas P. 'The Anglican Doctrine of the Affectionate Marriage in *The Comedy of Errors*.' *Modern Language Quarterly* 47 (1986): 91–107.

Heschel, Susannah. 'From Jesus to Shylock: Christian Supersessionism and "The Merchant of Venice".' *The Harvard Theological Review* 99 (2006): 407–31.

Heschel, Susannah. '*The Merchant of Venice* and the Theological Construction of Christian Europe.' *Mediating Modernity: Challenges and Trends in the Jewish Encounter with the Modern*

*World*. Ed. Lauren B. Strauss and Michael Brenner. Detroit: Wayne State University Press, 2008. 74–92.

Hilliard, Nicholas. 'A Treatise Concerning the Arte of Limning.' *The Volume of the Walpole Society* 1 (1911–12): 1–54.

Hinman, Charlton. *The First Folio of Shakespeare*. New York: W. W. Norton and Co., 1968.

Hirsch, Bret D. 'Counterfeit Professions: Jewish Daughters and the Drama of Failed Conversion in Marlowe's *The Jew of Malta* and Shakespeare's *The Merchant of Venice*.' *Early Modern Literary Studies* 19.4 (2009): 1–37. At https://extra.shu.ac.uk/emls/si-19/hirscoun.html#, accessed 14 September 2021.

Hirsch, Bret D. 'From Jew to Puritan: The Emblematic Owl in Early English Culture.' *'This Earthly Stage': World and Stage in Late Medieval and Early Modern England*. Ed. Bret D. Hirsch and C. J. Wortham. Turnhout, Belgium: Cursor Mundi: Brepols Publishers, 2011. 131–72.

Hockey, Dorothy. 'A World of Rhetoric in *Richard II*.' *Shakespeare Quarterly* 15 (1964): 179–91.

Hoeniger, F. D., ed. *Shakespeare, Pericles*. Second Arden edition. London: Methuen & Co. Ltd, 1977.

Hoenselaars, A. J. *Images of Englishmen and Foreigners in the Drama of Shakespeare and His Contemporaries*. Rutherford: Fairleigh Dickinson University Press, 1992.

Hoenselaars, A. J. 'The Other in the Mirror: Prejudice and Stereotypes on the English Renaissance Stage.' *Cahiers Charles V* 24 (1998): 85–101.

Holmer, Joan Ozark. '"Draw, if you be Men": Saviolo's Significance for Romeo and Juliet.' *Shakespeare Quarterly* 45 (1994): 163–89.

Honigmann, E. A. J. *Shakespeare: The 'Lost Years'*. Manchester: Manchester University Press, 1985.

Honigmann, E. A. J. '"Was William Shakespeare William Shakeshafte?" Revisited.' *Shakespeare Quarterly* 54 (2003): 83–6.

Hopkins, Lisa. 'Is Paris Worth a Mass? *All's Well that Ends Well* and the Wars of Religion.' *Shakespeare and the Culture of Christianity in Early Modern England*. Ed. Dennis Taylor and David N. Beauregard. New York: Fordham University Press, 2003. 369–81.

Huffman, Clifford Chalmers. 'Coriolanus and His Poor Host: A Note.' *Etudes Anglaises* 35 (1982): 173–6.

Humphries, A. R., ed. *Shakespeare, King Henry IV Part 1*. Second Arden edition. London: Methuen & Co. Ltd, 1968.

Hunt, John Dixon. 'Shakespeare and the Paragone: A Reading of *Timon of Athens.*' *Images of Shakespeare*. Ed. Werner Habicht, D. J. Palmer, and Roger Pringle. Newark: University of Delaware Press, 1988. 47–63.

Hunt, Maurice. 'Slavery, English Servitude and *The Comedy of Errors.*' *English Literary Renaissance* 27 (1997): 29–56.

Hunt, Maurice. *Shakespeare's Religious Allusiveness: Its Play and Tolerance*. Aldershot: Ashgate, 2004.

Hyman, Stanley Edgar. *Iago: Some Approaches to the Illusion of his Motivation*. London: Elek, 1971.

Jack, R. D. S. 'Petrarch in English and Scottish Renaissance Literature.' *Modern Language Notes* 71 (1976): 801–11.

Jardine, Lisa. 'Cultural Confusion and Shakespeare's Learned Heroines: "These are old paradoxes".' *Shakespeare Quarterly* 38 (1987): 1–18.

Jenkins, Harold, ed. *Shakespeare, Hamlet*. Second Arden edition. London: Methuen & Co. Ltd, 1982.

Jewell, Helen M. *Education in Early Modern England*. Basingstoke: Macmillan, 1998.

John, Ivor B., ed. *Shakespeare, The Tragedy of King Richard II*. First Arden edition. London: Methuen & Co. Ltd, 1912.

Jones, Ernest. 'The Oedipus-Complex as an Explanation of Hamlet's Mystery: A Study in Motive.' *The American Journal of Psychology* 21.1 (1910): 72–113.

Jonson, Ben. *Bartholomew Fair*. Ed. E. A. Horsman. The Revels Plays. Manchester: Manchester University Press, 1979.

Jonson, Ben. *Poems of Ben Jonson*. Ed. George Burke Johnston. London: Routledge & Kegan Paul, 1980.

Jonson, Ben. *The Cambridge Edition of the Works Online*. Ed. David Bevington, Martin Butler and and Ian Donaldson. Cambridge: Cambridge University Press, 2015. https://universitypublishingonline.org/cambridge/benjonson/reference/, accessed 3 March 2020.

Jorgensen, Paul A. 'Honesty in Othello.' *Studies in Philology* 47 (1950): 557–67.

Kahneman, Daniel. *Thinking, Fast and Slow*. London: Allen Lane, 2011.

Kaplan, M. Lindsay. 'Jessica's Mother: Medieval Constructions of Jewish Race and Gender in "The Merchant of Venice".' *Shakespeare Quarterly* 58 (2007): 1–30.

Karim-Cooper, Farah. *The Hand on the Shakespearean Stage: Gesture, Touch, and the Spectacle of Dismemberment*. London: Bloomsbury Arden Shakespeare, 2016.

Karim-Cooper, Farah, and Eoin Price. 'Shakespeare, Race and Nation: Introduction, a Conversation.' *Shakespeare* 17 (2021): 1–5.

Kehler, Dorothea. 'King of Tears: Mortality in "Richard II".' *Rocky Mountain Review of Language and Literature* 39 (1985): 7–18.

Kennedy, Roger. *Tolerating Strangers in Intolerant Times*. London: Routledge, 2019.

Kilgour, Raymond Lincoln. *The Decline of Chivalry as Shown in the French Literature of the Late Middle Ages*. Cambridge, MA: Harvard University Press, 1937.

Kingsley-Smith, Jane. *Cupid in Early Modern Literature and Culture*. Cambridge: Cambridge University Press, 2010.

Kingsley-Smith, Jane. '"Let me not to the Marriage of True Minds": Shakespeare's Sonnet for Lady Mary Wroth.' *Shakespeare Survey* 69 (2016): 277–91.

Klause, John. *Shakespeare, the Earl, and the Jesuit*. Madison, NJ: Fairleigh Dickinson University Press, 2008.

Klein, Emanuel. 'The Reluctance to Go to School.' *Psychoanalytic Study of the Child* 1 (1945): 263–79.

Klein, Melanie. *Envy and Gratitude*. First published 1957. London: Tavistock, 1977.

Klein, Melanie. 'A Contribution to the Psychogenesis of Manic-Depressive States.' *The Selected Melanie Klein*. Ed. Juliet Mitchell. Harmondsworth: Penguin, 1986a (1935). 116–45.

Klein, Melanie. 'Notes on Some Schizoid Mechanisms.' *The Selected Melanie Klein*. Here in revised version 1952. Ed. Juliet Mitchell. Harmondsworth: Penguin, 1986b (1946/1952). 176–200.

Koppenfels, Werner von. 'Eros and Anteros: Shakespeare's Dark Lady Sonnets and Some Metamorphoses of Love Debased.' *Elizabethan Literature and Transformation*. Ed. Sabine Coelsch-Foisner. Tubingen: Stauffenburg Verlag Brigitte Narr GmbH, 1999. 5–17.

Kullmann, Thomas. 'Shakespeare and Peace.' *Shakespeare and War*. Ed. Ros King and Paul Franssen. Basingstoke: Palgrave Macmillan, 2008. 43–55.

Lane, Robert. '"The sequence of posterity": Shakespeare's *King John* and the Succession Controversy.' *Studies in Philology* 92 (1995): 460–81.

Laslett, Peter. *The World We Have Lost: Further Explored.* Revised edition. London: Methuen & Co. Ltd, 1983.

Latham, Agnes, ed. *Shakespeare, As You Like It.* Second Arden edition. London: Methuen & Co. Ltd, 1975.

Lear, Jonathan. *Happiness, Death and the Remainder of Life.* Cambridge, MA: Harvard University Press, 2000.

Lear, Jonathan. 'Rosalind's Pregnancy.' *Raritan* 34.3 (2015): 66–85.

Lear, Jonathan. *Wisdom Won from Illness.* Cambridge, MA: Harvard University Press, 2017.

Leverenz, David. 'The Woman in Hamlet: An Interpersonal View.' *Representing Shakespeare: New Psychoanalytic Essays.* Ed. Murray M. Schwartz and Coppèlia Kahn. Baltimore: Johns Hopkins University Press, 1980. 110–28.

Levy, F. J. 'Savile, Henry, of Banke (1568–1617).' *Oxford Dictionary of National Biography.* Ed. H. C. G. Matthew and Brian Harrison. Oxford: Oxford University Press, 2004. Online edition.

Lewis, C. S. *English Literature in the Sixteenth Century.* New York: Oxford University Press, 1954.

Lewkenor, Lewis. *The Commonwealth and Gouernment of Venice: Written by the Cardinall Gasper Contareno.* London, 1599.

Lindsay, Tom. '"Which first was mine own king": Caliban and the Politics of Service and Education in The Tempest.' *Studies in Philology* 113 (2016): 397–423.

Linthicum, M. Channing. 'Malvolio's Cross-Gartered Yellow Stockings.' *Modern Philology* 25 (1927): 87–93.

Lisak, Catherine. 'In Search of Richard II: Shakespeare's Use of Eyewitness Accounts of the Revolution (1399–1400): Conflicting Tales and the Dramatic Structure of the Play (III.2–3).' *Shakespeare et le Moyen Age.* Ed. Patricia Dorval. Paris: Société Française Shakespeare, 2002. 95–128.

Little, Arthur L., Jr. *Shakespeare's Jungle Fever: National-Imperial Re-Visions of Race, Rape, and Sacrifice.* Stanford Stanford: University Press, 2000.

Little, Arthur L., Jr. 'Re-Historicizing Race, White Melancholia, and the Shakespearean Property.' *Shakespeare Quarterly* 67 (2016): 84–103.

Lothian, J. M., and T. W. Craik, eds. *Shakespeare, Twelfth Night.* Second Arden edition. London: University Paperbacks, 1984.

Macfarlane, Alan. 'Review of *The Family, Sex and Marriage in England 1500–1800* by Lawrence Stone.' *History and Theory* 18 (1979): 103–26.

Maguire, Laurie E. 'The Girls from Ephesus.' *The Comedy of Errors: Critical Essays*. Ed. Robert S. Miola. New York: Garland, 1997. 355–91.

Maley, Willy. '"A Thing Most Brutish": Depicting Shakespeare's Multi-Nation State.' *Shakespeare* 3 (2007): 79–101.

Maley, Willy. '"Let a Welsh connnection teach you a good English condition": Shakespeare, Wales and the Critics.' *Shakespeare and Wales: From the Marches to the Assembly*. Ed. Willy Maley and Philip Schwyzer. Burlington: Ashgate, 2010. 177–89.

Mallett, M. E., and J. R. Hale. *The Military Organization of a Renaissance State: Venice c. 1400 to 1617*. Cambridge: Cambridge University Press, 1984.

Marotti, Arthur F. 'Shakespeare and Catholicism.' *Theatre and Religion: Lancastrian Shakespeare*. Ed. Richard Dutton, Alison Findlay and Richard Wilson. Manchester: Manchester University Press, 2003. 218–41.

Martin, Randall. 'Economies of Gunpowder and Ecologies of Peace: Accounting for Sustainability.' *Shakespeare Survey* 72 (2019): 16–31.

Marshall, Gail, and Anne Thompson. 'Mary Cowden Clarke.' *Great Shakespeareans*. Ed. Gail Marshall. Vol. 7. London: Continuum, 2011. 58–91.

Marvell, Andrew. *Poems and Letters*. Ed. H. M. Margoliouth. Third edition revised by Pierre Legouis. 2 vols. Oxford: Clarendon Press, 1971.

Marx, Steven. 'Shakespeare's Pacifism.' *Renaissance Quarterly* 45 (1992): 49–95.

Mathew, Gervase. *The Court of Richard II*. London: John Murray, 1968.

Matthews, David. 'Public Ambition, Private Desire and the Last Tudor Chaucer.' *Reading the Medieval in Early Modern England*. Ed. Gordon McMullan and David Matthews. Cambridge: Cambridge University Press, 2007. 74–88.

Maus, Katherine Eisaman. 'Horns of Dilemma: Jealousy, Gender, and Spectatorship in English Renaissance Drama.' *ELH* 54 (1987): 561–83.

Mazzola, Elizabeth. 'Failure to Thrive.' *Shakespeare Survey* 72 (2019): 183–99.

McCutcheon, Elizabeth. 'The Education of Thomas More's Daughters: Concepts and Praxis.' *Moreana* 52(2015): 249–68.

Melchiori, Giorgio, ed. *Shakespeare, The Merry Wives of Windsor.* Third Arden edition. London: Thompson Learning, 2000.

Meltzer, Donald. 'The Delusion of Clarity of Insight.' *International Journal of Psycho-Analysis* 57 (1976): 141–6.

Meltzer, Donald. *The Claustrum: An Investigation of Claustrophobic Phenomena.* London: Karnac Books Ltd, 1990.

Meron, Theodor. 'Shakespeare: A Dove, a Hawk, or Simply a Humanist?' *American Journal of International Law* 111 (2017): 936–56.

Merriam, Thomas. 'Shakespeare's Supposed Disillusionment with Chivalry in 1599.' *Notes and Queries* 54 (2007): 285–7.

Merrill, Robert V. 'Eros and Anteros.' *Speculum* 19 (1944): 265–84.

Middleton, Anne. 'The Idea of Public Poetry in the Reign of Richard II.' *Speculum* 53 (1978): 94–114.

Milton, John. *Areopagitica and Other Prose Works.* London: J. M. Dent & Sons Ltd, 1941.

Milton, John. *Complete Poems and Major Prose.* Ed. Merritt Y. Hughes. Indianapolis: Bobbs-Merrill, 1957.

Milward, Peter. *Shakespeare's Soliloquies.* Tokyo: Shinkosha, 1979.

Miyazaki, Mariko. 'Misericord Owls and Medieval Anti-semitism.' *The Mark of the Beast: The Medieval Bestiary in Art, Life, and Literature.* Ed. Debra Hassig. New York: Taylor & Francis, 1999. 23–50.

Money-Kyrle, Roger. 'On Prejudice: A Psycho-Analytic Approach.' *The Collected Papers of Roger Money-Kyrle.* Ed. Donald Meltzer. Perthshire: Clunie Press, 1978. 354–60.

Moore, Peter R. 'Hamlet and Piers Plowman: A Matter of Conscience.' *Cahiers Elisabethains* 65 (2004): 11–24.

Moran, Jo Ann Hoeppner. *The Growth of English Schooling 1340–1548.* Princeton: Princeton University Press, 1985.

Morse, Ruth. 'Othello: White Skin, Black Masks.' *Shakespeare: Préjugés et tolérance.* Ed. Ruth Morse. Paris: Publications de l'Université Paris 7-Denis Diderot, 1998. 65–83.

Morse, Ruth. 'Some Social Costs of War.' *Shakespeare and War.* Ed. Ros King and Paul Franssen. Basingstoke: Palgrave Macmillan, 2008. 56–68.

Mulcaster, Richard. *Positions ... for the training up of children.* London, 1581.

Mulcaster, Richard. *First Part of the Elementarie*. London, 1582.
Neill, Michael. '"Ampitheatres in the Body": Playing with Hands on the Shakespearian Stage.' *Shakespeare Survey* 48 (1995): 23–50.
Nevo, Ruth. *Comic Transformations in Shakespeare*. London: Methuen & Co. Ltd, 1980.
Newton, Dorris Elizabeth. 'The Boy Actors of the Elizabethan Period 1558–1610.' MA thesis, Boston University. 1933. At https://hdl.handle.net/2144/13078, accessed 18 November 2018.
Norbrook, David. 'Rehearsing the Plebeians: Coriolanus and the Reading of Roman History.' *Shakespeare and the Politics of Commoners*. Ed. Chris J. Fitter. Oxford: Oxford University Press, 2017. 180–216.
Novy, Marianne. *Shakespeare's Outdsiders*. Oxford: Oxford University Press, 2013.
Nuttall, A. D. '*A Midsummer Night's Dream*: Comedy as Apotrope of Myth.' *Shakespeare Survey* 53 (2000): 49–59.
Oliver, H. J., ed. *Shakespeare, The Merry Wives of Windsor*. Second Arden edition. London: Methuen & Co. Ltd, 1979.
Orme, Nicholas. *Medieval Schools from Roman Britain to Renaissance England*. New Haven: Yale University Press, 2006.
Ormrod, W. M. 'Knights of Venus.' *Medium Aevum* 73 (2004): 290–305.
Orvis, David L. 'Eros and Anteros: Queer Mutuality in Milton's Doctrine and Discipline of Divorce.' *Early Modern Culture* 10 (2018): 24–44.
Orwell, George. 'Shooting an Elephant.' Published in *New Writing*, 2 (Autumn 1936). At https://www.orwellfoundation.com/the-orwell-foundation/orwell/essays-and-other-works/shooting-an-elephant/, accessed 14 September 2021.
Ovens, Michael. 'France and the Norman Lamord in Hamlet.' *Cahiers Elisabethains* 97 (2015): 79–86.
Palmer, Kenneth, ed. *Shakespeare, Troilus and Cressida*. Second Arden edition. London: Methuen, 1982.
Panofsky, Erwin. *Studies in Iconology*. Originally published 1939, Oxford University Press. New York: Harper & Row, 1972.
Parks, George B. 'The First Draft of Ascham's "Scholemaster".' *Huntington Library Quarterly* 1 (1938): 313–27.
Parten, Anne. 'Masculine Adultery and Feminine Rejoinders in Shakespeare, Dekker, and Sharpham.' *Mosaic* 17 (1984): 9–18.

Pater, Walter. 'Shakespeare's English Kings.' *Appreciations, with an Essay on Style*. Ed. Alfred J. Drake. 1889. 185–204. At http://www.gutenberg.org/files/4037/4037-8.txt, accessed 14 September 2021.

Patterson, Annabel. *Shakespeare and the Popular Voice*. Oxford: Basil Blackwell, 1989.

Patterson, Annabel. '"No Meer Amatorious Novel?".' *Politics, Poetics, and Hermeneutics in Milton's Prose*. Ed. David Loewenstein and James Grantham Turner. Cambridge: Cambridge University Press, 1990. 85–101.

Patterson, Annabel. 'Afterword.' *Shakespeare and the Politics of Commoners: Digesting the New Social History*. Ed. Chris J. Fitter. Oxford: Oxford University Press, 2017. 253–62.

Peltonen, Markku. 'Francis Bacon, the Earl of Northampton, and the Jacobean Anti-Duelling Campaign.' *The Historical Journal* 44 (2001): 1–28.

Peltonen, Markku. *The Duel in Early Modern England: Civility, Politeness, and Honour*. Cambridge: Cambridge University Press, 2003.

Pentland, Elizabeth. 'Shakespeare, Navarre, and Continental History.' *Interlinguicity, Internationality, and Shakespeare*. Ed. Michael Saenger. Ithaca, NY: McGill-Queen's University Press, 2014. 23–45.

Pettet, E. C. '*The Merchant of Venice* and the Problem of Usury.' *Essays and Studies* 31 o.s. (1945): 19–33.

Pettet, E. C. 'Coriolanus and the Midlands Insurrection of 1607.' *Shakespeare Survey* 3 (1950): 34–42.

Phialas, Peter G. 'The Medieval in *Richard II*.' *Shakespeare Quarterly* 12 (1961): 305–10.

Pinto, Vivian de Sola. *The English Renaissance, 1510–1688*. London: The Cresset Press, 1966.

Pittock, Malcolm. 'Widow Dido.' *Notes and Queries* 33 (1986): 368–9.

Plato. *Collected Dialogues*. Ed. Edith Hamilton and Huntington Cairns. New York: Pantheon Books, 1966.

Plautus, Titus M. *Menaechmi*. Trans. William Warner. London, 1595.

Plotz, John. 'Coriolanus and the Failure of Performatives.' *ELH* 63 (1996): 809–32.

Plutarch. 'The Life of Julius Caesar.' *The Parallel Lives*. Vol. VII. Trans. Bernadotte Perrin. Loeb Classical Library 99.

Cambridge: Harvard University Press, 1919. At penelope. uchicago.edu/Thayer/E/Roman/Texts/Plutarch/Lives/Caesar*. html, accessed 14 September 2021.

Plutarch. 'Life of Coriolanus.' *Shakespeare, Coriolanus*. Trans. Thomas North. Appendix in Second Arden edition. Ed. Philip Brockbank. London: Methuen & Co. Ltd, 1978 (1579). 313–68.

Plutarch. *The lives of the noble Grecians and Romanes ... translated ... out of French into Englishe, by Thomas North*. London, 1579.

Potter, Lois. '"Scenes and acts of death": Shakespeare and the Theatrical Image of War.' *Shakespeare et la guerre*. Ed. Marie-Thérèse Jones-Davies. Paris: Belles Lettres, 1990. 89–100.

Potter, Lois. *The Life of William Shakespeare: A Critical Biography*. Oxford: Blackwell Publishing, Ltd, 2012.

Proctor, Thomas. *A Gorgeous Gallery of Gallant Inventions*. London, 1587. Ed. Hyder Edward Rollins. Cambridge, MA: Harvard University Press, 1926.

Puttenham, George. *The Arte of English Poesie*. Ed. Gladys Doidge Willcock and Alice Walker. Cambridge: Cambridge University Press, 1936 (1589).

Raleigh, Sir Walter. *Poems*. Ed. Agnes M. C. Latham. Cambridge, MA: Harvard University Press, 1951.

Raleigh, Walter. *Shakespeare*. Originally published 1907. London: Macmillan and Co., Ltd, 1953.

Raylor, Timothy. '"Pleasure reconciled to virtue": William Cavendish, Ben Jonson, and the Decorative Scheme of Bolsover Castle.' *Renaissance Quarterly* 52 (1999): 402–39.

Robbins, Rossell Hope. 'A Gawain Epigone.' *Modern Language Notes* 58 (1943): 361–366.

Robbins, Rossell Hope. 'The Poems of Humfrey Newton, Esquire, 1466–1536.' *PMLA* 65 (1950): 249–81.

Robbins, Rossell Hope. 'Geoffroi Chaucier, Poète Français, Father of English Poetry.' *The Chaucer Review* 13 (1978): 93–115.

Rosenfeld, Herbert. 'On the Psychopathology of Narcissism a Clinical Approach.' *International Journal of Psycho-Analysis* 45 (1964): 332–7.

Rosenfeld, Herbert. 'A Clinical Approach to the Psychoanalytic Theory of the Life and Death Instincts: An Investigation Into the Aggressive Aspects of Narcissism.' *International Journal of Psycho-Analysis* 52 (1971): 169–78.

Rosenfeld, Herbert. *Impasse and Interpretation: Therapeutic and Anti-Therapeutic Factors in the Psychoanalytic Treatment of Psychotic, Borderline, and Neurotic Patients*. London: Tavistock, 1987.

Rosenstein, Roy. 'Richard the Redeless: Representations of Richard II from Boccaccio and Polydore to Holinshed and Shakespeare.' *Travels and Translations in the Sixteenth Century*. Ed. Mike Pincombe. Aldershot: Ashgate, 2004. 137–49.

Rutter, Carol Chillington. 'Shakespeare and School.' *Shakespeare beyond Doubt: Evidence, Argument, Controversy*. Ed. Paul Edmondson and Stanley Wells. Cambridge: Cambridge University Press, 2013. 133–44.

Ryan, M. K., and P. Buirski. 'Prejudice as a Function of Self-Organization.' *Psychoanalytic Psychology* 18 (2001): 21–36.

Saintsbury, George. 'Introduction to King Richard II.' *The Complete Works of William Shakespeare in Forty Volumes, Volume XXI*. Ed. Sidney Lee. New York: G. D. Sproul, 1907. ix–xxv.

Saintsbury, George. *A History of English Literature: Elizabethan Literature*. Reprint of London: Macmillan and Co., Ltd, 1902. New York: Cosimo, Inc., 2005 (1902).

Salerno, Luigi. 'Seventeenth Century English Literature on Painting.' *Journal of the Warburg and Courtauld Institutes* 14 (1951): 234–58.

Saul, Nigel. 'Chaucer and Gentility.' *Chaucer's England: Literature in Historical Context*. Ed. Barbara A. Hanawalt. Minneapolis: University of Minnesota Press, 1992. 41–55.

Saul, Nigel. *Richard II*. New Haven: Yale University Press, 1997.

Saul, Nigel. *Richard II and Chivalric Kingship: An Inaugural Lecture*. London: Royal Holloway, University of London, 1998.

Saul, Nigel. 'The Kingship of Richard II.' *Richard II: The Art of Kingship*. Ed. Anthony Goodman and James Gillespie. Oxford: Clarendon Press, 1999. 37–57.

Scattergood, V. J. 'Literary Culture at the Court of Richard II.' *In English Court Culture in the Later Middle Ages*. Ed. J. W. Sherborne and V. J. Scattergood. London: Duckworth, 1983. 29–44.

Schiefele, Eleanor. 'Richard II and the Visual Arts.' *Richard II: The Art of Kingship*. Ed. Anthony Goodman and James Gillespie. Oxford: Clarendon Press, 1999. 255–71.

Schoenbaum, S. *William Shakespeare: A Compact Documentary Life*. New York: New American Library, 1986.

Shakespeare, William. *The Complete Works*. Ed. Stanley Wells and Gary Taylor. Electronic edition. Oxford: Oxford University Press, 1989.

Shapiro, James. *Shakespeare and the Jews*. New York: Columbia University Press, 1992.

Sherborne, J. W. 'Aspects of English Court Culture in the Later Fourteenth Century.' *English Court Culture in the Later Middle Ages*. Ed. J. W. Sherborne and V. J. Scattergood. London: Duckworth, 1983. 1–27.

Shin, Hiewon. 'Single Parenting, Homeschooling: Prospero, Caliban, Miranda.' *SEL: Studies in English Literature, 1500–1900* 48 (2008): 373–93.

Showalter, Elaine. 'Representing Ophelia: Women, Madness, and the Responsibilities of Feminist Criticism.' *Shakespeare and the Question of Theory*. Ed. Patricia Parker and Geoffrey H. Hartman. New York: Methuen & Co. Ltd, 1985. 77–94.

Sidney, Philip. *Apology for Poetrie*. Ed. J. C. Collins. Oxford: Clarendon Press, 1961 (1595).

Sidney, Philip. *The Poems of Sir Philip Sidney*. Ed. William A. Ringler. Oxford: Clarendon Press, 1962.

Siemens, Raymond G. 'Henry VIII as Writer and Lyricist.' *Musical Quarterly* 92 (2009): 136–66.

Silvayn, Alexander. 'Declamation 95 of *The Orator*.' *Shakespeare, The Merchant of Venice*. Appendix in Second Arden edition. Ed. John Russell Brown. London: Methuen & Co. Ltd, 1977 (1596). 168–72.

Simon, Joan. *Education and Society in Tudor England*. Cambridge: Cambridge University Press, 1966.

Skinner, Quentin. *Forensic Shakespeare*. Oxford: Oxford University Press, 2014.

Smith, Emma. 'Was Shylock Jewish?' *Shakespeare Quarterly* 64 (2013): 188–219.

Snyder, Susan. '"Othello" and the Conventions of Romantic Comedy.' *Renaissance Drama* 5 (1972): 123–41.

Snyder, Susan. 'Ourselves Alone: The Challenge to Single Combat in Shakespeare.' *SEL: Studies in English Literature, 1500–1900* 20 (1980): 201–16.

Snyder, Susan. 'Ideology and the Feud in Romeo and Juliet.' *Shakespeare Survey* 49 (1996): 87–96.

Soens, Adolph L. 'Tybalt's Spanish Fencing in Romeo and Juliet.' *Shakespeare Quarterly* 20 (1969): 121–7.

Sokol, B. J. 'Numerology in Fulke Greville's *Caelica*.' *Notes and Queries* 27 (1980): 327–9.

Sokol, B. J. 'A Spenserian Idea in *The Taming of the Shrew*.' *English Studies* 66 (1985): 310–16.

Sokol, B. J. 'The Symposium, Two Kinds of "Definition," and Marvell's "The Definition of Love".' *Notes and Queries* 35 (1988): 169–70.

Sokol, B. J. '"Tilted Lees," Dragons, Haemony, Menarche, Spirit, and Matter in Comus.' *Review of English Studies* 41 (1990): 309–24.

Sokol, B. J. 'Holofernes in Rabelais and Shakespeare and Some Manuscript Verses of Thomas Harriot.' *Etudes Rabelaisiennes* 25 (1991): 131–5.

Sokol, B. J. '*The Merchant of Venice* and the Law Merchant.' *Renaissance Studies* 6 (1992): 60–7.

Sokol, B. J. *Art and Illusion in The Winter's Tale*. Manchester: Manchester University Press, 1994.

Sokol, B. J. 'Constitutive Signifiers or Fetishes in *The Merchant of Venice*?' *International Journal of Psycho-Analysis* 76 (1995): 373–87.

Sokol, B. J. 'Macbeth and the Social History of Witchcraft.' *Shakespeare Yearbook* 6 (1996): 245–74.

Sokol, B. J. 'Prejudice and Law in *The Merchant of Venice*.' *Shakespeare Survey* 51 (1998) ed. Stanley Wells: 159–73.

Sokol, B. J. *Shakespeare and Tolerance*. Cambridge: Cambridge University Press, 2008.

Sokol, B. J. 'A Warwickshire Scandal, Sir Thomas Lucy, and the Date of *The Merry Wives of Windsor*.' *Shakespeare* 5 (2009): 355–71.

Sokol, B. J. 'Inverted Biblical and Religious References and Shylock's Word "suffrance" in *The Merchant of Venice*.' *Notes and Queries* 57 (2010): 368–72.

Sokol, B. J. 'Shylock and Marsyas.' *Shakespeare* 11 (2015): 337–61.

Sokol, B. J. *Shakespeare's Artists: The Painters, Sculptors, Poets and Musicians in his Plays and Poems*. London: Bloomsbury Arden Shakespeare, 2018.

Sokol, B. J. 'The "rule of three" and the "callback": How Comic Form in The Merry Wives of Windsor 4.1 May Help to Date its Folio Text.' *Ben Jonson Journal* 26 (2019a): 97–112.

Sokol, B. J. 'Why Does Shakespeare give his Windsor Schoolmaster a Double Occupation as an Educator and as a Parson?' *Notes and Queries* 66 (2019b): 430–5.

Sokol, B. J. 'Three Notes on Faulty Bilingualism in Shakespeare's *The Merry Wives of Windsor* and Middleton's *A Chaste Maid in Cheapside*.' *Ben Jonson Journal* 27 (2020): 253–62.

Sokol, B. J. '"Sans 'sans' I pray you", a serious Shakespearian joke.' *Essays In Criticism* 71 (April 2021): 174–82.

Sokol, B. J., and Mary Sokol. 'Shakespeare and the English Equity Jurisdiction: *The Merchant of Venice* and the Two Texts of *King Lear*.' *Review of English Studies* 50 (1999): 417–39.

Sokol, B. J., and Mary Sokol. *Shakespeare, Law and Marriage*. Cambridge: Cambridge University Press, 2003.

Sokol, B. J., and Mary Sokol. *Shakespeare's Legal Language*. Paperback reprint, corrected. London: Continuum, 2004.

Sowell, Thomas. *Discrimination and Disparities*. New York: Basic Books, 2018.

Spenser, Edmund. *Minor Poems*. Ed. E. De Selincourt, 1910. Oxford: Clarendon Press, 1966.

Spillius, Elizabeth Bott, et al. *The New Dictionary of Kleinian Thought*. London: Routledge, 2011.

Spring, Eileen. 'The Family, Strict Settlement and Historians.' *Law, Economy and Society, 1750–1914: Essays in the History of English Law*. Ed. G. R. Rubin and David Sugarman. Abingdon: Professional Books, 1984. 168–91.

Staley, Lynn. 'Richard II, Henry of Derby, and the Business of Making Culture.' *Speculum* 75 (2000): 68–96.

Steel, Anthony. *Richard II*. Cambridge: Cambridge University Press, 1941.

Steiner, John. 'Man's Inhumanity to Man: Confrontations and Prejudice.' *Psychoanalytic Inquiry* 36 (2016): 285–94.

Stephens, Lyn. '"A Wilderness of Monkeys": A Psychodynamic Study of *The Merchant of Venice*.' *The Undiscover'd Country*. Ed. B. J. Sokol. London: Free Association Books, 1993. 91–129.

Stephenson, Craig E. *Anteros, a Forgotten Myth*. Hove: Routledge, 2012.

Sternfeld, Frederick W., and Mary Joiner Chan. 'Come Live with Me and Be My Love.' *Comparative Literature* 22 (1970): 173–87.

Stockholder, Kay. 'The Other Coriolanus.' *PMLA* 85 (1970): 228–36.

Stoller, Robert J. 'Shakespearean Tragedy: Coriolanus.' *Psychoanalytic Quarterly* 35 (1966): 263–74.

Stoller, Robert J. 'Hooray for Love.' *Journal of the American Psychoanalytic Association* 39 (1991): 413–36.

Stone, Lawrence. *The Family, Sex and Marriage in England 1500–1800*. London: Weidenfeld and Nicolson, 1977.

Stone, Lawrence. *Broken Lives: Separation and Divorce in England 1660–1857*. Oxford: Oxford University Press, 1993.

Stow, Kennith. *Jewish Dogs*. Stanford: Stanford University Press, 2006.

Strier, Richard. 'Paleness versus Eloquence: The Ideologies of Style in the English Renaissance.' *Explorations in Renaissance Culture* 45.2 (2019): 91–120.

Tambling, Jeremy. *Allegory and the Work of Melancholy: The Late Medieval and Shakespeare*. Amsterdam: Rodopi, 2004.

Tassi, Marguerite A. 'O'erpicturing Apelles: Shakespeare's Paragone with Painting in Antony and Cleopatra.' *Antony and Cleopatra: New Critical Essays*. Ed. Sara Munson Deats. London: Routledge, 2005. 291–307.

Thomas, D. L., and N. E. Evans. 'John Shakespeare in The Exchequer.' *Shakespeare Quarterly* 35 (1984): 315–18.

Thompson, Ayanna. *Passing Strange: Shakespeare, Race, and Contemporary America*. Oxford: Oxford University Press, 2011.

Thompson, Ayanna. 'Introduction.' *Othello: Revised Edition*. Ed. E. A. J. Honigmann. London: Bloomsbury Arden Shakespeare, 2016. 1–116.

Thompson, Ayanna. *Blackface (Object Lessons)*. London: Bloomsbury, 2021.

Thompson, Edward Maunde. 'A Contemporary Account of the Fall of Richard the Second. Part II.' *The Burlington Magazine for Connoisseurs* 5 (1904): 267–77.

Tiffany, Grace. 'Rank, Insults, and Weaponry in Shakespeare's Second Tetralogy.' *Papers on Language and Literature: A Journal for Scholars and Critics of Language and Literature* 47 (2011): 295–317.

Traub-Werner, D. 'Towards a Theory of Prejudice.' *International Review of Psycho-Analysis* 11 (1984): 407–12.

Tribble, Evelyn B. *Early Modern Actors in Shakespeare's Theatre: Thinking with the Body*. London: Bloombury, 2017.

Tuck, Anthony. 'Richard II (1367–1400).' *Oxford Dictionary of National Biography*. Ed. H. C. G. Matthew and Brian Harrison. Oxford: Oxford University Press, 2004.

Tudeau-Clayton, Margaret. '"This is the strangers' case": The Utopic Dissonance of Shakespeare's Contribution to *Sir Thomas More*.' *Shakespeare Survey* 65 (2012): 239–54.

Ure, Peter, ed. *Shakespeare, King Richard II*. Second Arden edition. London: Methuen & Co. Ltd, 1961.

Van Doren, Mark. *Shakespeare*. Originally published 1939 by Henry Holt. Undated paperback reprint. New York: Doubleday Anchor Books, 1939.

Vasari, Giorgio. *Lives of the Most Eminent Painters, Sculptors and Architects*. Trans. Mrs Jonathan Foster. 5 vols. London: Henry G. Bohn, 1855.

Vickers, Brian. *Coriolanus*. London: E. Arnold, 1976.

Vickers, Brian. 'Shakespeare's Hypocrites.' *Daedalus* 108 (1979): 45–83.

Vickery, Amanda. *The Gentleman's Daughter: Women's Lives in Georgian England*. New Haven: Yale University Press, 1998.

Wells, Robin Headlam. 'John Dowland and Elizabethan Melancholy.' *Early Music* 13 (1985): 514–28.

Wells, Robin Headlam. *Elizabethan Mythologies*. Cambridge: Cambridge University Press, 1994.

Wells, Robin Headlam. '"Manhood and chevalrie": Coriolanus, Prince Henry, and the Chivalric Revival.' *Review of English Studies* 51 (2000a): 395–422.

Wells, Robin Headlam. *Shakespeare on Masculinity*. Cambridge: Cambridge University Press, 2000b.

Wells, Stanley, and Paul Edmondson. 'The Plurality of Shakespeare's Sonnets.' *Shakespeare Survey* 65 (2012): 211–20.

White, R. S. 'Pacifist Voices in Shakespeare.' *Parergon* 17 (1999): 135–62.

Williams, Meg Harris. 'The Undiscovered Country: The Shape of the Aesthetic Conflict in Hamlet.' *The Apprehension of Beauty: The Role of Aesthetic Conflict in Development, Art, and Violence*. Ed. Donald Meltzer and M. H. Williams. London: Karnak Books Ltd, 1988. 84–133.

Wilson, Richard. *Shakespeare in French Theory: King of Shadows*. Abingdon: Routledge, 2007.

Wilson, Richard. '"A stringless instrument": Richard II and the Defeat of Poetry.' *Shakespeare's Book: Essays in Reading, Writing, and Reception*. Ed. Richard Wilson, Jane Rickard and Richard Meek. Manchester: Manchester University Press, 2008. 103–19.

Winnicott, D. W. 'Transitional Objects and Transitional Phenomena: A Study of the First Not-Me Possession.' *International Journal of Psycho-Analysis* 34 (1953): 89–97.

Winstanley, Michael. 'Shakespeare, Catholicism, and Lancashire: A Reappraisal of John Cottom, Stratford Schoolmaster.' *Shakespeare Quarterly* 68 (2017): 172–91.

Wrightson, Keith. *English Society 1500–1680*. London: Hutchinson, 1982.

Yaffe, Martin D. *Shylock and the Jewish Question*. London: Johns Hopkins University Press, 1997.

Yates, Frances. *A Study of Love's Labour's Lost*. Cambridge: Cambridge University Press, 1936.

Yeats, W. B. 'At Stratford-on-Avon.' *Ideas of Good and Evil*. New York: The Macmillan Company, 1903. 142–67.

Young-Bruehl, Elisabeth. *The Anatomy of Prejudices*. Cambridge, MA: Harvard University Press, 1998.

Zender, Karl F. 'The Humiliation of Iago.' *SEL: Studies in English Literature, 1500–1900* 34 (1994): 323–9.

Zimmermann, Heiner. 'Macbeth and Hercules.' *Renaissance Studies* 20 (2006): 356–78.

# INDEX

Adelman, Janet 166, 203–5
Allport, Gordon 89–90, 103–4, 105
'Alma Mater' 26–7
Anglin, Jay Pascal 33, 142
Animals, comparisons with
    as insults 41, 100, 113, 116–17, 124, 126, 161, 164
Anteros, myth of 182–91
Anterotic love 5–6, 99, 121, 149, 151, 177–224
Aristotle 163, 177
Art, definitions of 47–8
Ascham, Roger 22–3, 31, 38
Augustine, Saint 145

Bacon, Francis 140–1, 144
Barber, C. L. 54
Barton, Anne 158, 168
Baxandall, Michael 21
Bennett, Michael 61–3
Bion, W. R. 10–11, 17, 19, 21, 22, 216, 227, 233
Bowers, John 78
Britton, Ronald 35, 44, 157, 172, 232, 243
Brockbank, Philip 79–80
Burrow, Colin 24

Carlson, Donald 52–55
Castration motif 117–18, 120
Cervantes 122
Chambers, E. K. 75

Chaucer 54, 62–5, 73
Chesterton, G. K. 54–5
Coke, Edward 111
Cressy, David 32
Creton, Jean 68–9, 77

Davids, M. Fakhry 7–8, 89
Donne, John 100
Dowland, John 222
Duelling 33–4, 134–44

Einstein, Albert 11, 222
Eliot, T. S. 48
Envy 12, 35, 40–1, 103, 127–8, 130, 167, 172, 178, 179, 193, 218, 226, 231, 233
Equity v Law 110–11
Erasmus 23, 24, 30
Ewbank, Inga-Stina 78, 79

Fairbairn, Ronald 130, 233
Fiedler, Leslie 201–2
Fischlin, Daniel 76
Floyd-Wilson, Mary 122
Ford, Thomas 223–4
Fraunce, Abraham 185, 190
Freedman, Barbara 98–9
Freud, Sigmund 11, 90–1, 93–4, 96–7, 105–6, 118, 206
Froissart, Jean 67–8

Gawain Poet 62, 63, 64
Geohumoural theory 122–3
Gombrich, Ernst 53

Gordon, D. J. 189
Gower, John 54, 62, 63, 64, 65, 73
Gratitude/ingratitude 20, 24, 37, 81, 118, 163, 206, 213, 217, 218
Greville, Fulke 149–50, 196, 222–3

Hackett, Helen 23–4
Hardy, Barbara 35
Hilliard, Nicholas 59
Homer 59, 68
Honour 57, 64, 134–5, 137–40, 142, 144, 149–50, 154–7, 171, 173, 192, 208, 222
  types of 156–7, 170

Ideology 145–8

Jacob (in Bible) 115–16, 117
Jonson, Ben 23, 49, 114, 185–9, 190

Klein, Melanie 12–13, 172, 174, 179, 204–6

Lambarde, William 74–5
Langland 62, 64
Law Merchant, the 113–14
Lear, Jonathan 171, 179
Lending and borrowing 108–10, 114, 119
  on a 'sealed bond' 111–13
*Love Affair* (1939 film) 91–3, 101

Marlowe, Christopher 23, 34, 36, 49
Marsyas (mythical musician) 107–8, 115, 116

Marvell, Andrew 178
Masculinity, (mistaken) views of 49–50, 64, 173, 191–3, 196–7, 202–3
Meltzer, Donald 233
Meron, Theodor 150
Militarism vs. civilian life 59, 63–4, 71, 73, 83–5, 131–3, 137–8, 149–52, 161–2, 168–9
Milton, John 103, 185, 189–90
Money-Kyrle, Roger 90
Montaigne 76
More, Sir Thomas 29
Mulcaster, Richard 2–3, 4, 6, 29, 35, 42–3, 44–5, 225, 226, 227, 229–33

Narcissism 91, 105–6, 126
  destructive 124, 157, 172
  libidinal 117, 157, 162, 172
  thick skinned 124
  thin skinned 125
New Learning, the 18–19

Ovid 18, 189, 196–7

Panofsky, Erwin 184
Paragone 48
Pater, Walter 70–1
Peltonnen, Markku 156
Petrarch / Petrarchan / Petrarchism 26, 57–8, 65, 78, 147, 177–8, 194
Plato 177, 178, 182–3, 184, 189
Plutarch 28, 152–3, 155, 160, 163, 164, 168, 169, 174
Pol Pot 38

Prejudice
  and deficiencies of thinking
    or knowledge 2–3, 4, 6,
    10–11, 44–5, 94, 101,
    168, 227, 229–33
  and intellectual
    pretentiousness 5, 25–6,
    43–5, 193–8, 208, 231
  and values 3–5, 42–3, 133,
    172, 229–31
  definitions of 2–3, 6–7,
    9–11, 13, 89–90
  vs. tolerance 9–10, 44
Presentism 8–9
Priests not usually Elizabethan
  schoolmasters 31–3
Psychological concepts
  depressive position 13, 172,
    179, 204–6
  hysterical traits 105–6, 206–7
  latency 191
  manic defences 172, 179, 211
  paranoid schizoid position
    12–13, 174, 205–6, 226,
    227
  projection 2, 3, 13, 90, 91–3,
    100–1, 102–4, 115, 120,
    125, 126–30, 166, 172,
    205, 216, 226
  reparation 13, 178, 205–6,
    213
  repression / denial 94, 97–9,
    101, 117, 227
  splitting 12–13, 106, 125,
    157, 171–2, 174, 205–7,
    214–15, 218, 220, 226
  triangular relations 12, 214
Psychoanalytic theory and
  literary studies 11–13, 232–3
Puttenham, George 64–5, 78,
  79

Queen Elizabeth I 31, 66, 72–5,
  78, 108, 110, 111

Racialism, early modern
    anticipations of (or not)
    8, 87, 106, 116, 122–4,
    125, 126
  Jews 88–9, 103, 104, 106,
    108–10, 122
  Moors 116, 123–4, 125–7,
    133, 207
  'Negro' 116
  Spaniard / Spanish 122, 143,
    149, 196, 209
Raylor, Timothy 190
Ricardian poetry 54, 60–8,
  72–3, 76, 77–8, 83–4
're-fencing' 103–4, 106, 107
  *also see Silencing or ignoring*
Richard II, realm of 60–6
Robbins, Rossell Hope 68–9, 77
Roper, Margaret 29–30
Rosenfeld, Herbert 125, 157

Saul, Nigel 72–4
Saviolo, Vincentio 134, 143–4
Shakespeare, William
  his own education 20–4,
    25, 32
  his own (falsely) alleged
    prejudices 9, 87–8,
    180–1, 201–2
  his works
    *All's Well That Ends Well*
      108, 151, 192–3, 201,
      209
    *Antony and Cleopatra*
      28, 136, 182
    *As You Like It* 18, 21,
      25–6, 59, 138, 179.
      182, 211, 217

# INDEX

*Coriolanus* 116, 137, 149, 151–75
*Cymbeline* 18, 21, 49–50, 151, 191, 199, 201
*Hamlet* 64, 66, 109, 135, 138–9, 200–1, 206–13, 214
*Henry IV, part 1* 80–1, 82–5, 136–7, 151, 225
*Henry IV, part 2* 25, 80–2, 134, 136
*Henry V* 68, 70, 80–1, 88, 131, 134, 138
*Henry VI, part 1* 133, 136, 138, 162, 181
*Henry VI, part 2* 37–44, 133, 136, 138, 181, 192, 225, 232
*Henry VI, part 3* 1, 6, 29, 133, 181
*Julius Caesar* 28, 58–60
*King Lear* 104–5, 110–11, 136, 181, 192, 200–1, 206–7, 214
*Love's Labour's Lost* 18, 19, 26, 28, 50, 57–8, 66, 143, 193–8, 208–11, 223, 228
*Macbeth* 152, 181, 191–2
*Measure for Measure* 45
*Midsummer Night's Dream* 47, 50–55, 182, 221
*Much Ado About Nothing* 22, 151, 198–9, 201
*Othello* 89, 102–3, 107, 123–30, 133, 199–202, 214, 225, 226
*Pericles, Prince of Tyre* 29, 63, 135, 182
*Richard II* 22, 26–7, 60–83, 85, 135
*Richard III* 131, 152, 181
*Romeo and Juliet* 25, 49, 57, 71, 133, 140–9, 151, 156, 225, 226
*Shakespeare's Sonnets* 120, 131–2, 181
*Sir Thomas More* 88
*The Comedy of Errors* 27, 93–101, 104, 116, 226
*The Merchant of Venice* 6, 88–9, 104, 106–22, 123, 211, 223
*The Merry Wives of Windsor* 22, 31–7, 51, 66, 138, 139
*The Taming of the Shrew* 4–5, 18, 25, 26, 27, 28, 193
*The Tempest* 21–2, 29, 131, 182
*The Winter's Tale* 50, 56, 169–70, 182, 199–200, 213–22, 226
*Titus Andronicus* 18, 123, 181, 192
*Troilus and Cressida* 20, 136, 137, 151, 157–8, 164–5, 225–6
*Twelfth Night* 33, 49, 55–6, 57, 66–7, 104, 139, 211
*Two Noble Kinsmen* 22, 27, 56–7, 64, 135
*Venus and Adonis* 190–1

Showalter, Elaine 207–8
Sidney, Sir Philip 65, 67, 78, 81, 137, 152, 180
Silencing or ignoring 29, 48, 89, 101–2, 103–5, 106–8, 112, 115, 143, 163, 166, 212
Single combat 134–9, 166
Snyder, Susan 136, 137, 145–8, 150
Social hierarchies ('class' distinctions) 23, 41, 56–7, 59, 128–9, 138, 148, 150, 154, 156, 160, 161–2, 164, 192, 195–6, 197–8, 208–10, 219, 223
Soens, Adolph L. 142
Southwell, Robert 53
Sowell, Thomas 4, 7–8, 232
Spenser, Edmund 23, 65
Steiner, John 13
Stephens, Lyn 118, 119
Stoller, Robert J. 178–80, 198, 202–5, 223
Stone, Lawrence 203–4
'Strangers', ridicule of or attacks on 5, 7, 9, 33, 39–40, 87–130, 143, 194, 196, 226–7
Strier, Richard 78
Surrey, Earl of 64–5

Themistius 184–5
Thrift / Thriving 109–10, 115–16, 118, 120, 121, 126, 129, 132, 184–5, 186, 188

Titian (cover image) 17
Tottel, Richard 66–7
Trial by combat 134–6, 186

Vasari 75
Vives 23

Wells, Robin Headlam 66
Westminster Abbey x, 60–1, 68
Williams, Meg Harris 212
Winnicott, Donald 215–16
Women (in Shakespeare or his age)
  education of 18–19, 25, 29–31, 35
  agency of 73, 121–2, 151, 181, 191–2, 210–11
  misogyny 5, 31, 49–50, 89, 126, 181, 192, 193, 194–5, 198–203, 211–12, 213–15, 217, 225–6
  oppression of, and resulting complaints or responses 105, 120–1, 121–2, 150, 210
Wyatt, Sir Thomas 64–5, 66–7

Yaffe, Martin 109, 110, 114–15, 121
Yeats, William Butler 69–70
Young-Bruehl, Elisabeth 105–6, 206, 207

www.ingramcontent.com/pod-product-compliance
Lightning Source LLC
Chambersburg PA
CBHW070749020526
44115CB00032B/1601